# GREAT
# VACATIONS
# WITH
# YOUR KIDS

# About the Authors

DOROTHY JORDON is the founder and managing director of TWYCH, Travel with Your Children, a resource information center for parents planning successful and fun family vacations across the country or around the globe. This information is disseminated to thousands of families via a monthly newsletter, *Family Travel Times,* and two annually updated information guides: *Skiing with Children* and *Cruising with Children*. Ms. Jordon, mother of two boys, age 7 and 10, appears regularly on television and radio shows, encouraging and supporting parents with advice on family travel, understanding that today's parents and their children are a unique breed who want to spend these very special times together.

MARJORIE A. COHEN is a freelance writer, author of six previous books: *Work, Study, and Travel Abroad: The Whole World Handbook; Where to Stay USA; The Teenagers Guide to Study, Travel and Adventure Abroad; Volunteer: The Comprehensive Guide to Voluntary Service in the U.S. and Abroad; The Budget Traveler's Latin America;* and the *Shoppers' Guide to New York*. She is also a contributing editor to *Family Travel Times*. She lives with her husband and two daughters, age 6 and 12, in New York City.

# GREAT

# VACATIONS

## WITH

# YOUR KIDS

### The Complete Guide
### to Family Vacations
### in the U.S.

DOROTHY ANN JORDON
AND
MARJORIE ADOFF COHEN

E. P. DUTTON | NEW YORK

Published in the United States by E. P. Dutton,
a division of NAL Penguin Inc.,
2 Park Avenue, New York, N.Y. 10016.

Published simultaneously in Canada by Fitzhenry and Whiteside
Limited, Toronto.

Library of Congress Cataloging-in-Publication Data

Jordon, Dorothy.
  Great vacations with your kids.

  Includes index.
  1. United States—Description and travel—1981–
—Guide-books.  2. Family recreation—United States—Guidebooks.  I. Cohen, Marjorie Adoff.  II. Title.
E158.J8  1987      917.3'04927       87-13595

ISBN: 0-525-48338-1

Designed by Stanley S. Drate

10 9 8 7 6 5 4 3 2

*This book is dedicated
to our own wonderful kids—
Elizabeth, Lucy, Jordon, and Russell.*

# ACKNOWLEDGMENTS

We have lots of people to thank. First, there are all the people who took the time to answer our questions, the experts who were so willing to share their knowledge with us, and the friends who told us about their own "great vacations" with their kids.

More specifically, we want to thank Nancy Bolick and Cindy Lake Thomas for help with the city chapters, and Sandra Soule, our editor, for her patience and good advice every step of the way.

# CONTENTS

# GREAT VACATIONS WITH YOUR KIDS

# INTRODUCTION

Trust us: you are going to have a wonderful vacation with your family this year. We've had a great time putting this book together, sorting through the possibilities, uncovering all kinds of great places to go. If we had all that fun just doing the paperwork, imagine how great it's going to be when you actually get to try it all out.

Some of you may have a little trepidation about traveling with your kids; others are seasoned family travelers. For the wary: you need, want, and deserve a family vacation. Think of how rare it is for all three, four, five, or six of you to be together at once. Think about those wild mornings when everyone's running off to school, to work, to the babysitter. Think of those nights—the rushed dinners, the meetings, the homework, the "stuff" of everyday life. Now think of how wonderful it would be to step out of the routine, to leave all of the hectic, tightly scheduled time behind and spend time together, not worrying about the clock, maybe even forgetting what day of the week it is. This really can happen.

Traveling with your kids has three advantages over other kinds of travel: with your kids along you get an entirely new perspective on what you're seeing, kids make friends for themselves and for you, and the adventurous spirit of your kids often leads you to experiences you may not have anticipated.

Although we think that family travel is great, we also know that it's different from other kinds of travel. Traveling with the kids requires a different approach to planning—it involves a different kind of travel than you did on your own, with your friends, or with your spouse before you had the kids. That's exactly why we have written this book: so that we can present first what's different and then, more importantly, show you how to cope with the differences.

**1**

We cover the generalities of travel in the first part, the specifics in the second. What you'll read in the first section can be applied to any trip you take no matter how long, how far, or how elaborate. And each successive trip will become easier. We promise.

The second section gives you some specific suggestions of places to go and things to do. We admit it: we are trying to be all things to all people. We have included vacations that appeal to the rugged, outdoorsy types and vacations that appeal to the more sedentary among us. We talk about skiing down mountains, backpacking in wildernesses, and lying on beaches. There are vacations here that cost a lot, others that are quite inexpensive. Some of our suggestions take you thousands of miles from home, others only an hour or two away. Whatever you need or want in a family vacation, we think you'll find it here.

Fortunately, people in the travel industry are beginning to recognize and address the needs of families traveling together, but it's not always easy to find out just what they're up to. We have done all that for you. We have researched and uncovered information that's not easy to come by, so that you can spend your time on the parts that are fun—the choosing, the planning, and the doing.

Remember, too, that when we refer to a family vacation, we don't just mean mom, dad, and their 2.4 kids—we're talking about single parents plus their children; grandparents and their grandchildren; grandparents, parents, and kids together; and any other "family" configurations that are possible.

Time together as a family is precious time. Don't think we're naïve, though. We know that it's not going to be fun and games and laughter every minute (real life is not, after all, the "Cosby Show"), but the collective memories of a vacation together are very special for each member of a family and last a long, long time after the vacation is done.

All prices were correct at press time.
Changes may have occurred since.

# 1

# GETTING READY

Ask 20 people what makes a great family vacation and you may very well get 20 different answers. But all great family vacations have some common denominators: they should be fun, they should be relatively carefree, they should include something of interest for every single member of the family, and they should provide lots of time together, away from the pressures of everyday life.

We've thought a lot about family vacations, and we've come up with what we call the six keys to great vacations. Everything in this book is related in one way or another to the six following principles:

1. Planning: Of all the six principles, this one is probably the most important. Planning your vacation with the individual needs of each member of your family in mind is the key to success. Begin with your youngest child and work your way up. Consider what each person's needs are and then how you can blend them all and make one smashing vacation out of it all. Work on all the details ahead of time. Be sure there are cribs, find out whether there's a children's program where you're going, ask whether you can warm the baby's bottle on the plane, and so on.
2. Participation: Be sure to include every member of your family in the planning process. The kids should be actively involved from the very beginning. There are many

reasons for this, but one of the most important and often overlooked is that kids have problems with "unknowns"—change and new places can be upsetting to them. And don't succumb to the fallacy that you should wait until the kids are old enough. One couple we know did that, and by the time they got to it, the kids were 13 and 15 and totally uninterested in a family vacation. By including your kids in the planning process from the beginning, many of the "unknowns" can be eliminated. We'll give examples of how to do this further on.

3. Alternating time together/time apart: You can't spend every minute of every day together on vacation any more than you can at home. Parents need time to be with each other without the kids, kids need to be off with other kids or adults, one parent may want to spend some time with just one kid—all kinds of configurations are possible and desirable. We've done lots of research on resorts and hotels with children's programs. We feel that it is through these programs that parents can best budget their time, but these programs aren't the only solution.

4. Go where you're wanted: You don't want to spend any time at a place where you're merely tolerated. You want to be welcomed. Some hotels just don't encourage families, and that's okay, too, but you want to avoid them. You want to be sure that the place you're going to stay will welcome you—that they're glad to have children, like them, and are able to handle their special needs.

5. Plan days that everyone is going to enjoy: Each day should be special and fun, and each day should have something for everyone. You don't have to spend day after day at a theme park; kids can enjoy all sorts of different things as long as their own needs relating to the activity are considered. Museum visits can be fun for kids as long as they don't involve endless hours of walking from painting to painting. And kids should have a chance to run around whenever possible. Stop at a playground on your way to a sightseeing attraction; let them scramble up and down a public statue and run in a park.

6. Attitude: Be realistic about what you can and can't expect on family vacations. Don't set yourself up for disappoint-

ment by having to cover every inch of a city. Choose what you plan to see and do carefully, and remember that it's not how much you do but how good it feels doing it. Slow down. You rush around enough during your regular life. Adopt a vacation pace, and, even if it goes against your nature, force yourself to be flexible. Things are going to go wrong—everything will not be exactly as you planned. Anxiety is infectious; if you lose control, the kids probably will, too.

## TRAVEL AGENTS

This leads us to our next topic—travel agents: Should you or shouldn't you use them?

As in most other areas, we have a definite opinion on the subject: we are very definitely pro–travel agent. The best thing about using a travel agent is that it gives you the luxury of "one-stop shopping": if the agent is a good one, you can have all your questions answered, fares and packages researched, reservations booked in minutes. Although much that you need to know as a parent traveling with children is not available to the travel agency network, with the information in this book you and your agent should be able to plan a great vacation.

Remember that even the best agents haven't been everywhere. But if they are good, they will have learned a lot from past clients and their colleagues. Although it might take you weeks to track down certain information, a good agent can accomplish miracles in five minutes to an hour with a computer and all the special resources available to the industry. A good example is airfares. Since deregulation of the airlines, the proliferation of airfares has been mind-boggling. While this is good for the consumer, it's enormously confusing. A good agent can sift through all of this with you and come up with the best deal. Sure, you can call airlines and get their lowest fare, but they're not going to tell you anything about what the competition has. Agents can advise you on the reliability and general reputation of the travel wholesalers; they can decipher some of the fine print of packagers' brochures. Using travel agents won't cost you anything, and very often will save you money because they are paid their commissions by suppliers (airlines, hotels, car rental companies, tour operators). Don't be surprised, though, if a travel agent adds a service charge for booking some of the smaller hotels or resorts, which may not give commissions.

Good agents are able to work within your budget. They know whom to go to for special fares, which tour operators have packages to your destination, plus unpublicized specials. Agents can be a great help with airfares. They can use their clout to get a "booked" seat and can have a wait list cleared much faster than you. Most agents' computers have something called *shopper's fares,* which provides a quick review of all the airlines that travel to any given destination. Think of all the time that one service can save. Another time saver: if you're stopping at more than one place, an agent can repeat the same information requests to the various hotels along your route.

You should pick your travel agent as carefully as you would your doctor or your car mechanic. How? One of the best ways is to ask for recommendations from friends whose opinions you trust and whose values you share. Consider factors such as destination or type (whether the agent specializes in the type of trip you're planning), accessibility and policies of the agency, and personality and qualifications of the individual agent.

Another factor to consider is whether the agency is a member of ASTA, the American Society of Travel Agents. Although there are good agencies who are not members, ASTA is a professional organization whose members have been in operation for at least three years. It has a tour payment protection plan (in case tour operators default) and is a ready resource for problems and complaints. More and more agents are now becoming certified travel consultants (CTCs), indicating at least five years' experience and completion of a two-year intensive study program. Although *CTC* after the agent's name is no guarantee, it does indicate that you're dealing with a professional—someone who is serious about what he is doing, serious enough to commit himself to a vigorous program of study. It would be nice, of course, if the agent were a traveling parent, like you, but it's certainly not a must.

While you're considering the choice of an agent, take a look at the agency itself. Is it a pleasant place? What are their policies on service charges, refunds, payments? Are they an appointed agency of the airlines, Amtrak, and the cruise lines? Airline appointments indicate a certain basic financial investment and staff experience, plus the ability to write airline tickets.

You must like and respect the person you entrust your trip to and have confidence in his ability. You should feel able to ask questions, even the same ones repeatedly, no matter how silly they may seem. When working with an agent, be specific. "Sometime in August" will not get the same response from an agent as "one week beginning between August 2 and 8." A prepared client simplifies the task for the agent. On the other hand, if you can be flexible about dates, a good agent may be able to arrange some savings.

A good agent will begin with a broad outline of your trip, respond and listen to your ideas and needs, and give specific suggestions. The agent should have an idea of your life-style, your "ideal vacation" and budget. He should ask, or you should volunteer the information, about what is an essential part of your vacation. Is a crib necessary? Do you want to be able to walk out your door onto the beach? Do you want daily maid service in an apartment? What do you like to do on vacation? A good agent can analyze these needs and pull them all together. A good agent can advise you on the amount of travel insurance you need, only enough to insure the part you may lose. For instance, if you're only liable for 50 percent of the ticket, only buy insurance for that amount.

All travel agents have a limited amount of time, so some of the detail work must be your responsibility. Check Appendix 3 for the tourist offices of each state you plan to visit and write to them. If you're an AAA member, use their guides and Triptik service. (See page 16.) Travel books and articles are fun for the family and often have good advice on "extras" or little-known area attractions. They can also help you to select your destination. Again, talk with friends who have been there.

Janet Tice, co-author of *What to Do with the Kids This Year* (see page 170), operates a travel service called "Families Welcome!" that arranges vacations especially for individual families. Call 212-861-2500 or 800-472-8999 for information.

Another special travel service is one called *Grandtravel,* which is designed to cater to grandparents and grandchildren traveling together. Itineraries are planned to appeal to both generations and to include time together and time with peers. All tours include predeparture counseling—on what to do if the child gets homesick or the grandparents get tired—and tour escorts. Longer trips are scheduled for the summer; shorter trips coincide with school vacations. Some of Grandtravel's choices for trips in the United States include a 4-day trip to Disney World, Sea World, and the Kennedy Space Center; a 9-day tour called "The American Indians of the Southwest" that begins in Albuquerque and ends in Phoenix; and a 16-day trip to Alaska to explore its glaciers and wildlife. For details, contact Grandtravel, The Ticket Counter, 6900 Wisconsin Avenue, Suite 706, Chevy Chase, Maryland 20815.

Two other family-oriented travel services are the American Institute for Foreign Study (AIFS) and Schilling Travel Service. AIFS caters primarily to groups of families traveling together. For details, contact AIFS, 102 Greenwich Avenue, Greenwich, Connecticut 06830.

Schilling Travel Service specializes in educational travel for families. For example, they recently arranged a trip to the U.S.S.R. for a group of grandparents and their grandchildren. For information, contact Schilling Travel Service, 722 Second Avenue South, Minneapolis, Minnesota 55402, Telephone: 612-332-1100, 800-328-0302.

And for parents with handicapped children, a group called Rainbow Horizons coordinates workshops and trips for families with a member who has special needs. For information, contact P.O. Box 5231, New York, New York 10185.

### A Word About Problems

Even the best agent can make mistakes. Check your documents carefully for dates, arrival and departure times, correct airports, guaranteed reservations at hotels and car rental agencies. Because the agent often acts as the middle person, it may not be his fault if you get a window instead of an aisle seat, a small hotel room, or water in the trunk of your rental car. If you feel you have a legitimate complaint, first go to the supplier, and then to the agency owner or manager to see what his response is. If you are still not satisfied, write to ASTA, the Better Business Bureau, or a local newspaper. As a last resort, you can go to your local small claims court.

## PLANNING

Just as soon as you know where you're going, get the whole family involved in the planning. Not only is this fun, but it eliminates the children's wariness about the unknowns of travel. Think about it for a moment from your children's point of view. They are about to set out for a place they've never seen; to be surrounded by people they've never met; to sleep in a new room, in a new bed; and to eat foods cooked differently from what they're used to. Planning together, discussing what can be expected, will accomplish a great deal in allaying the fears of children. Preparation is the key. Take out a map and show the kids where you're going and the route you're going to take. Talk about distances in terms they can understand: "We'll be driving for four hours—that's like going to Grandma's house and back home again." Help them compose and address letters to tourist offices asking for information on the places you'll be visiting. (See Appendix for list of addresses.) Have them put their own names on the return address so that the responses can come to them. Kids love getting their own mail. Even if your children aren't old enough to read, they can enjoy the colorful pictures from a very early age. Let them point to or circle what they'd like to do. We give our kids different colored markers and let them go at it. From what's been circled, make up a list of what you're going to do, and don't forget your own desires.

Take a trip to the library with the kids and get some books that have some connection to an aspect of your trip. *Family Travel Times,* published monthly by Travel with Your Children (TWYCH), 80 Eighth Ave., New York, New York 10011, runs a monthly column called "Bookshelf" with lots of suggestions for suitable books on whatever topics are discussed in that particular month's issue.

When we were getting ready to go to a dude ranch out west, we all headed for the card catalogue and looked up Wyoming, dude ranches, and Custer. Each of the kids took out four books; the favorite turned out to be a textbook about Wyoming. We read a piece every night at bedtime: we read about the mountains, the towns we'd pass through en route to the ranch from the airport, rodeos, Indians, reservations, and horses. Ask your child's teacher whether there's anything that the class is studying that can be related to your travels. Whether or not the answer is yes, you can be sure that the trip will have invaluable educational value. Kids absorb so much. Even the youngest will learn.

Another great benefit of advance planning is that it's the best way we know to combat the "When are we going on vacation?" syndrome that can drive parents crazy. From the minute your kids find out about an upcoming vacation, they start asking, "Is today vacation?" or, if they're a bit older, "How many more days until we go?" One of the best ways, not to avoid the question, but to channel all that anticipation and excitement, is to involve the kids in the planning. One friend came to us and said that she was going to Walt Disney World with the family but that the kids were driving her wild asking about when they'd get going. We gave her a handful of brochures for her nonreader and a guidebook for her older child. When we saw her two days later, she was overflowing with gratitude. Between the two of them, the kids had planned exactly what they wanted to see and do. A pretrip calendar is good, too. Little ones can cross off the days; the older ones can plan final chores and packing.

Remember, as you plan a trip, that kids love to repeat the things they like; they like to go back to the places they enjoy. Be flexible enough in your planning so that repeats will be possible.

## DECIDING WHERE AND FOR HOW LONG

If we can believe the statistics we've been hearing, families are now taking shorter but more frequent vacations. People no longer pin all of their vacation hopes on one vacation per year. How long and how frequent your vacations are really depend on your own circumstances. No matter what the situation, the length of your vacation depends a great deal on how much money you can afford to spend. If you can afford two weeks at a certain ski resort as long as you don't opt for the children's program or ten days if you do, you probably should choose the shorter vacation with the children's program and enjoy the luxury of having a place where they can go to have fun and meet people their own age. It's value, not just bargains, that you have to consider.

Determining where you should go is more complicated than deciding how long. We advise parents to start out by asking themselves where they'd like to go if they didn't have kids. You can go practically any place you've ever wanted to go as long as you make the right arrangements and can be sure that your kids' needs can be met as well as your own. Let's take, as an example, a friend we know who always wanted to take a trip along the California coast. "If I were alone," she told us, "I'd be happy to ride in the car for four hours, but how can I do that with a 15-month-old?" Obviously, she can't. But she can cover the same territory by finding a good base for her travels and taking short day trips from that place. If she's determined to go someplace four hours from her "base," she can make sure that there is someone who can take care of her toddler for the day.

In spite of the extraordinary variety of vacation choices, when you think about it there are only three basic vacation types: (1) on the move, (2) staying in one place, and (3) a little of each. Which would you like?

One of the first things all of your family have to ask themselves is what they want from a vacation. If you have four people involved, there may be four answers. One person may love the beach; one may hate it; one may love to sightsee and be on the go; another may want to relax by the side of a pool. It's really not that difficult to accommodate everybody's tastes. Let's give some examples: A friend of ours is an avid sailor, but his kids and his wife despise boating. They like to be near water but not on it. They spent a week at a resort where the mother could relax on the beach while the father enjoyed unlimited sailing and the kids went to morning sports activities. Every day when the father came back from the sail, the whole family took a hike or a bike ride or went shelling. Everyone got to do what he or she liked separately, and they all did something they enjoyed doing together. A cardinal rule of successful vacations—no martyrs, *please*.

Another family we know is made up of ski-crazy kids, a mother who can take it or leave it, and a father who never liked skiing but has developed back problems that would prevent him from going even if he wanted to. The solution: a resort where the mother can ski, play tennis, and go to the spa while the kids are at ski school, and where the father can swim in the indoor pool and catch up on his reading.

Another success story is the family of a mother, a father, and a teenage son who didn't want to do anything with his parents. The solution: two weeks at a spot where the father could play tennis, the mother could horseback ride, and the teenager could go off on a five-day wilderness trek with expert guides and other kids his own age.

And finally we cite the family who had always dreamed of going to Alaska. When they checked on the airfare for six to and from their home city, their dream ended abruptly. But they were clever: they asked themselves what it was that so appealed to them about Alaska, and when they determined that it was the quiet, the wilderness, and the closeness to nature, they went camping in the Grand Tetons, only a four-hour car ride from their home.

The moral of all this is simple: All travel problems have solutions. All it takes is determination, some creative thinking, and research.

## BOOKS THAT HELP

Throughout *Great Vacations* we refer to books that can help you with your planning—from choosing a place to go, to organizing your trip, to knowing what you want to do along the way or upon arrival. To begin with, we recommend the following books, which do not fit neatly under any specific chapter. Some are guidebooks; others are how-to books. We've looked through them all and think that they're worth your consideration. Most are available at bookstores, but some from smaller publishers may have to be ordered directly by mail. See the list of publishers in Appendix 2 for addresses. You'll notice that our list is heavily weighted toward New England, so let us know about any good books you find on some of the other parts of the country.

> *Trips with Children in New England* by Harriet Webster published by Yankee Books, publishers of *Yankee* magazine ($9.95). Webster's attitude is reflected in the dedication of her book: "For Ma who gave me the joy of travel, and for Jonathan who helps me pass it on to our kids." Her book is thorough and thoughtfully written and includes nature centers, hiking trails, science museums, animal farms, train and plane rides, and more. She's aimed her book at the 5-to-14 set, but families with younger kids can benefit from it just as much.
>
> *Favorite Weekends in New England,* also by Harriet Webster

and published by Yankee Books ($8.95). Although not specifically for kids, this book has a lot to interest them.

*Favorite Daytrips in New England* by Michael Schuman, published by Yankee Books ($8.95). A good book to use if you decide to base your vacation somewhere in New England. You can easily stretch most of the trips into a full vacation.

*The Great Weekend Escape Book* by Michael Spring, published by E. P. Dutton ($10.95). We can't keep this one on the shelf. In it, Spring gives you 26 choices from Tangier Island to Mt. Monadnock. His taste is excellent; as he explains: "I wrote this as though you were a close friend who sat me down and said, 'Tell me about 26 glorious weekends.' " Every chapter includes a section called "For Kids" that gives some ideas on topics of special interest to families traveling together. It has our highest recommendation.

*Daytrips, Getaway Weekends and Budget Vacations in the Mid-Atlantic States* by Patricia and Robert Foulke, published by the Globe Pequot Press ($10.95). There are eight itineraries to choose from, ranging from the Adirondacks to Washington, D.C. The book is well organized, and the itineraries are appealing, with lots that are suitable for kids. The same authors have written *Daytrips and Budget Vacations in New England*, also published by Globe Pequot Press ($8.95), with six itineraries from the coast to mountains, from cities to villages.

*America's Greatest Walks* by Gary Yanker and Carol Tarlow, published by Addison-Wesley Publishing Company, Inc. ($10.95). No matter how old your kids are, walks are wonderful family activities. The authors have picked their favorite 100 walks—long walks and short walks, walks in cities, walks in woods, mountain hikes and strolls along beaches. A nice little book.

*Family Vacations: USA* by Diane Torrens, published by Fielding Travel Books, William Morrow and Company, Inc. ($12.95). This book, too, chooses 100 resorts and describes them, including a little on children's activities for each. Not as good as the book we recommend in Chapter 8.

*Directory of Free Vacation and Travel Information* edited by Raymond Carlson, Pilot Books ($3.95). An often overlooked source of good, free travel information are the local, state, and federal government tourism agencies in this country. This directory has them all and is available from the publisher, 103 Cooper Street, Babylon, New York 11702, for $3.95 plus $1 for postage and handling.

*Traveling With Your Baby*, by Vicki Lansky, published by Bantam ($2.95). This is a compendium of practical and ingenious suggestions together with helpful checklists. Filled with hints, both from the author and other parents, this book gives you the tools to plan a happier trip the first time out. Lansky is a true student of family life, an observant parent, and, as such, provides information unavailable elsewhere.

---

## ABOUT OUR LISTINGS:

The properties we list in this book all welcome kids and all willingly responded to our many, many questions. We're relying on you, our readers, to let us know about your own experiences with our choices—good and bad—and to tell us about any new places we can list in the next edition.

## ONE MORE REMINDER:

If you're looking for a place to play tennis, check the tennis and golf chapter but don't overlook Chapter 8 on resorts, Chapter 10 on skiing (many ski resorts turn into tennis and golf spots once the snow melts), and Chapter 11 on farms and dude ranches.

And don't forget the None of the Above listings beginning on page 289.

NOTE: Rates quoted here were accurate at press time but are subject to change.

NOTE: Be sure to check pages 297–99 for a list of publishers' addresses. Some books published by smaller publishers may not be readily available in bookstores but can be ordered directly from the publisher.

Send us your cards and letters. We want to hear from you about your great vacation choices so that we can include them in the next edition.

# 2

---

# GETTING THERE

Whether you decide to travel by car, plane, train, or bus, preparation is the key. You can start, with younger children, by getting library books about the kind of transportation you'll be using. If this is your child's first airplane ride, try Pat and Joel Ross's *Your First Airplane Trip* or Dinah L. Moché's *We're Taking an Airplane Trip*. For car trips, scout out *The Car Trip* by Helen Oxenburg, Anne Alexander's *ABC of Cars and Trucks,* or Richard Scarry's *On Vacation*. In preparation for the first plane trip you can play a game of setting up rows of chairs in the configuration of a plane and taking turns being the pilot, the passenger, and the flight attendant. Be especially sure not to put any of your own fear of flying into your child's mind; most children are excited, not frightened by the idea of flying. Don't ruin it.

Talk to the kids about the distance you're traveling and the time it will take to get there. If you're going to visit relatives or friends, get out photos and talk about them. However you decide to travel, don't start packing the night before you leave. Even if you're not the organized type, force yourself this once. Start making lists of everything you need to take a week ahead of time. Remember, too, that you don't have to keep your kids entertained every single minute of their trip, but that you do have to provide them with things that will keep them busy, involved, and comfortable. They need toys and games to play with alone and some they can play with you or their brothers and sisters.

Fatigue and hunger are the two things you want to avoid on any trip. It's always best to start a long trip with a nap: we like late flights so that the kids are nice and tired when they board the plane. We like to start car trips early, early in the morning: get up at 5:00, bundle the kids into a prepacked car, get going, and hope they'll go back to sleep.

Hunger is easy enough to avoid. Just be sure to pack a variety of snacks and let the kids carry their own food. Since it is vacation time we let them eat their snacks whenever they want. They like that! Even if there's going to be a meal on board your flight, even if there's a dining car on the train, you can be sure that your kids are going to get hungry long before anything is officially served. There are lots of possibilities for snacks—dry cereal, oranges (great for thirst, hunger, and even deodorizing a stuffy car), bananas, apples, cheese, crackers, unsalted popcorn and pretzels, and individual packages of apple sauce. As a parent you've probably realized that one of the greatest inventions of the 20th century is juice-in-a-box. What genius came up with it? If we knew, we'd dedicate this book to him or her. Just freeze the box the night before the trip, and it will stay cold for a long time. It will even serve as a refrigerator pack for the other food. (We used it once to keep our kids' antibiotics cold during a flight.)

## BY CAR

We don't have to tell you about having your car tuned up before you go. And if you're not a member of the American Automobile Association, this is the time to sign up. For the chapter nearest you, check your phone book or write to their headquarters, 8111 Gatehouse Road, Falls Church, Virginia 22047. Not only will you be able to call someone if you're stuck on the road but you'll also be able to take advantage of their trip planning service called "the Triptik," which highlights the easiest, quickest, or most scenic routes. When the inevitable "Are we there yet?" comes, the Triptik gives a good graphic answer. (Other automobile clubs that offer trip planning services are the ALA Auto and Travel Club, 888 Worcester Street, Wellesley, Massachusetts 02181; Allstate Motor Club, 34 Allstate Plaza, Northbrook, Illinois 60062; Amoco Motor Club, P.O. Box 9049, Des Moines, Iowa 50369-0010; Chevron Travel Club, P.O. Box P, Concord, California 94524; and Montgomery

Ward Auto Club, P.O. Box 2463, One Shell Plaza, Houston, Texas 77001.)

Let each of your kids take a turn being the "navigator." Give the navigator a special hat or badge to make the assignment even more impressive. As we've said before, it's best to start your car trip early in the morning. Not only will you get a few hours of sleep from the kids, but you will also be able to avoid rush hour traffic and arrive wherever you're going well before bedtime. This last part is important: kids who have some time to look around the new place a bit before dark will be less apprehensive when bedtime comes. If you can end your driving day early enough to do something active before bed—a swim or a romp in a playground— all the better. When you're planning your travel in the car, make a driving pit stop schedule and stick to it. Don't make the kids wait 25 extra minutes for a stop; that breaks your part of the bargain. You can expect a car trip with kids to take one-third longer than without; for example, a four and one-half hour trip becomes a six-hour drive. When you take your breaks, have them accomplish as much as possible—picnic; sightsee; get some exercise. Give the kids a signal ten minutes before you're going to stop so that they can put away their toys and find their shoes. When you stop, look for a shady spot and cover the seats so they won't overheat. When it's time to get back into the car, announce the change of navigator, rotate the seating positions, and so on.

Car seats are, of course, a given. You must use your seat belts, and your younger children need car seats. If you haven't bought your car seat, you can get a reprint of *Consumer Reports* magazine's article "Child Safety Seat" for $2 from Consumer Reports, P.O. Box 2485, Boulder, Colorado 80322. If you buy a new car seat for the trip, give it a trial run before takeoff. In cold weather, tuck blankets around your baby *after* the belt is buckled.

In Chapter 3 we talk about what to take along with you in a car or on any kind of transportation. That's where we suggest toys, games, first aid kit, clothing, and so on.

Arrange the car so that your kids can get at the toys or games they want without having to undo their seat belts. Take pillows and blankets, and don't forget premoistened paper towels and dry paper towels.

Before you leave, talk to your children a bit about exercising caution with strangers. The easiest rule to follow is probably "talk to anyone you'd like to when you're with me, but avoid strangers when you're alone." Two New York women, Pamela McDonnell and Tamar Hosansky, cofounders of the Safety and Fitness Exchange (SAFE), an organization that gives nationwide workshops and seminars on the subject of personal safety, have written an article called "Travel Tips for Parents and Children—Having Fun the SAFE Way." For a copy, send $1 to SAFE, 541 Avenue of the Americas, New York, New York 10011, 212-242-4874.

### When Things Go Wrong

We've been told that a high-carbohydrate, low-fat diet a few days before a trip diminishes the incidence of car sickness. Sometimes car sickness can be caused by drinking too much milk or soft drink, reading in the car, being overdressed, having no air in the car, or just plain being overexcited. Ask your pediatrician for advice. If you're traveling during the summer in a hot climate (such as New York City!) prevent sun sickness by keeping your children's arms and heads covered.

### Meal Stops

When it's time to eat a real meal, our first choice is a picnic. Picnics avoid waiting to be served, and the chance to go shopping gets rid of some pent-up energy. If you're not going to picnic, choose a restaurant with an outdoor café or terrace on the beach or lakeside so that the kids can play while you wait for your food. Places that offer a serve-yourself buffet or a salad bar are good for immediate gratification, which in turn avoids premeal crankiness. Lots of times we let our kids sit in a booth right behind ours so that they can eat by themselves. They really do rise to the occasion. This really works best when you're traveling with another family, because the kids from both families can sit together.

While you're at the restaurant, you can refill your thermos and make bathroom stops.

### Some Gadgets You May Want

A company called Children on the Go manufactures fine products that we think are quite clever. They include the Secure View Mirror ($7.95), which attaches to the windshield and gives you a view of your child in the back seat as you drive; a Totty Seat ($8.95), which is a portable potty seat that folds to five and a half square inches, comes in a vinyl travel pouch, and fits any regular toilet seat; a Beam Screen ($9.95), which attaches to the window next to your child to block out heat and glare from the sun; Hands-Free Diaper Pack ($24.95), which can be worn like a backpack or carried and has a fold-down changing pad and pockets for bottles, wipes, and so on; Splat Mat ($9.95), a three-foot by four-foot vinyl mat that can go under high chairs to catch the splats; and Travel Beams ($4.95), a battery-operated light that attaches to the car window for night reading or game playing. To order any of these products, you can write directly to the company: P.O. Box 396, Arlington Heights, Illinois 60005.

## Car Rentals

There are a few basic points to consider when you're choosing a car rental company:

How easy is it to get 24-hour service when you break down?

What *exactly* is the cost of liability insurance? (Don't pay for more than you need; check your own coverage with your insurance company.)

In plain English, what are the mileage charges? What does "unlimited" mileage really mean? What are the drop-off fees?

If you're going to ski country, will the car have snow tires and a ski rack? If you're going to be in Florida, will it be air-conditioned?

Ask ahead of time what will happen if the budget car you reserve is not available and a sleek, luxury model has to be substituted. Make *sure* you're not liable for the difference.

And, finally, check on the availability of car seats.

On this last point: although many people will use their own car seats (if you take them on a plane to your car rental destination, you can just check them through as baggage), many people will prefer not to carry them along. We surveyed the major car rental companies to ask about car seat availability and came up with the following:

*Alamo*

Car seats are available for $3 per day and should be reserved when you reserve your car. Call 800-462-5266 for reservations.

### Avis

Many of Avis's locations have car seats to rent. The seats are Century 200's, and for a confirmed car seat rental you need to allow 48 hours' advance notice; for two car seats you need 72 hours. The charge is either $2 per day or $10 per week per car seat; if the rental is only one-way, there's an additional $15 charge. Avis can also send you a booklet called *U.S. Child Safety Seat—Child Restraint Laws* so that you know what's required in each state you plan to travel in. Call 800-331-1212 for reservations.

### Budget Rent a Car Corporation

Since Budget is a franchise operation, the availability of car seats varies. But according to a printout sent by one of the public relations people at Budget, many franchises do make them available. (Some that have children's seats do not have what they call "baby seats.") Seats are free at some locations, $2 to $5 per day at others. Some locations require deposits; others do not. Call 800-527-0700 for information on individual locations.

### Hertz

Hertz guarantees child safety seats—the Century 200 model—at all of their U.S. corporate locations and at some licensee locations with a 48-hour advance reservation. The seats are $3 per day, $15 per week, and $40 for 18 to 30 days. Call 800-654-3131.

### National

Most National locations have AstroSeats, good for kids up to 42 inches and 42 pounds. Two days advance booking is necessary to confirm, and the cost is $2 per day, $10 per week for local returns. Call 800-328-4567.

## BY PLANE

When you're traveling by air, you'll have to be a bit more strict about what to bring along. You won't have as much room as you would in the car, and you won't be able to spread out as much. Air travel is exciting for kids and has its own set of pleasures and pains. We've already outlined the importance of preparing kids for flying with storybooks and games. You'll also have to prepare them for the possibility their ears will hurt when they take off and land. If you explain why this happens, it won't be so frightening. Explain, too, that you will be carrying some gum or their bottle to keep at takeoff and landing. If your child tends to have ear problems, try to arrange nonstop flights to avoid compounding his or her discomfort. Whenever you fly, get to the airport early so that the preflight process can be orderly and unhurried.

### Airfares: What's Best

A travel agent can be an enormous help with airfares. He or she knows what the deals are and can help you sort out whether certain restrictions are really worth the money you save. Just about every airline has a special fare for kids 2 to 11 years (those 2 years and under fly free on their parents' laps, one lap child allowed per adult). Occasionally, a Kids Fly Free program will pop up. Again, your travel agent should know about it.

### Where to Sit

Try to reserve your seat as early as you can. Sometimes it is possible to reserve when you book; other times you must wait until just before flight time. Everyone has a theory about what are the best seats, it seems. The one we hear so often is to reserve the bulkhead seat, the one up in front of the cabin with all the leg room. We don't agree because in the bulkhead seats the armrests don't move up, so the youngest children can't comfortably lie on your lap to rest. We prefer aisle seats for kids. If you ask, your child will probably request a window seat, but the fascination of the window seat is limited to takeoff and landing—the four hours of clouds and blue sky in between is not very entertaining. The aisle seat lets them get in and out at will. We have a friend who reserves one aisle seat and one window seat when traveling with her 2-year-old. The premise is simple: she figures no regular travelers want to reserve the middle seat, and she ends up with an empty seat for her baby. We like to book two seats for us and two seats right behind us for our kids. That way the kids can sit together, we can sit together, or one of us can alternate sitting with each of the kids. The flexibility is nice.

For some suggestions on what to take so that the kids can amuse themselves on the plane, see Chapter 3.

### Car Seats on the Plane

Practically all airlines we surveyed allowed passengers to use their approved car seat on flights. All seats manufactured after January 1, 1981 (the date that federal safety standards took effect) and bearing the proper label can be used on an airplane. Seats manufactured between January 1981 and February 26, 1985, should have a label that reads "This child restraint system conforms to all applicable Federal motor vehicle safety standards." A seat manufactured after February 26, 1985, should have a second label that reads "This restraint is certified for use in motor vehicles and aircraft." There is no question that having your child in a car seat is the safest way to fly. We also understand that it is not very convenient or economical since, unless there is an unused seat on the plane, you're going to have to pay for the seat for your child— even a lap-sized child. We repeat our advice: When you book your seats, book a window seat and an aisle seat where there are three across. Unless the flight is packed, that middle seat will remain empty. For children over 2 years who require a paid seat, just take your car seat on board. If you have any problem, just ask to see a supervisor. All of these car-seat-on-airplane regulations are relatively recent, so be patient with anyone who is confused. For a free copy of *Child/Infant Safety Seats Acceptable for Use in Aircraft* you can write to Community and Consumer Liaison Division, APA-400, Federal Aviation Administration, Washington, D.C. 20591, or you can call the Federal Aviation Administration's toll-free number, 800-FAA-SURE.

## What the Airlines Have for You

We took a survey of the various domestic airlines and compiled the following rundown on each airline. We asked the public relations/marketing department of the airlines to tell us about their children's fares (be aware that they are always subject to change), any special food and beverage service they have for kids, in-flight services, and so on. Our questionnaire asked about the availability of disposable diapers and bibs, bottles, bassinets, bottle warming, special seating, advance boarding, toy or game packets, cockpit visits, changing table in the bathroom, special arrangements for nursing mothers, and airport facilities for kids. If we don't mention any of these in the airline's listing, they aren't available. Armed with the information that follows, you may well know more than your travel agent or the reservationist you speak to. If the airline you're going to fly has kids' or infants' meals, you'll of course have to order them in advance. Go one step further, too. A few days before your flight, call and make sure your special order made it into the computer. No matter whether there'll be a meal or not, take your own snacks and drinks. The kids will be hungry before anything is served.

Some airlines make special arrangements for nursing mothers; flight attendants help you find a comfortable spot. Baby bassinets can be reserved on some flights for infants up to about 20 pounds.

### Alaska Airlines

Children aged 2 to 11 pay two-thirds of the fare; anyone 12 or over is considered an adult. At press time, Alaska Airlines has a "Kids Fly Free" program in conjunction with their flights to Disneyland (Long Beach or Los Angeles). One child, aged 2 to 11, flies free for every adult who buys the package. Alaska also has special kids' meals: for breakfast, orange juice and a banana, cold cereal and milk, and blueberry crumb cake. The snack for kids is orange juice, ham and cheese sandwich, potato chips, and a cookie; for lunch and dinner, there's a hamburger, potato chips, and a cookie. Order the kids' meals 24 hours in advance. There's no infant food, but milk is always available. Parents can order a birthday cake *free* with 24 hours notice. If a seat is free, car seats can be used at no charge. You can expect disposable diapers, bottle warming service, advance boarding, a changing table in the bathroom, and a toy/game packet. Cockpit visits while the plane is on the ground can be arranged.

### American Airlines

Certain markets have children's fares that are 25 percent lower than adult fares. There's a children's menu—hamburgers, hot dogs, fried chicken, and spaghetti. Give them six hours advance notice to arrange it. Car seats must fit under the seat or in an overhead bin. Expect special seating with advance notice, bottle warming, and advance boarding. If you ask ahead, a cockpit visit is possible.

### Braniff

Kids 2 to 17 pay three-fourths the published fare. There are no kids' or infant meals available, but there is milk. Sometimes families can get special seating; they can always board early. A cockpit visit is sometimes possible, but don't plan on any sky cots (infant beds) when you fly Braniff.

### Continental Airlines

There are no kids' or infants' meals available. Special seating and advance boarding are okay, and sometimes there's a game packet. Cockpit visits may be possible. Continental has a "Young Travelers Club" for children 12 and under with "clubrooms" in Houston and Denver airports. The clubrooms, for unaccompanied minors, are stocked with television, books, and games and provide "constant adult supervision."

### Delta

Delta offers baby, toddler, and child meals. They are as follows: for baby, three jars of baby food (vegetable with meat, vegetable and fruit, oatmeal and milk); for toddlers, corn flakes with banana and milk, an orange, and toast for breakfast, and peanut butter and grape jelly sandwich with a banana and animal crackers for lunch. For older children, breakfast is corn flakes, orange, melon, and a Danish. Order the special meals when you make your reservation, but if you forget, you can ask for them up to three hours before flight time. Parents may use any FAA-approved car seat. Advance boarding is available, and children traveling with an adult (anyone 12 years or over) pay a 75 percent fare unless there's a special kids' fare at the time.

### Eastern Airlines

Children's fares are available, and promotional fares, especially to Orlando and Disney World, come and go. Special children's meals are available with eight hours advance notice. Bottle warming, special seating, and advance boarding are always offered; game packets and changing tables in the bathroom are sometimes provided.

### Midway Airlines

In some markets, Midway offers a "Family Coach Plan." Parents pay full price and half for the child. There are no children's or infants' menus. If there's an extra seat, you can use your own car seat. Bottle warming, advance boarding, and cockpit visits are all possible.

### Mid Pacific Air

There's no meal service on these Hawaiian interisland flights for anyone, but there are cookies for infants. Families can board in advance.

### New York Air

New York Air has a number of special fare arrangements for kids. Reduced fares are available for children 2 to 11—they vary according to when kids fly—one fare for weekends and another for weekdays. At press time, New York Air's family fares enable one full-paying family member to take along up to three other relatives for $39 from New York to Washington and $49 to other destinations. Bottle warming and advance boarding are available. Cockpit visits are sometimes possible.

### Northern Airlines

Some fares allow a 25 percent discount for children 2 to 11, but on round-trip, 30-day advance purchase fares there are no special children's fares. Infants are allowed one carry-on bag. Infant meals consist of strained beef or chicken, vegetable, and fruit. Children's meals are usually available: banana, orange juice, Danish, cereal and milk for breakfast; for lunch or dinner, peach and cottage cheese salad or Jell-O or a hamburger or a hot dog, potato or corn chips, cake or ice cream, and milk. Snack time brings back the peach/cottage cheese salad or Jell-O, peanut butter and jelly sandwiches, chips, the dessert of the week, and milk. Six hours' advance warning is needed. Car seats may not be used without paying for an extra seat. You can board early and have your bottle warmed; sometimes there are available disposable diapers, a bassinet, and the chance to visit the cockpit.

### Piedmont

Periodically, Piedmont offers special children's and family plan fares. The standard children's discount (ages 2 to 11) is 25 percent off the regular adult fare. The children's menu, which should be ordered 24 hours ahead, is a hot dog, baked beans, and apple sauce; infants can have baby cereal, strained fruit, and a vegetable/meat combination. There's no charge for using an FAA-approved seat for a child under 2 years as long as there's an adjacent seat available. Sometimes you'll be able to have your baby's bottle warmed or visit the cockpit, and you can always count on advance boarding with your family.

### United

Kids (2 to 11 years) are entitled to discounts. For example, on a standard coach ticket, the child's fare is 75 percent of the adult fare. Bassinets are available at bulkhead seats only. Children's meals—hot dog, hamburger, chips, peanut butter and jelly, or spaghetti and meat balls—can be arranged with at least 24 hours' notice. Bottles may be warmed and a "Fun in Flight" kit is available. Cockpit visits are possible before take-off.

### U.S. Air, Inc.

Children's fare (2 to 11 years) is 25 percent off the regular coach or discount fares. In selected markets, a special family fare is available: one adult pays full fare, other adults get a discount, and the children's fare is extended to any child 17 and under. An example at press time: Pittsburgh to Orlando: first adult pays $572 round-trip, and each additional adult and each child pays $98. Family fare is not an advanced purchase plan, so it can be used at the last minute and for one-way or round-trip travel. Children's meals are available with 24 hours' advance notice. Car seats in vacant seats are fine. Bottle warming, advance boarding, a game packet, and a cockpit visit are all possible.

## BY TRAIN

We go to Washington, D.C., every year to visit relatives, and the kids *love* the train trip. Train travel—as long as it is not for too long a distance—is great for kids. It's more of an adventure than the family car, there's enough room to move around during the trip, there are usually snacks to be had, there's a bathroom on board, and there's a lot to see out the window. The kids always seem to meet other kids on the train, too, and have fun going from seat to seat, playing with their new companions. And the fares are excellent for families. With Amtrak's Family-Plan Fare, the "head of the household" pays full fare, the spouse and children 12 to 21 years half fare, and children 2 to 11 pay 25 percent of the full fare; children under 2 years may travel free. We are all going to Washington for $156 round-trip. The Family-Plan fare applies to all trains except some Metroliners and the Florida Auto Train (the Auto Train goes from the Washington, D.C., area to Florida near Disney World three times per week) and is not valid in conjunction with other special promotional fares. (Even when Family-Plan doesn't apply, children 2 to 11 never pay more than 50 percent of the adult fare.) Amtrak dining cars have children's portions and an excellent game book called *Happy Time Fun Book* that's good for kids 3 years and older. On long-distance western trains, passengers get route guides with a map and description of what they're going to pass. These trains also have movies and games in the lounge car. The Chicago–San Francisco–Oakland, California *Zephyr,* the Chicago–Los Angeles *Southwest Chief,* the Chicago–Seattle–Portland *Empire Builder,* and the Seattle–Los Angeles *Coast Starlight* also feature Sightseer Lounge cars with picture windows from floor to ceiling. For information on any of Amtrak's trains or services, call 800-USA-RAIL; ask them to send you a National Train Timetable.

And, if you really want to know about exploring the United States by train, we recommend William G. Scheller's *Train Trips,* published by East Woods Press, 429 East Boulevard, Charlotte, North Carolina 28203. The book costs $9.95 and includes a listing of passenger trains, a rundown on equipment, and a route-by-route guide. Scheller is crazy about trains. We quote him: "The real delight of a train trip lies in its peculiar combination of motion and stasis: you know that you are moving, that you are headed somewhere, but you are also living . . . in a separate, self-contained world in which time may as well have stopped."

Another book by and for train aficionados is Ira Fistell's *America by Train* ($8.95), published by Burt Franklin, 235 East 44th Street, New York, New York 10017.

## BY BUS

We don't think buses are a great way to travel with kids. They are cramped, and kids can't really walk up and down the aisle for exercise. For short trips, when there's no other alternative, the bus experience will be improved if you're sure to pack food and take games, toys, and a tape recorder/radio for the kids. They'll have to sit near the window for good radio reception. Bus fares are generally inexpensive: children 5 to 11 pay half fare, and one child under 5 years can travel free for each fare-paying adult.

Once more, we refer you to Chapter 3 for details on what to take with you on your trip, whether you go by car, plane, train, or bus.

---

### ABOUT OUR LISTINGS:

The properties we list in this book all welcome kids and all willingly responded to our many, many questions. We're relying on you, our readers, to let us know about your own experiences with our choices—good and bad—and to tell us about any new places we can list in the next edition.

### ONE MORE REMINDER:

If you're looking for a place to play tennis, check the tennis and golf chapter but don't overlook Chapter 8 on resorts, Chapter 10 on skiing (many ski resorts turn into tennis and golf spots once the snow melts), and Chapter 11 on farms and dude ranches.

And don't forget the None of the Above listings beginning on page 289.

NOTE: Rates quoted here were accurate at press time but are subject to change.

NOTE: Be sure to check pages 297–99 for a list of publishers' addresses. Some books published by smaller publishers may not be readily available in bookstores but can be ordered directly from the publisher.

Send us your cards and letters. We want to hear from you about your great vacation choices so that we can include them in the next edition.

# 3

---

# WHAT TO TAKE

Although the particulars of what to take with you vary with the age of your children, the place you're going, and the way you plan to get there, the basics remain the same. Try not to overload yourself with unnecessary equipment, but don't forget the essentials: a portable crib may not be absolutely necessary, but a stroller will be. Think about the pieces of equipment you use each day—baby food grinder, for example—and take whatever will make your travels easier. And, unless you're heading into the wilderness, you will probably be able to rent, buy, or borrow whatever you need wherever you are going.

The basic rules for choosing clothes to take along is simple enough: take clothes that are comfortable, sturdy, and dark-colored with tops and bottoms that can easily be mixed and matched. Keep in mind that polyester and cotton shirts dry a lot faster than pure cotton, and forget about taking anything along that you love and your child doesn't. You don't want arguments about clothes while you're on vacation.

One suggestion from a friend seems particularly clever: pack a "nighttime bag" with pajamas, toothbrushes, toothpaste, favorite toys, and favorite blanket and put it all on top of the suitcase so that when you arrive at a place, you don't have to go through the entire bag looking for the night things. Always take rain gear, too, unless you're desert-bound. We spent three very soggy days in Vermont in June with no boots, no raincoats, and no umbrellas. It was *miserable*.

## A Word About Health

We advise taking along a basic first aid kit. Unless you have some valid reason to worry about your child's health, don't. Again, unless you're going deep into the wilderness, there will always be medical help nearby. If it will make you feel more relaxed, call ahead to wherever you are going and check out medical facilities or ask your pediatrician to recommend someone who practices in the place you're going.

Our multipurpose first aid kit contains the following:

- Band-Aids
- gauze pads and tape
- antiseptic cream (something like Neosporin or Bacitracin)
- thermometer and Vaseline
- vitamins
- children's acetaminophen
- insect repellent
- needle and tweezers for splinter or tick removal and matches for sterilizing
- sunscreen
- first aid book

Be sure to have your medical/hospital insurance card with you, and if it will make you feel more secure, a copy of your favorite baby care book.

## For Infants

If your child is 2 or under, here's a checklist of things to bring along:

- disposable diapers
- some kind of baby wipes
- diaper rash ointment or cream
- pacifier (and plenty of spares if your child is addicted)
- food
- formula or juice and lots of extra bottles and nipples
- bibs
- blanket

- waterproof sheet (we've always preferred a small plastic tablecloth to double as a changing "table" and at night, as a mattress protector)
- some plastic bags for dirty laundry

## Some Things You May Not Have Considered

Through the years, we've found that there are a few things that we wished we had had, but didn't, so we pass the list on to you:

- a can opener
- a jackknife (one of our kids wears braces and needs apples, bagels, and other snacks cut up)
- flashlight with batteries
- sewing kit (all this has to be is one spool of black thread, one of white, a few needles, and a few safety pins)
- plastic bags in various sizes that close tight for toothbrushes, bits of wet soap, wet bathing suits and towels, sandy beach shoes

## TOYS AND GAMES: WHAT TO TAKE AND WHERE TO PUT IT

Probably the most important point to remember about getting together toys, games, and assorted travel equipment is that your kids should be the ones who ultimately decide what goes. When you travel, your children have very little control over what they're going to see, what they'll do, where they'll sleep, and where they'll eat. This uncertainty can unnerve them. Children like structure, and when they travel, structure all but disappears. Giving them control over what toys and games they'll take with them will be a great comfort to them.

Several days before you leave (*please* don't wait for the last minute), have the kids choose a container for their goodies; a backpack is one of the best choices. Follow one simple rule—if you can carry it, you can take it. One friend has her kids carry their packed bags around their backyard for ten minutes, just long enough for them to see whether they can manage them. When they go back into the house they invariably eliminate a few things.

Although the kids should choose their own toys and games, you are still in a good position to lobby for some of the things that you know will keep them busy and happy. You want them to take toys that will serve more than one purpose, toys and games that they can play with by themselves, as well as some that require your participation. Encourage your kids to avoid games with small bits and pieces; they'll only get lost or roll under the seat. Have them take some new toys and some old favorites, too. Younger children should have a stuffed animal and a blanket, for sure. Even if your child doesn't seem particularly attached to any one blanket or teddy the time will come when he or she will need the comfort of a familiar object. Trust us on this one.

With our own experience in mind and after talking to friends who travel a great deal with their families, we've come up with the following "recommended" list. Pick what seems best from it, taking into account, of course, your children's individual interests:

### Magic Markers

Make sure magic markers are washable; if they come in a box, transfer them immediately into a plastic bag with a zipper or a box with a tight-fitting lid. The original containers are guaranteed to disintegrate in the course of the trip. When our youngest was still in a car seat, we put the markers in a drawstring bag and tied the bag to the car seat so that she'd be able to get them easily.

### Spiral Notebook

A spiral notebook will serve many purposes. It can be a travel diary for an older child, a drawing pad for any age, a scrapbook for the collecting types, and a workbook for others. One friend buys her kids hardcover artist's sketch books, different sizes for different ages. The hard cover serves as a good lap tray and prevents it from being mashed on the floor of the car. A clipboard is another good choice. A travel editor friend of ours makes a few match-up games for her 3-year-old in a notebook. Even very young children can draw a line between two apples or two chairs, and doing it makes them feel very grown up.

### Glue Stick or Tube

What a wonderful invention the glue stick is—perfect for collages and scrapbooks as you go.

### Geometric Plastic "Snake"

Some kids love geometric snakes—there are no pieces to lose, and they can play for a long, long time creating new shapes.

### Cards

Take a regular deck of cards and/or any of the special card games such as Fish or Crazy Eights.

### Books

Books are a must (paperbacks preferred), no matter what the age of your child. Take some new ones and some old favorites. Take some that the kids can read themselves and some that you can read to them. (A collection of fairy tales is a good idea.)

### Tape Recorder

A tape recorder runs a close tie with books as the greatest boon to travel with children. Think of the possibilities: you can take tapes with the kids' favorite stories on them or with stories they've never heard before. Song tapes (Wee Sing is the brand name of a series of 60-minute tapes that include "Nursery Rhymes and Lullabies," "Children's Songs and Finger Plays," "Silly Songs," and "Around the Campfire"; lyrics are included and each costs $7.95) and tapes of Broadway shows ("My Fair Lady" and "Annie" took one family we know from Alsace–Lorraine all the way to Paris) are great entertainment during trips. Two excellent tapes meant especially for use with kids while traveling are "Traffic Jams" and "Imagination." The first is a collection of songs for the car written and performed by Joe Scruggs. We all loved listening to the tape; the musical arrangements are terrific, real toe-tapping stuff. Copies are available from Educational Graphics, P.O. Box 180476, Austin, Texas 78718, 512-251-9620. Two other tapes by the same people, although not specifically for travel, "Late Last Night" and "Abracadabra," also deserve our highest recommendation. All three tapes cost $9.95 each plus $1.25 for postage and handling. "Imagination" is the creation of Lulu and Shelly Richardson; it is a 40-minute tape with background music and sound effects—of what the creators call "interactions and travel games." "Imagination" is meant to be used by kids and adults together. The Richardsons think that 5- and 6-year-olds can enjoy the tape as long as there are older brothers and sisters participating. Otherwise, kids should be about 7 years old. The Richardsons have also put together a travel tape called "Christmas" that is especially designed to use en route at holiday time. "Imagination" ($9.95) and "Christmas" ($7.95) are available from Family Travel Tapes, 9220 A-1 Parkway East, Suite 125, Birmingham, Alabama 35206, 205-836-0638. Add $1 for one tape, $1.50 for two for postage and handling.

Another independent producer, Golden Glow Recordings, offers two tapes that are nice for travel, although not specifically for trips. The two tapes are "Nitey-Nite," which helps put kids to sleep with lullabies accompanied by harp, guitar, recorder, flute, and keyboard, and "Good Morning Sunshine," with a side that helps wake kids up gently and another that is more up-tempo for the "wide-awake and raring-to-go." These tapes are $8.95 each and are available from Golden Glow at 317 Pleasant Street, Yellow Springs, Ohio 45387.

And finally for tapes of children's stories, usually two to two and one-half hours long, we recommend the catalog of Listen for Pleasure, One Columbia Drive, Niagara Falls, New York 14305. Tapes cost $13.95 each plus $1 postage, and the selection includes lots of favorites such as *Grimm's Fairy Tales, Little Women, Black Beauty,* and *The Secret Garden.*

Take blank tapes, too, so that the kids can be creative. Have them interview each other, the flight attendants, the people sitting next to them on the plane. One friend turned what might have been a boring visit to a sculpture show into a real adventure for her two boys by letting them tape a running commentary on what they saw as they went around the exhibit. Or try a sightseeing tape; it will bring back the whole trip when you play it a few months later.

It's best to let each kid have his or her own tape recorder, ear plugs, and microphone to avoid conflicts. Take extra batteries, too.

### Hand-held Video Games
Video games are great for passing time. Our kids like to trade with other kids on the plane.

### Workbooks
There are lots of good activity books on the market. A few are reviewed here. If the place you're going to has a related coloring book or workbook (for instance, a coloring book of colonial Williamsburg), it would be great to get it ahead of time. Local tourist offices should be able to tell you what's available.

### Action Figures
The category of action figures includes a variety of crea-

tures—GI Joe's, He-Men, Barbie dolls, and My Little Pony, to name a few. Kids can stay happy and busy for hours making up adventures for their plastic friends.

### Puppets
Even the youngest child can have fun with puppets, and they can substitute for stuffed animals.

### Magnetic Letters and Numbers
Taking magnetic alphabet and numbers breaks the rule about small pieces, but some kids may really enjoy taking these along. A cookie sheet makes a good stick-on surface.

### Press-on Games
Colorforms makes kits that are widely available, but we much prefer the kind made in Denmark by Uniset and distributed in the United States by International Playthings, Inc., Bloomfield, New Jersey 07003. Colorforms are more like commercials than toys, but Uniset makes an airport stick-on set, a construction site, a doll's house, dinosaurs, and a map of the United States (unfortunately, the map is a little too big for lap play).

### Lego or Bristle Blocks
These are another exception to the bits and pieces rule, but these toys are excellent for even the youngest children. If you're going to be traveling in Europe, buy your Lego as you travel. By the end of your trip you'll have a wonderful collection for much less than it would ever cost at home.

### Active Toys
If you're traveling by car, don't forget to pack a few things for the rest stops to get the kids moving. Consider an inflatable beach ball, bat and mitt, a jump rope, or, for the littlest ones, a bottle of bubbles to blow and to chase.

### Surprise Package
Hide a "surprise" or "crisis" bag somewhere in your hand luggage, something to pull out when the going gets rough. It should be wrapped—comic papers make a good wrapping—and should have some minitreats in it: maybe some candy, a hand-held game,

a new book, stickers, or a story tape. Consider picking up something at a tag sale to put into the surprise bag, all that matters is that it's new to your kids.

It's a good idea, too, to tell the kids that you'll buy them something new at the airport or bus or train station. We like those booklets with the invisible ink pens. Or have the children buy some postcards to write en route. They can even cut them up to make puzzles for their friends that can be mailed in an envelope.

Here let's take a very subjective look at some specific take-along toys, games, and books.

One company that puts out an excellent catalog of toys and games, "Toys to Grow On," reserves a page for toys especially suited for travel: a Miles of Smiles Travel Box with games, cards, activity books, and so forth ($12.95), and "The World's Greatest Travel Game" ($14.95), which consists of 25 six-sided cubes. It has instructions for seven game variations and is suitable for kids as young as 3 years. Send for a Toys to Grow On catalog from 2695 East Dominguez Street, P.O. Box 6261, Carson, California 90749, 213-537-8600.

### Mad Libs

Our whole family loves "Mad Libs." It's a fill-in-the-blank game published by Price/Stern/Sloan and costs about $2 per pad. The pad is filled with stories with missing words; players supply the words, and the result is a convoluted, usually very amusing tale. My youngest has been able to play since she was 3 years old, although it's most fun for older kids.

### Travel Yahtzee, Travel Connect Four, Travel Battleship, Travel Mastermind, Travel Shut-the-Box

All of the games listed are good for kids; most of the ones we talked to, though, thought Travel Scrabble was a drag.

### Are We There Yet?

The *Are We There Yet?* activity book put together by Rand McNally ($2.95) claims to be for all ages, but we'd recommend it for ages 6 and up. Rand McNally also packages a travel kit with *Are We There Yet?*, another coloring-activity book, crayons, a tape, and matching song sheet of "Songs for the Car." All of this is packed in a plastic tote bag and priced at $9.95.

### The Kids Book of Games for Cars, Trains and Planes
The *Kids Book,* by Rudi McToots, published by Bantam Books ($4.95), has 160 suggestions for keeping children amused. It's a clever book with lots of workable ideas clearly explained.

#### Creative Kits
Two women in St. Louis, Peggy Umansky and Joan Present, have made a business of assembling kits for special occasions. Their travel kit contains workbook and crayons, arts and crafts materials, laminated sheets for coloring, and a toy. Meant for kids aged 3 to 6, the kits cost $6.95 and can be ordered from P.O. Box 27603, St. Louis, Missouri 63146. If your child has a special learning problem or interest in a particular subject, Peggy and Joan can individualize kits.

#### Sealed with a Kiss
Julie Winston handpicks the items she puts in her travel-toy collection, called "Sealed with A Kiss." We ordered one with ten items, all individually wrapped, and our kids were kept busy for hours. The charge is $25. Write to her at 6709 Tildenwood Lane, Rockville, Maryland 20852.

### My Holiday Away Scrapbook: A Souvenir for Me to Keep
*My Holiday Away Scrapbook*, a booklet published in Great Britain by Longman, is written by two good friends of ours, Herb Mack and Ann Cook, which is not widely available here but should be. It's a kind of personal diary that helps kids keep track of their trip, think about what they're seeing and what they've done, and, when completed, serves as a very personalized record of their adventure. It includes graphs to make, travel games, a record of how money was spent, a food log, a place to record the best and worst things about the trip, and more. The illustrations are delightful, and the idea is a terrific one. Copies are available for $2.50 in the United States through Eeyore's Books for Children, 2212 Broadway, New York, New York 10024.

### Best Travel Activity Book Ever
Despite a bit of hyperbole by the publishers, Rand McNally's

*Best Travel Activity Book Ever* is thick—320 pages—and would be best for kids 4 to 6 to use with the help of an older brother or sister or parent ($6.95).

### Games to Play in the Car

Written by Michael Harwood and distributed in the United States by St. Martin's Press ($6.95), *Games to Play* is a little book that has some old and some new, all quite playable games for car rides. The suggestions for games for little ones are especially useful.

### Questron Books

Random House publishes 24 *Questron* workbooks that are sold with an electronic wand. The books teach reading and number skills; the wand signals right and wrong loudly enough for the kids to hear but not loudly enough to bother anyone around them.

## Games People Play

There are many games to play as you go that require no equipment whatsoever. Some are classics—"20 questions," "G-H-O-S-T," "Geography"—your kids will like playing them as much as you did when you were their age. Here are a few that may be new to you:

### Alphabet Sentences

Make up sentences with at least five words that begin with the same letter, more words per sentence for older kids.

### How Many Bridges?

Kids guess how may bridges you'll cross between two points, how many hills you'll climb, how many haystacks or horses or billboards you see. A certain number of points is given for the best guess, and points can add up to an ice cream cone or sticker reward.

### Memory Game

The first person says, "I'm going on a trip and packing a toothbrush." The second repeats the sentence and adds an item, and on and on, until someone forgets.

### Alphabet Game

We compete with each other to find each letter in the alphabet, in sequence, on road signs, license plates, and billboards: only one letter per sign per person. The first to finish the alphabet is the winner.

### Similes

You can slip a little poetry by the kids without their knowing it. Have them finish sentences like "rain sounds like . . ." "tears taste like. . . ." For older kids, get more abstract with "anger feels like . . ." "joy feels like. . . ."

### Navigator

The kids take turns being the navigator. One friend gives the navigator a special hat, a map, and special privileges. It's the navigator's job to follow the route on the map, estimate when the next exit will occur, figure a good spot for lunch, and answer the question "When are we going to be there?"

### String-along Story

One person starts the story, then stops after about ten sentences, and the next person adds a piece. You may want to tape record the tale to play later.

### The (World's First Ever) Pop-Up Games Book

By pop-up book superstar Ron van der Meer, it's great for train and plane trips. It's not a book, or a game, but both. Almost any age can play, but some simple math and reading skills make it even more fun to play without the help of parents. Published by Delacorte Press, the book is $9.95.

### Just Plain Singing

It's fun to just sing together. Let everyone have a chance to choose a song! Try a round or some harmony.

### Toy Libraries

Years ago we walked into the children's room of a library along the Connecticut shore and saw a bookcase filled with fabulous toys, puzzles, and games that were there to be borrowed like books. We couldn't believe our good luck, and the kids were thrilled. We've since discovered that there is an association of toy libraries called, appropriately enough, the U.S. Toy Library Association. They publish a directory of toy libraries in the United States; it costs $5 and is available from the Association's headquarters, 1800 Pickwick Avenue, Glenview, Illinois 60025-1377.

# 4

# WHERE TO STAY

When it comes to choosing a place to stay with your kids, there are lots of variables to consider, variables that you may never have thought about when you were traveling alone. For example, when you're traveling by yourself, it rarely matters whether the room you stay in has a bathtub or just a shower. But if you're traveling with a 3-year-old who is used to a bath and who has never taken a shower, the absence of a bathtub can be a real issue.

Because kids feel most secure when they can sleep in the same bed every night, if at all possible, try to arrange to stay in one place and travel from there. If that's not possible, do what you can to make them secure in their new surroundings by taking their own portable crib or at least by setting up a corner of the room just for them.

Some questions you should ask when choosing a place to stay are the following:

- How much space do you need? If you're accustomed to having a lot of space, don't cram yourself into a tiny room for your vacation. One room for a family of four is okay for a night or two, but for anything longer, consider two rooms or find a hotel with suites or rent a condo or an apartment. If budget is a problem, think about cutting a day or two off your vacation for the sake of more space; it really may be worth it. If you want two rooms in a hotel where kids stay free, try to book two singles. You may well save 25 to 40 percent over the cost of two doubles.

- What amenities do you want? If you're staying in a hotel, look for one that has a swimming pool, a nearby playground, a game room—a place where your kids can get rid of some of their excess energy. Indoor pools are wonderful in winter. Ask whether the hotel or motel will help find a baby-sitter. Many do. And find out whether room service is possible. We love to order breakfast from room service—two large breakfasts are usually plenty for a family with two small children—and then take our time to eat and plan our day. Find out whether there's a refrigerator in the room. Being able to store juice and milk and to make your own breakfast will save you quite a bit of money.

- What's the best location for your room? If you're in a motel, ask for the first floor. Ideally, the kids should be able to step outside to play where you can see them. Avoid rooms with balconies. We try to limit the number of required no's and don't's on a vacation; to that end we avoid stairs and try to get rooms at the ends of halls or near the soda or ice machine, where the kids don't have to be quite so restricted about making noise.

- Are there bathtubs or only showers? This is worth repeating. Vacation is no time to introduce little ones to a shower. If a room without a bath is unavoidable, try to make your child comfortable with showers before you leave for vacation.

- Are there restaurant facilities for kids? Determine whether there are high chairs or booster seats available in the restaurant of the hotel or motel. Even if you carry your own booster seat or one of those great collapsible infant chairs that attach to any table, ask about the availability of high chairs. Whether or not the restaurant supplies high chairs will give you a good idea of just how eager they really are to have kids there.

- Are there laundry facilities? It's great to have access to a washing machine and dryer, not just for getting clothes clean, but also for drying them after getting caught in the rain.

- Is the place you are considering near where you're going to sightsee? If you're going to be in a city and plan to do a lot of sightseeing, it's nice to stay at a well-located hotel. The extra money you may pay for a room may be what you save in transportation to and from another hotel.
- Are there special rates for kids? Most accommodations have special rates for children; most often kids can stay in a parent's room at no extra cost. Always ask about family plans or, in cities, about special weekend rates.
- Is there a children's program? More and more resort hotels are offering children's programming to their guests. We're delighted by this. We feel that even if you have no intention of taking advantage of the program— if your child is too young or you insist on complete family togetherness every minute of the day—you should still seek out accommodations with children's programs. The reason: if there's a children's program there are bound to be other kids, and one of the nicest parts of a vacation for kids is meeting new friends.

## A Very Special Word About Children's Programs

We have a very definite philosophy about children's programs. It can best be introduced by quoting from a letter we received in response to a questionnaire we sent to a couple who run a dude ranch in the Ozarks:

Your questionnaire asks for activities for the children. It concerned me that if you are writing a book about "Great Vacations with Your Kids," why in the world would you be so concerned about activities where the child would be supervised by someone other than the parent? We try to set up an atmosphere where parent and child can relate to each other. Granted our parents love the idea that the kids can go on a supervised trail ride and they don't have to go every time, but that is not the intent and purpose of the vacation. Yes, they love to be able to have a person to watch their toddler for a few hours while they canoe, go shopping or just lie in the sun, but that isn't the main point of the trip! Familes that come here, especially if they are from metropolitan areas, usually take three days to just unwind! If the kids are teenagers, in those three days they go from nagging, complaining "nothing to do" syndrome creeps, to real people! It is truly astounding! The parents who have spent more money than time with their children find out who their kids really are.

As soon as we read the letter, we wrote back explaining that we agree completely. Children's programs are not meant to be places where parents "dump" their kids. They should be places where kids can go to have fun with other kids, where they can do things they enjoy alongside their peers. That doesn't mean a full day away from their parents—maybe just an hour or two at a time is all you want. The author of the letter says herself that parents like the idea of having the kids go off on a supervised trail ride. That's the kind of thing we like, too. It's great to have a choice, to have the option of a supervised children's activity.

Besides being fun for the kids, a good children's program, we feel, is safer than a private baby-sitter, especially on a beach holiday. Also, in the case of an emergency, there is additional staff to turn to. Other advantages of places with children's programs is that these places are most likely to have ideas about family activities in the area.

## Hotels

In our city section (Chapter 7) we have some specific hotel suggestions and then, further on, in the very end of the book, Appendix 1 suggests some hotels. We've listed the hotels because they welcome children and, in some cases, because they have children's programs. If you are looking for a hotel on your own, you can certainly contact the tourist office of the place you're going, you can leave it to your travel agent, or you can consult a good guidebook that features accommodations. We list some of the best at the end of this chapter. When choosing the hotel, keep in mind the criteria we have already noted. And try to get to wherever you're going to stay by 5:00 P.M. so that there'll be a chance to acclimate the kids long enough before bedtime. Also, once you've arrived at the hotel of your choice, here are some simple things to do to prevent your kids from going crazy with boredom while they wait for you to check in. Have something in your bag that they haven't seen yet for them to do while they wait. Or let them sit down with some hotel brochures and circle what they want to see. If your kids are old enough, let them explore the lobby, but tell them to be sure that wherever they go, they can still see you.

As soon as you've checked in, take a walk around the hotel with the kids, teach them how to call the operator themselves, and choose a meeting place to use in case you get separated. If it's a large hotel, go to the room then back to the lobby, and then ask the kids whether they can lead the way back to the room. The more comfortable the kids feel with their surroundings, the easier bedtime will be.

## ALL-SUITE HOTELS

There's something new happening in the hotel industry—the all-suite hotels—and they're great for traveling families. Although they were originally designed to attract business travelers, they've got what families need: extra space. Most of these all-suite hotels feature a separate bedroom or even two bedrooms, a living room, a dining area, and, almost always, a completely equipped kitchen, all for the cost of a standard hotel room. The price is usually calculated per suite, and weekend specials are common. Also, because these new accommodations have been well received, new ones are appearing all the time and competition is keen. That is all the better for us since the competition forces the hotels to offer more and more amenities: free breakfasts and local newspapers, prestocked refrigerators, and help in finding baby-sitters. Here we list some of the larger all-suite chains, with a short profile of each one. For more information on each—directories, rates, reservations, and so on—just call the toll-free numbers listed.

### Aston Hotels and Resorts
2255 Kuhio Avenue
Honolulu, Hawaii 96815-2658
Telephone: 800-367-5124

Formerly the Hotel Corporation of the Pacific, this group of 24 hotels in California and Hawaii offers a choice from studios to three-bedroom villas. Children under 18 are free, the charge for a crib is $10. Each suite has a full kitchen, and high chairs and booster seats can be arranged through the concierge. Some properties have market facilities, and most have children's camps that run through the summer for children aged 5 to 12. Activities include sand sculpture, making shell jewelry, scuba lessons, Hawaiiana classes, and snorkeling. A sample rate: an oceanfront two-bedroom, two-bath suite at the Sands of Kahana costs $165 per day for one to four guests.

**Beacon Hospitality Group**
One Post Office Square
Boston, Massachusetts 02109
Telephone: 800-EMBASSY or 800-424-2900

This corporation has bought what was formerly the Guest Quarters hotel chain and owns and operates three of the Embassy Suites hotels. Their Embassy properties are franchised and include one all-suite hotel in Boston and two in Pennsylvania. These hotels have one- and two-bedroom suites with family rates available. A complimentary full American breakfast is included in the overnight rate, and each of the properties has an indoor pool, a whirlpool, and a game room. Baby-sitting can be arranged when reservations are made.

Beacon's Guest Quarters properties number nine, all in cities, and include one- and two-bedroom suites with family rates available. The suites have complete kitchens, booster seats, a shopping service to stock the refrigerator, and room service; all but two of the properties have restaurants as well. All have outdoor pools, and VCRs can be rented; game cartridges are stocked by the hotels. Laundry can be done for you or you can do it yourself, and baby-sitting is usually possible with 24-hour notice.

**Embassy Suites**
Xerox Centre
Suite 1700
222 Las Colinas Boulevard
Irving, Texas 75039
Telephone: 800-EMBASSY

This is the largest all-suite system in the United States and includes what used to be the properties of the Granada Royale chain. There are 65 hotels now, with 200 planned by 1990. This company is ambitious. Suites are one- and two-bedroom, including a living room with a sofa and armchair, a dining/work area, a color television, refrigerator, wet bar, and in some places, ice makers, microwave ovens, or ranges. Included in the nightly rate, which averages about $75, is a complimentary full breakfast with eggs, pancakes, sausages, hash browns, cereals, juices, pastries, tea, or coffee. Guests are treated to complimentary cocktails each evening, too, if local laws allow. Breakfasts and drinks are served in the central atrium, a courtyard with ponds, pools, and tropical plants. All Embassy Suites have maid service, and the choice of laundry service or self-service laundry. Baby-sitting can be arranged; sometimes advance notice is required. We thought you'd like to know, too, that Embassy received a very high rating recently from *Consumer Reports*.

### Paradise Management
Kukui Plaza C-207
50 South Beretania Street
Honolulu, Hawaii 96813
Telephone: 800-367-5205

Another Hawaiian-based company, Paradise Management has 168 properties available ranging from condos to hotel suites to apartments to homes. Accommodations range from studio-size to three-bedroom, and there's no charge for children staying with parents; cribs are available for $6 per day. Most properties have outside pools, children's pools, and jungle gyms; some even have a children's playground. Baby-sitting can be arranged.

### Pickett Hotel Company
555 Metro Place North
Dublin, Ohio 43017
Telephone: 800-PICKETT

At present there are Pickett properties in Ohio, Georgia, Florida (one in Walt Disney World), and North Carolina. Suites have one or two bedrooms, and rates are reasonable—children 17 and younger stay free with their parents. Cribs cost $15 extra. Each suite has a refrigerator stocked with juices, soft drinks, mixes, and snacks; a wet bar and dining table, and a microwave oven on request. Built-in hair dryers, a coffee maker, garment steamers, bathrobes, and three televisions (one in the bathroom!) are also included. There's a complimentary full breakfast served every day. Baby-sitting can be arranged, and you can either do your own laundry or have it done for you. Properties have outdoor pools and whirlpools, and there's a children's playground at the Walt Disney World Resort.

### Potomac Hotel Group
1901 North Fort Myer Drive, Suite 400
Arlington, Virginia 22209
Telephone: 800-468-3532

The Potomac people have 13 properties in the area surrounding Washington, D.C. They offer studios on up to two-bedroom suites. Cribs are available at no charge, and children under 18 stay free in a room with parents. The properties feature kitchens, restaurant facilities, room service, high chairs, and booster seats. At four of the properties there are outdoor pools; at three the pool is indoors. Baby-sitting can be arranged; just let them know what you need when you make your reservations.

### The Residence Inn Company
257 North Broadway
Wichita, Kansas 67202
Telephone: 800-331-3131

By the time this book appears, Residence Inn plans to have 115 properties; some are in cities; most are in suburban areas; and they cover 30 states in all. The Residence Inns are very deliberately designed to remind you of a quiet, residential neighborhood. One- and two-bedroom suites are available, and all have a separate living room area. Suites have kitchens, and a shopping service to stock the refrigerator is available. All include a complimentary "hospitality hour" and a free breakfast of rolls and pastries, cereal, juice, milk, tea, and coffee and a free local newspaper. Practically all of the properties have an outdoor pool, a whirlpool, and a "Sport-Court," and they have a lounge. Other nice features are wood-burning fireplaces in most suites and reduced rates for extended stays (anything over a week is reduced about 20 percent); baby-sitting can be arranged, and there's free popcorn for everyone who checks in.

## BUDGET MOTELS

On the basis of the logical premise that travelers were getting tired of paying high prices for motel rooms, a few entrepreneurs dreamed up the idea of the no-frills motel. All the basic amenities—air-conditioning, television, even swimming pools—still remain, but often the coffee shop is across the street or there's no wall-to-wall carpeting on the floor. The budget motel phenomenon has spread, and now there are lots of low-cost facilities all across the United States. For a listing of what's available, state by state, you may want to send for a copy of Pilot Books' *National Directory of Budget Motels,* which lists over 2,200 such facilities. The book costs $4.95 and may be ordered from the publisher at 103 Cooper Street, Babylon, New York 11702.

You can also call any of the following 800 numbers and ask for a free directory of the chain's properties. Rates of the various low-cost motels vary from chain to chain, often even from motel to motel within a chain, but, in general, the more people you fit into one room, the more money you'll save. Following is a list of some of this country's budget motel chains. Call for reservations or for a directory. Whenever there's a special children's discount, we note it here.

### Allstar Inns, Inc.
2020 De La Vina
P.O. Box 3070
Santa Barbara, California 93130-3070
Telephone: 805-687-3383
Locations: Arizona, California, Idaho, Nevada, New Mexico, Oregon, Texas, and Washington.

### Budget Host Inns
2601 Jacksboro Highway
Caravan Suite 202
P.O. Box 10656
Fort Worth, Texas 76114
Telephone: 800-835-7427
Locations: In 31 states
For kids: All motels have cribs, charges range from $2 to $5 per night.

**Chalet Suisse International, Inc.**
Chalet Drive
Wilton, New Hampshire 03086-0657
Telephone: 800-258-1980 (in New Hampshire, 800-572-1880)
Locations: In nine states, primarily eastern
For kids: Baby-sitting service.

**Days Inns of America, Inc.**
2751 Buford Highway, N.E.
Atlanta, Georgia 30324
Telephone: 800-325-2525
Locations: In 44 states and the District of Columbia
For kids: Often children are free with an adult; some motels have
    "Kids Eat Free" plan (a free meal for every child under 12
    accompanied by an adult, for instance).

**Econo Lodges of America, Inc.**
6135 Park Road, Suite 200
Charlotte, North Carolina 28210-9981
Telephone: 800-446-6900
Locations: In 43 states
For kids: Kids under 12 are free; cribs are free.

**Excel Inns of America**
4706 East Washington Avenue
Madison, Wisconsin 53704
Telephone: 800-356-8013 (in Wisconsin, 800-362-5478)
Locations: In Texas, Iowa, Minnesota, Michigan, Illinois, and
    South Dakota
For kids: Free under 12 years and no charge for cribs.

**E-Z 8 Motels**
2484 Hotel Circle Place
San Diego, California 92108

Telephone: 619-291-4824 (Reservations must be made with
   individual motels, no central number.)
Locations: In California, Nevada, and Arizona
For kids: Cribs are available.


**Friendship Inns International, Inc.**
2627 Paterson Plank Road
North Bergen, New Jersey 07047
Telephone: 800-453-4511
Locations: In 34 states and Canada
For kids: The policy for children's rates varies from place to place
   because each inn is individually owned.


**Hampton Inns**
6799 Great Oaks Road, Suite 100
Memphis, Tennessee 38138
Telephone: 800-HAMPTON
Locations: In 29 states
For kids: Under 18, stay free; free continental breakfast and
   in-room movies.
Note: This chain is the budget arm of Holiday Inns and is
   expanding rapidly.


**Hospitality International (Scottish, Red Carpet, and
Master Hosts Inns)**
1152 Spring Street, Suite A
Atlanta, Georgia 30309
Telephone: 800-251-1962
Locations: Southeastern states


**Imperial 400 National, Inc.**
1000 Wilson Boulevard, Suite 820
Arlington, Virginia 22209
Telephone: 800-368-4400 (in Virginia, 800-572-2200)
Locations: In 40 states

**La Quinta**
La Quinta Plaza
P.O. Box 790064
San Antonio, Texas 78279
Telephone: 800-531-5900
Locations: In 29 states
For kids: Usually no charge for kids 18 and under in parents'
room.
Note: This chain received the highest budget rating in *Consumer
Reports'* study of budget hotel chains.

**Motel 6, Inc.**
51 Hitchcock Way
Santa Barbara, California 93105
Telephone: 805-682-6666
Locations: In 42 states, most in California

**Quality International**
10750 Columbia Pike
Silver Spring, Maryland 20901
This is the umbrella company for Quality Inns 800-228-5151 and
Comfort Inns 800-228-5150
Locations: All over the United States
For kids: Children under 16 stay free in parents' room.

**Red Roof Inns, Inc.**
4355 Davidson Road
Hilliard, Ohio 43026-9699
Telephone: 800-848-7878
Locations: In 30 states
For kids: Free cribs and free in-room service.
Note: This chain recently received a very favorable rating from
*Consumer Reports.*

**Regal 8 Inns**
P.O. Box 1268
Mount Vernon, Illinois 62864
Telephone: 800-851-8888
Locations: In 22 states
For kids: All have indoor or outdoor pools.


**TraveLodge/Viscount Hotels**
Corporate Headquarters
1973 Friendship Drive
El Cajon, California 92090
Telephone: 800-255-3050


**Thrifty Scot Motels, Inc.**
One Sunwood Drive
P.O. Box 399
St. Cloud, Minnesota 56302
Telephone: 800-258-1980; in Nebraska and Canada, call collect:
    402-493-0333.


**Vagabond Inns**
Box 85011
San Diego, California 92138
Telephone: 800-522-1555
Locations: In California, Nevada, and Arizona
For kids: Kids 18 or younger stay free in their parents' room. A
    roll-away bed or crib is provided, when available, at no extra
    charge.

## HOME EXCHANGES AND RENTALS

Exchanges and rentals are a possibility to consider well in advance of your trip because arranging a house, apartment, or condo swap or a rental is a lot more complex than just reserving a hotel room. But think of the advantages: you'll have your own base of operations with all the comforts of home, or even more comforts in some cases. Exchanging homes means you'll certainly save money; all you pay for is transportation. If you rent, you may also save, compared to the cost of a hotel room.

Home exchanging means trading your home, your vacation home, boat, or recreational vehicle with another family. It requires research and energy, but it can be a wonderful option. We have found two books on the subject. The first, *Home Exchanging: A Complete Sourcebook for Travelers at Home or Abroad,* by James Dearing covers the generalities, gives lots of advice, and includes an appendix listing agencies and newspapers good for advertising a swap. Copies are available for $9.95 from the publisher, East Woods Press, 429 East Boulevard, Charlotte, North Carolina 28203. The second is a more homespun approach to the subject, written by Cindy Gum, a Georgian who has exchanged her homes with families in Brussels, Miami, Copenhagen, and Alexandria, Virginia. She writes this book with enthusiasm, including what to consider before embarking on an exchange search, ways to go about it, and lots of practical advice for the actual exchange. Copies of Gum's booklet cost $4.95 plus $1 postage and handling and are available from the author, 15195 El Camino Grande, Saratoga, California 95070.

### How to Find an Exchange

Using the services of an exchange club is the easiest and most efficient way to go about swapping or renting. (Many clubs arrange either trades or rentals.) Most of the clubs publish periodically updated directories listing subscriber properties with or without photographs and information on location, the family that lives there, and details of a variety of options such as a car or boat that may come with the house. Once you've found something that interests you in a directory, it's time for a letter of inquiry. Your letter should include a detailed description of your family, home, and community; nearby activities; climate; and your preferred dates of exchange. Ask questions about the things that are important to you. Is there a washing machine, a cozy place to read, a backyard for the kids to play in safely? Enclose a stamped, self-addressed envelope to make it easier for the people on the other end.

Once you've decided on the exchange, write everything down—the dates, number of participants, car insurance information, details of pet care, cleaning procedures, the way the telephone bill will be handled, and any instructions for care of any special equipment you may have. When you leave, Cindy Gum suggests leaving a personalized household information booklet as a guide to the newcomers; include auto repair numbers, emergency numbers, your pediatrician's number, names of friends and neighbors who can answer questions, some suggested restaurants, nearby sightseeing attractions, baby-sitters, and so on. Suggest that the exchange family do the same for you.

If you don't want to work through an exchange club, you can go the word-of-mouth route: tell all the people you know about what you're looking for and ask whether they have any connections. Or you can advertise in a professional journal, a college alumni magazine, or a newspaper in the location where you're headed. If you're planning a summer exchange, start the fall before.

Here we list some of the organizations that can facilitate exchanges and, in many cases, rentals. To find the best for you, contact several and compare. What would be ideal, of course, would be to find someone with kids the same age as your kids so that there'll be some toys and games for them and maybe even a jungle gym out in the backyard.

**International Home Exchange Service/ INTERVAC U.S.**
P.O. Box 3975
San Francisco, California 94119
Telephone: 415-382-0300

This organization arranged what was probably the most publicized home exchange in history: a San Francisco couple and their two children traded homes with the governor of Colorado for a week at Christmastime. Use of the Denver mansion included a holiday dinner cooked by the governor's personal chef; the governor got a three-story contemporary home five blocks from the marina. IHES publishes three directories each year—January, March, and May—containing 4,000 listings in over 20 countries. The listings are in a coded format, and the directory we looked through had some fabulous possibilities. There are two kinds of subscriptions available—one for people who list their own homes, another for those who do not. The latter is more expensive, $45 as opposed to $35, because the people at IHES want to encourage listings. Hospitality exchanges are also offered; for example, extra rooms in a home are listed. For families who want to "swap" children on a cultural, student, or vacation exchange basis there's even a Youth Exchange option.

**Interservice Home Exchange, Inc.**
Box 387
Glen Echo, Maryland 20812
Telephone: 301-229-7567

Interservice publishes three catalogs per year. Deadline for the first catalog of the year is November 22. Once the third catalog is printed, in April, it's too late to be listed, but you can still join and receive the catalogs. Annual membership is $29, which includes a listing and three catalogs; unlisted membership costs $23. Photos cost $8 more, and a second home can be listed for an additional $5. If you don't find a swap you like, you can return the catalogs and get your money back. Besides home swapping, you can rent through Interservice, be a guest in someone's home in a "hospitality exchange," or even arrange to house-sit.

**Hideaways International**
15 Goldsmith Street
P.O. Box 1464
Littleton, Massachusetts 01460
Telephone: 617-486-8955.

Hideaways publishes a guide twice a year for its members—the cost is $49 annually—which lists condos, cottages, chalets, and chateaux for rent, exchange, and/or sale. Rental prices start at

$350 and average about $750 per week. Listings include photos of the property, usually inside and out; detailed descriptions of features such as landscaping; nearby sports, and so on; price; and the name and telephone number of the contact person. The catalog also includes some travel articles and details on "Preferred Access"—a plan whereby Hideaway members save 10 percent on bookings at condos in Florida, the Caribbean, Hawaii, and New England. Hideaways offers an elaborate array of travel services as well. Friends who have used Hideaways found that the prices of some of their rentals were *much* less than the same properties through other agents.

### Global Home Exchange and Travel Services (GHETS)
P.O. Box 2015
South Burlington, Vermont 05401-2015
Telephone: 802-985-3825.

This organization, run by teachers, is a matchmaking service. There's no directory; rather, prospective exchangees contact GHETS, and they search for the right match. GHETS interviews all applicants, inspects prospective homes, and requires personal references. To arrange an exchange within the United States costs $250, $25 of which is a nonrefundable lifetime application fee. European-American exchanges cost $300. Applicants fill out a form providing details of their home and 10 to 12 interior and exterior color photos, and the GHETS area coordinator gets to work finding a match. If a proposed exchange is rejected, GHETS tries a second time. GHETS also offers travel services and an optional vacation insurance plan.

### Home Exchange International
185 Park Row
P.O. Box 8781
New York, New York 10038-0272
Telephone: 212-349-5340

This is another matching organization; there's no directory. Applicants fill out a form and supply a set of photographs of both the inside and the outside of the house. Fees are based on the category of home you choose. Homes are rated by the staff in the

United States; the ratings are, in ascending order, "quality," "superior," and "luxurious." The ratings are based on three factors—location (from easy access to a major resort or urban area to central location in a highly desirable area); furnishings (from comfortable with some modern conveniences to elegant with most modern conveniences); and availability of a car. Fees for exchanges within the United States are for stays of 14 days or less, $150 to $250; 15 days to 3 months, $200 to $300; and over 3 months, $275 to $375. International exchanges are slightly higher. Home Exchange International has offices in New York, London, Paris, Milan, and Los Angeles.

### Loan-a-Home
2 Park Lane, 6E
Mount Vernon, New York 10552
Telephone: 914-664-7640

Designed primarily to serve the academic and business communities, this organization helps people find homes to exchange or rent. Many teachers anticipating a sabbatical contact Loan-a-Home as soon as they know when their leave will begin. A check for $25 will get you a current directory and a supplement; there's one in December and another in June, with supplements in March and September. For $35 you'll get four issues: two directories and two supplements. There's no charge to have your own home listed. Subscribers handle all the details of the exchange themselves. For an additional $5 you can list a "housing wanted" notice in the directory.

### Vacation Exchange Club
12006 Eleventh Avenue, Unit 12
Youngtown, Arizona 85363
Telephone: 602-972-2186

VEC publishes two issues per year of what they call *The Exchange Book,* one in February and another in April. Approximately half the listings are in the United States, and half abroad. Even if you don't want to be listed, you can order copies of the books. If you're listed, your cost is $24.70; if you're unlisted, it is $16. Each additional home listed costs $6, and photos are $9 extra.

(For first-class mail, add $3.50; otherwise, the books will be sent third class and will take three to six weeks to get to you.) Deadlines are December 15 for the February issue and February 15 for the April version. All follow-up home exchange details have to be arranged by the exchangees.

Some other possibilities with the VEC directory include renting from a subscriber (although the VEC people warn that their experience shows that subscribers take better care of exchanged homes than rented ones); a "double exchange"—two families from one area exchange with two from another; "hospitality"—staying as paying guest in a home; "exchange hospitality"—a stay in your home is swapped for a stay somewhere else at another time; "youth hospitality"—you and your teenagers offer hospitality to a younger person from another country; bed and breakfast; and a request for a travel companion.

### Vacation Home Rentals, Worldwide
235 Kensington Avenue
Norwood, New Jersey 07648
Telephone: 201-767-9393

VHR has a seductive brochure with photographs of what they call "the best in homes away from home. . . ." They specialize in renting homes in resort areas and "secret hideaways" all over the world. Included in VHR's repertoire are villas, condominiums, townhouse apartments, houses, chateaux, and estates. Rates range from $300 to $20,000 (yes, that's the right number of zeroes) per week, depending on quality, size, staff, location, season, and amenities. When the services of household personnel are not included in the rental, help can usually be arranged at extra cost with enough advance notice. VHR can also make related travel plans—airline reservations, car rentals, and so forth. The people at VHR sent us a batch of description sheets for some of their properties, and here's a sampling: a country estate in the Berkshires of Massachusetts with a house that accommodates 12, a deck that runs the full length of the "view side" of the house, 72 acres of virgin forest surrounding it, and a pond for fishing, boating, or ice skating. The rent is $1,400 per week. Other possibilities are the condos and villas at Orange Lake Country Club, located four miles from the entrance to Walt Disney World. The choices are studio condominiums in the Club House complex, or two-bedroom villas on the golf course. The studios rent for $65 to $93 per night, depending on season; the villas from $107 to $157, which includes hotel-style maid service.

## CONDOMINIUMS

One of the best choices for families are *condos,* the name we've given to what the travel industry may call villas, leisure homes, vacation rentals, or apartments. With a condo you have space, kitchen facilities, often laundry facilities, and privacy. For ski families with young kids, slope-side condos are great: at naptime you can just pick up your kids at the nursery, take them "home," and tuck them in for their naps. If you have older kids, you may prefer the "sociability" of a hotel or lodge to the privacy of a condo, and the option of having the kids go down to the lobby or to the restaurant by themselves.

In many of our chapters—Chapters 9 and 10, in particular— we list condo possibilities. And Vintage Books has published four regional guides to condos, all under the name *The Condo Lux Vacationer's Guide to Condominium Rentals* ($9.95 each). The guides, one each for *The Southeast, The Bahamas and Caribbean Islands, The Mountain States and The Southwest,* and *Hawaii,* are written by Jill A. Little. Each volume contains information on rentals, including policy toward children, details of the accommodations, a description of activities on site, and special facilities and services. Each listing has an accompanying photo.

Hideaways International publishes a "how-to" report that answers the most frequently asked questions about condo rentals. Copies are $7.50 and can be ordered from 15 Goldsmith Street, Box 1464, Littleton, Massachusetts 01460.

Other sources for condo rental information are local tourist offices, classified newspaper and magazine ads, airlines (for air and condo packages), travel agents, and vacation clubs that publish property directories listing exchanges and/or rentals. (See Hideaways International and other listings under the Home Exchanges and Rentals section of this chapter.)

A few words of advice on the subject of condo rentals:

- Property owners who rent directly may offer the lowest accommodation rates and the most personal service, comparable to a home exchange.

- Check with off-site management firms or with the owner if you're "dealing direct" on how frequently they visit their properties and whether they have on-site managers to help out once you're there.
- Begin planning at least two months in advance, four or more if you're going at a peak time to a prime location.
- As with a vacation home exchange, be sure you get, in writing, your dates and an exact description of what is included in your rental in terms of facilities, service, insurance, and so on.

## BED AND BREAKFASTS

In 1975 Betty Rundback wrote the first edition of *Bed and Breakfast U.S.A.* We remember it well: 16 pages, 40 listings. Rundback's current edition is 650 pages long and lists 857 bed and breakfast spots and 145 reservation agencies. Bed and breakfast places—private homes opened to guests or small family-operated inns—have certainly caught on in the past few years. We're delighted, because a bed and breakfast place can be a wonderful alternative to a hotel or motel for a family on vacation. We like bed and breakfasts because of their homey feeling and because in our experience the hosts have been very welcoming and very helpful in orienting us to the surrounding area. There is one thing you must be sure of, though, when choosing a bed and breakfast: you must make certain that the hosts welcome—and we mean welcome, not tolerate—kids. Some bed and breakfasts like to be thought of as adult hideaways, and the idea of an early-rising, talkative 2-year-old would send chills up the spines of some proprietors. To find out whether children are welcome, don't just rely on what the listing in a guidebook says. Check on your own.

Here are a few questions you should ask about any bed and breakfast you are considering:

- Are there kids of similar age in the host family? This is the ideal situation because there will be instant friends for your kids as well as some play equipment to share. There'll also be a lot more understanding if you have to keep some milk in the family refrigerator or warm up a bottle on the family's stove.
- What are the rooms like? Are there cribs or cots for the kids? Are adjoining rooms for parents and children

possible? Ask about the bathroom; will you have to share it with other guests?

- Is breakfast included? Is it a continental or full breakfast? Are there booster seats and high chairs?
- Is there a play area inside or outside? Are there board games or some children's books? Is there a playground nearby?

## Reservations Services

With the increased popularity of the bed and breakfast, reservation networks have sprung up all over the country. These networks match hosts and guests. Many of these services have brochures describing the homes that have registered. Reservations are made through the services, and most charge no fee because they work on a commission for the bed and breakfasts. Some agencies are *membership-based:* they charge a basic fee and then send descriptive directories "free" to members. In larger cities, many reservation services include apartments, condominiums, and even houses without any hosts in them. In our city sections (Chapter 7) we include some bed and breakfast networks. Most of the bed and breakfast guidebooks include listings of these reservation services along with individual listings.

As you'd expect, the proliferation of bed and breakfasts has been accompanied by the proliferation of books about bed and breakfasts. See the listings at the end of the chapter for some suggestions.

## HOSTELS

According to the executive director of the New York Council of the American Youth Hostels (AYH), the trend at AYH is toward more and more family accommodations as the 250 hostels that cover the United States Hostels now set aside family rooms where families can be together and enjoy some privacy. No two hostels look alike—in the United States a hostel may be a lighthouse on the California coast, a dude ranch in the Rockies, or a converted lifeguard station in Cape Cod. Simplicity is the rule at hostels; everything is "do-it-yourself." Guests help with chores, and beds come with the basics: mattresses, pillows, and blankets. Sheet

sleeping sacks are often available for rent or can be purchased from
AYH at $12.25 for nylon or $13.25 for cotton blend.

It's the cost of a stay at a hostel that is most surprising. A
hostel in a converted ski lodge in the Catskills costs $9.00 for
adults and $4.50 for kids per night in high season. Some of the
family rooms even have private baths.

In order to stay at any hostel in the United States or abroad
(there are 5,000 in 61 other countries), you and your family will
have to be members of AYH. Family membership for parents and
children 17 and under costs $30. Members receive a directory
listing all hostels in the United States, a monthly newsletter from
their local council, and updates throughout the year on AYH
activities. For details, contact your local council or the national
headquarters, P.O. Box 37613, Washington, D.C. 20013.

## BOOKS TO READ

On the subject of where to stay there are lots and lots of books
that list recommendations. Here we list some we've reviewed:
All of the United States:

*Bed and Breakfast U.S.A.* by Betty Rundback and Nancy
Kramer, published by E. P. Dutton ($10.95). This is the
one we mentioned before, our favorite. It's well organized, covers the entire United States, and includes
information for each place listed and whether or not
children are welcome. We've used the book ourselves
and have never been disappointed. There's a new edition each year.

*America's Wonderful Little Hotels and Inns* by Sandra Soule,
published by St. Martin's Press ($12.95). This is a
comprehensive book full of great reader-recommended
inns, hotels, resorts, and lodges. Each listing indicates
whether children are welcome.

*Bed and Breakfast America: The Great American Guest
House Book* by John Thaxton, published by Burt Franklin and Company ($8.95). A no-nonsense guide to the
species. Each listing includes a notation about children.

*The Complete Guide to Bed and Breakfasts, Inns and Guest-
houses* by Pamela Lanier, published by John Muir

Publications, Inc. ($11.95). The write-ups are in a short-hand style (we like a bit more detail), but there's a useful appendix that includes a section called "Family Fun" with a list of accommodations that are particularly recommended for kids.

*Fielding's Havens and Hideaways* by T. Tracy and J. O. Ward, published by William Morrow Company ($7.95). The listings include notations on family suitability; local attractions are also included.

Regional:

*New England Bed and Breakfast* by Corinne Madden Ross, East Woods Press/Globe Pequot Press ($8.95). Most of the bed and breakfasts listed here welcome families, and the listings include the availability of cribs. We like this one and the same publisher's *California Bed and Breakfast Book*, by Kathy Strong ($8.95).

*Bed and Breakfast in the Northeast* by Bernice Chesler, published by Globe Pequot Press ($9.95). Another nice one, which includes 300 bed and breakfasts from Maine to Washington, D.C. One of the most useful parts of each listing is the "In-Residence" section, which gives you the names and ages of children who live there. Chesler includes reservation services, too, that extend beyond the Northeast.

*Guide to the Recommended Country Inns.* This is a series of three regional guides—one to the West Coast ($10.95) by Julianne Belote; one to the Northeast ($8.95) by Brenda Chapin; and one to New England ($9.95) by Elizabeth Squier. They're all published by Globe Pequot Press, and although some of the inns welcome kids, some are very definitely meant to be romantic getaways for adults.

*Best Places to Stay in New England* by Christine Tree and Bruce Shaw, published by Harvard Common Press ($9.95). The authors have two chapters of special interest to traveling families, "Family Finds" and "Family Resorts." All listings throughout the book indicate the hosts' attitude toward children.

*Budget Driving and Lodging in New England* by Frank and Franklin Sullivan, published by Globe Pequot Press ($8.95). There's no consistent indication of whether children are or are not welcome at the various listings, but it's a well-constructed book nevertheless.

*Bed and Breakfast Colorado and Rocky Mountains West* by Buddy Mays, published by Chronicle Press ($7.95). Here you'll find 50 places to stay, including lodges, ranches, and historic hotels. Loving descriptions give the mood of each place, and most of the places described welcome children.

---

## ABOUT OUR LISTINGS:

The properties we list in this book all welcome kids and all willingly responded to our many, many questions. We're relying on you, our readers, to let us know about your own experiences with our choices—good and bad—and to tell us about any new places we can list in the next edition.

## ONE MORE REMINDER:

If you're looking for a place to play tennis, check the tennis and golf chapter but don't overlook Chapter 8 on resorts, Chapter 10 on skiing (many ski resorts turn into tennis and golf spots once the snow melts), and Chapter 11 on farms and dude ranches.

And don't forget the None of the Above listings beginning on page 289.

NOTE: Rates quoted here were accurate at press time but are subject to change.

NOTE: Be sure to check pages 297–99 for a list of publishers' addresses. Some books published by smaller publishers may not be readily available in bookstores but can be ordered directly from the publisher.

Send us your cards and letters. We want to hear from you about your great vacation choices so that we can include them in the next edition.

# 5

## PLANNING YOUR DAYS AND NONE OF THE ABOVE

In this chapter we talk about how best to plan a day on vacation and then some of what we call "none of the above"—topics that are important but don't fit neatly into any other category: finding baby-sitters while you're away, some special advice for single parents traveling with their kids, and a word or two about theme parks.

### PLANNING A DAY

Here the password is underplan. When the kids are with you, don't expect to cover as much territory as you would without them. Allow plenty of time for eating, bathroom visits, and dawdling. Plan something especially for the kids each day, and let them in on the planning sessions. You can make lists with your sightseeing "goals." Clustered sightseeing is best: pick one area and explore it instead of dashing all over town. Find out where the nearest park is, and if the weather is nice enough, include a visit. Very young children find a full day of sightseeing boring and exhausting. How about half a day with you and then the rest of the day with other children? Go to informal restaurants as you sightsee, or, better still, have a picnic. Take along a stroller. Even if your kids seem too old for a stroller at home, it can be a lifesaver while you're sightseeing.

Part of the reason you should underplan when you've got your kids along is so that you don't ever have to feel rushed. When you're feeling pressured you get impatient, and when you get impatient you lose your temper. A leisurely pace will loosen things up enormously.

If there are some places you feel you must see and they are places that your kids really aren't going to like, arrange some baby-sitting. We'll give some advice on the subject later in this chapter.

Once your plans have been made, feel free to rearrange them. If the kids are really restless at a particular place, leave. There are some stalling tactics you can try in order to give a place a second chance, though: a lunch break (a picnic in the park would be nice), going out to the gift shop, or trying to find something else at the same place they might like. To be prepared for this, you should read the brochure beforehand and know some alternatives. If your kids are 6 years old or older, consider a guided tour or one of the taped guides.

When you are planning your day, don't dismiss the possibility of going to a movie. That can be fun, particularly on a rainy or snowy day.

Whenever you go to a place that's large or likely to be crowded, be sure to choose a central meeting spot just in case you get separated. We teach our kids to call our first names if they can't see us. If they call "Mommy" or "Daddy," it's less noticeable. Be sure the children know where they're staying; rehearse them on the name of the hotel or motel.

And don't forget to ask, just as soon as you arrive at a sightseeing attraction, where the bathrooms are located. Don't wait until you have a bathroom emergency to try wending your way through the halls of some enormous museum trying to find the restrooms.

## MUSEUM VISITS—MAKING THEM WORK

Museums really can be fun for kids just as long as you choose the right ones and prepare the kids for the visit. Here are some ideas that have worked for us: we start out early, before the crowds; we avoid mealtimes; and we plan to stay no more than two hours.

We visit the gift shop first. This may seem a bit peculiar, but we do it so that the kids can choose five or ten postcards they like best and then look for the originals as they walk through the museum. We return to the gift shop at the end of the visit, too; give the kids a limit as to how much they can spend; and let them get some kind of souvenir of the visit.

Since we want to avoid the "don't's" and "no's" as much as possible, we have the kids ask the guards whether something can be touched. This is the passing-the-buck theory, and it works.

Naturally, we want our kids to learn something from their visit, but we try not to overdo the pedantry. After one museum visit our daughter said, "That was great, but next time don't read to me so much. Let me just look at things."

We never take the kids to a museum we don't like. Martyrdom is unnecessary.

One of the things our kids like to do at a museum—or any sightseeing spot, in fact—is to take along their tape recorders, making narrative tapes of what they're looking at. The prerecorded tapes sold at museums are good, too, so long as your child is old enough to concentrate on them.

You shouldn't think of museums as merely places to view art; there are many other kinds as well. There are crafts museums, science museums, historical museums, ethnic museums, and a growing number of "hands-on" children's museums throughout the country. A book called *Special Museums of the Northeast* by Nancy Frazier lists museums from Maine to Washington, D.C., that include whaling museums, a motorcycle museum, doll museums, and one museum dedicated to the cranberry and another to the nut. The book is $9.95 and is published by the Globe Pequot Press, Old Chester Road, Chester, Connecticut 06412. In our city sections in Chapter 7, we describe the various children's museums. Our kids have spent many wonderful hours at many of these places, and we've enjoyed the visits as much as they have. Honestly.

If you're going to visit a large museum, such as the American Museum of Natural History or the Metropolitan Museum of Art in New York, choose just one or two areas of concentration—the rocks or the dinosaurs in the former, the armor or the mummies in the latter.

If there's something you desperately want to see in a museum and you know your kids aren't going to like it at all, or if you don't want any distractions, call the museum ahead of time and see whether you can coordinate your visit with a family or children's workshop. You'd be surprised at how often this is possible: even some of the most "serious" museums offer collage making, building with clay, origami, and so on. Prepare your children first, though. Don't just spring the idea of a drop-off on them. Stay with them for a few minutes at the beginning of the session, explain that you'll be in the museum the whole time, and be sure to find out exactly when the program is over so that you can be sure to be on time to pick them up and admire their work.

If you're traveling with a very young child, and you need to be able to use a stroller, be sure to check in advance whether strollers are allowed. Some places even rent strollers and back carriers, another detail to check.

Two books written especially to prepare kids to visit an art museum are *Let's Go to the Museum* by Virginia K. Levy and *Mommy, It's a Renoir,* by Aline D. Wolf.

*Let's Go* is written by an art teacher, Virginia K. Levy, who designed her book for 6- to 12-year-olds to use as a workbook with questions, spaces for answers, and room to compose some original works of art. The book is available from Veejay Publications, P.O. Box 1029, Pompano Beach, Florida 33061, for $6.95 plus $1 for postage and handling.

*Mommy, It's a Renoir* by Aline D. Wolf is meant for parents and teachers and presents the author's system of teaching art appreciation through the use of art postcards. The process becomes a game. Copies of the book are available for $10.95 plus $1.50 for shipping from the publisher, Parent Child Press, P.O. Box 767, Altoona, Pennsylvania 16603.

Our favorite, though, for reading to the kids before any trip to a museum is *Visiting the Art Museum,* published by E. P. Dutton and written by Laurene Krasny Brown and Marc Brown ($11.95). Animated characters and full-color reproductions of art selected from museums all over the world combine to present an amusing and instructional-without-being-pedantic look at a museum. We recommend it highly.

## FINDING BABY-SITTERS

Up to now we've talked about the time you're going to spend with your kids, but now it's time to discuss the time you're going to spend alone or with another adult. Be sure that you allow yourself some of this "grown-up" time; you really do deserve it. If you're staying at a place where there's a children's program, you'll have no problem arranging time for yourself to take a tennis clinic or visit a nearby museum or just go on a shopping spree. But particularly if you are in a city, you'll need to be more resourceful.

The first thing to do, before you leave, is ask people you know at home whether they have friends or relatives with children in the place where you're going. If so, you can call and ask about baby-sitting. Or maybe a business associate knows someone. Once you've arrived, you can try contacting the local college or university; often they have baby-sitting services as part of their student employment program. Nursing schools are good sources, as are senior citizen groups or churches or synagogues. Most hotels have access to sitters—either staff people who want extra work or an agency contact. Bonded baby-sitting agencies are also listed in the Yellow Pages. Of course, a baby-sitter must have references, and we suggest that you have any baby-sitter arrive an hour or so before you leave so that he or she can get to know the children and also see how you interact with them. They'll get a good idea of what your kids can and cannot do and what they're used to.

We think you should know, too, about a baby-sitting franchise that was begun by Nancy Ann Van Wie in 1979. Staffed by teachers, nurses, and other qualified adults, Sitters Unlimited offers baby-sitting services in hotels through franchises in Honolulu; Washington, D.C.; Chicago; Miami; Los Angeles and San Francisco; and other areas of southern California. Sitters Unlimited also sets up an on-site nursery school for the little ones and guided tours for older kids during conventions and meetings. For information on Sitters Unlimited, write to their headquarters, 23046 Avenida de la Carlota 653, Laguna Hills, California 92653.

## A SPECIAL WORD FOR SINGLE PARENTS

More and more single parents are traveling with their kids, and without a doubt, they face many problems that a two-parent family doesn't. Being the only adult can be lonely, and it can be exhausting; with no one to share the responsibility, a vacation can become a disappointment. To find out what advice to pass on to single parents, to find out how they can make their vacations fun and rewarding, we spoke to Phyllis Diamond, the founder and former president of a New York–based group called Kindred Spirits, an organization dedicated to arranging entertainment, travel, and education programs for single parents.

According to Diamond, you're not likely to meet a lot of other single parents while you travel, so it's best to arrange to team up with a friend and his or her kids and go as a group. Not only will you have more fun, but you will also be able to have the kids in one room and the adults in another so that there can be some private time. If your budget is really tight—and for many single parents this is the case—you can all share a room and save money. Diamond suggests that you set out on your vacation with the clear understanding that you will probably not meet other singles. If you have realistic expectations—if you aim to have a good time with your kids and forget about meeting Prince or Princess Charming—everything will work out fine.

Where should you go? Probably the best places are the ones where you'll find children's programs, and this book is crammed with suggestions. Diamond told us that many single parents think that Disney World is the greatest place to take their kids, but she says they're wrong: it is too lonely and too exhausting for one adult. One of the best things she thinks that single parents can do when vacation time comes around is rent a share in a beach house with other single parents and their kids. It's fun, it provides other kids and other adults, it needn't be too expensive, and it is usually not hard to arrange. Kindred Spirits sponsors such rental shares in the New York area, and it's likely that there are other similar organizations in other parts of the country that do the same. For information on Kindred Spirits, write to them in care of Group Services, the 92nd Street Y, 1395 Lexington Avenue, New York, New York 10128, 212-427-6000.

An official of the American Youth Hostels told us that his organization's ski trips are enormously popular with single parents and their kids. In fact, any "adventure"-type vacation is a good bet. See Chapter 6 for suggestions.

## THEME PARKS

Some of you may want to include a theme park visit on your vacation. If you're really wild for theme parks, you can plan your entire vacation around them and head for Orlando, Florida (Disney World, Wet'n'Wild, Sea World), or Anaheim, California (Disneyland, Marine Land, Knott's Berry Farm). But it's more likely that you'll just take a day or two out of a vacation and visit one of the theme parks that dot the country. For some advice on how to best arrange these kinds of visits, we spoke to two experts, Barry and Hermine Block, senior editors of the trade magazine *Tourist Attractions and Parks* and authors of a soon-to-be-published book called *America's Best Amusement Parks*. (To find out how to get a copy, write to the Blocks at P.O. Box 50, Island Station, New York, 10044.)

We asked the Blocks what some of their favorites are, and they told us that they're partial to the kind of parks that combine entertainment, education, and amusement, such as the ones run by the Busch group—The Dark Continent in Tampa, Sesame Place in Pennsylvania, and The Old Country in Williamsburg. They also like parks where there are lots of activities—water games and other features that require the active participation of the visitors. Action Park in New Jersey and Sesame Place are two good examples of this new trend in parks.

The Blocks gave us some good advice on how to make the most of any trip to a theme park, and we pass it on to you:

- Plan ahead. Send for brochures and find out as much as you can about the park to be sure that it is appropriate to the ages and interests of your kids.
- Allot the right amount of time to the park you're going to visit. Don't ever consider "doing" Disney World in less than two days; you should really allow at least three.
- Arrive at the park early. The lines will be shorter, and you won't be in danger of being closed out when the park

reaches maximum capacity. Have a map with your route outlined in order to save unnecessary walking.

- Decide which rides or activities are most important to you and head for them first.
- Eat properly. You can't survive happily on junk food for eight hours. Consider packing a lunch if the food available isn't the kind you or your kids like.
- Try breaking your day into two parts. Start out with a morning visit; go back to your hotel for lunch, a swim, a rest; and then return for the evening.

We have three suggestions of our own to add:

- Have one parent wait on line while others look around. Usually the theme parks have the wait time posted, and they're usually very accurate.
- If you're like us and can't get anywhere really early, wait until later and hit the popular rides when other people are eating.
- When you enter the park, go left. Most people go to the right, so there will be less crowds to the left.

# 6

# ADVENTURE

If you want to lie on a beach and soak up the rays, skip this chapter. But if you're in the mood for adventure, for getting out into the middle of the great outdoors with your family, consider some of the offerings here. Read on and you'll find out about rafting trips, llama treks, backpacking, and nature study and mountaineering.

Adventure vacations are "in" right now, so there are bound to be lots to choose from. Fortunately, more and more adventure tour operators are thinking "family." One woman who probably knows the most about adventure-type vacations is Pat Dickerman, author of *Adventure Travel North America,* who started writing on the subject long before it became trendy. In conjunction with her book, Dickerman operates a travel service that arranges family adventures. The book is available for $14 book rate or $16 first-class from Adventure Guides, 36 East 57th Street, New York, New York 10022. From the same address you can find out about the family adventures, or if you prefer, call 212-355-6334.

A well-known organization that you may want to contact about adventure travel is Outward Bound. With schools located throughout the United States, Outward Bound is dedicated to wilderness education; with Outward Bound, "you'll learn to trust your own abilities and instincts while you learn to live comfortably in the wilderness." Outward Bound is "serious" adventure—it doesn't ask for lots of experience, but it does demand commitment and willingness to try new experiences. Outward Bound's minimum age for participation is never less than 16, so this would be a possibility only for a family with teenage kids. For information and a brochure, contact the national offices, 384 Field Point Road, Greenwich, Connecticut 06830.

Before we go into descriptions of specific programs, here's a rundown of some of the questions to ask when you're researching adventure vacations for your family:

- Exactly what is included?
- Where will you spend the nights?
- How well established is the tour operator?
- Will the tour operator give you the names of some people who have gone before you?
- What are the qualifications and experience of the staff that's going along with you?
- What is the size of the group?
- Do they often have families?
- What special services are available for kids?

One final word: In order to get your family warmed up for your outdoor vacation, try some day hikes or canoe trips near home.

We've divided this chapter into five sections according to the type of adventure. Our categories are exploring nature, canoeing, rafting, pack trips, and sailing. We've included a variety of operators, all of whom expressed a willingness to accommodate kids. The listings are alphabetical, by state.

## PACK TRIPS

### McGee Creek Pack Station
Star Route 1, Box 100-A
Independence, California 93526
Telephone: Summer: 619-935-4324
　　　　　　 Winter: 619-878-2207
Owners: John and Jennifer Ketcham
Operating Season: June 1–October 15
Trips in: California

IN THEIR OWN WORDS: "A majority of our wranglers are women; most families like that. We specialize in dealing with families, with no minimum age. We use home bred, raised and trained Morgan horses which are not only gentle, trustworthy, and sure-footed, but a real pleasure to ride. Ours is a family-run operation that knows how a family likes to be treated."

THE TRIPS: The Ketchams recommend their High Sierra Weekend (three days) or their John Muir Wilderness Trail Ride (one week) for families. They'll also customize all-inclusive, everything provided, trips as well as spot trips—trips that include getting you to the campsite and a horse and a mule per person. The setting is the eastern High Sierra's McGee Canyon. The canyon is uncrowded and colorful with multihued wildflowers and marbleized red slate and granite peaks.

EQUIPMENT: This depends on the type of trip. The all-inclusive trips include tents, foods, a guide, cooking gear, and packhorses.

RATES: Cost for an all-inclusive trip for riders is $100 per person per day for three to four people; $90 per day for five or more.

### Holland Lake Lodge
Swan Valley
Box 2083
Condon, Montana 59826
Telephone: 406-754-2282
Owners: Howard and Loris Uhl, Dick and Carole Schaeffer
Operating Season: July 1–September 1
Trips in: Montana

IN THEIR OWN WORDS: "We customize our pack trips to fit the individual needs. Scenic beauty, quality stock and tack, and a knowledgeable staff all add up to a memory of a lifetime."

THE TRIPS: Kids have to be old enough to sit on a horse alone and hang on; children under 6 years are probably too young. A good trip for families who haven't done a lot of camping is a five- to seven-day trip with a base camp about 20 miles from the lodge in the Bob Marshall Wilderness. The trip includes swimming, fishing, and short hikes and a seven-mile ride to the South Fork of the Flathead River. Custom trips can be arranged for four or more people. (See page 276 for information on lodge.)

EQUIPMENT: Everything except sleeping bags, duffels, fishing gear, and life vests is provided. Food is home-cooked, not freeze-dried.

RATES: Customized trips cost $20 per day per person. A seven-day guided trip costs $840 per person and includes one night at the lodge.

### Hurricane Creek Llamas
Route 1, Box 123
Enterprise, Oregon 97828
Telephone: 503-432-4455
Owners: Stan and Lynn Daugherty
Operating Season: May 15–September 15
Trips in: Oregon

IN THEIR OWN WORDS: "Llama trekking is the ideal family vacation. Parents are free from camp chores and are able to spend time with their children exploring all that nature has to offer. . . ."

THE TRIPS: According to Daugherty, llamas are natural hiking companions for adults and children alike because of their gentle nature. On these treks, llamas carry all food and equipment, and the staff takes care of the cooking and the camp chores.

The trips that are recommended for families with kids age 6 or over are the end of June trip up Bear Creek, which includes a visit to Stanley Springs; the July trip up Hurricane Creek through flower-lined meadows along a mountain stream to its headwaters; and the August astronomy trip, led by an astronomer and featuring a viewing of the Perseid meteor shower from a high wilderness point. These trips last from three to six days.

Trips can also be customized for any family group. All trips are limited to ten participants and take place against the backdrop of the Eagle Cap wilderness and Wallowa Mountains in northeastern Oregon. Participants must be able to walk three to eight miles per day over trails that range from easy to moderate.

EQUIPMENT: Hurricane Creek provides tents, sleeping pads (take your own bag), food, the llamas, and pack equipment. You may take up to 25 pounds of personal gear for the llamas to carry.

RATES: The cost is $85 per person per day, 20 percent less for children 6 to 11 years old.

**Big Buffalo Trail Ride, Inc.**
P.O. Box 772
Gallatin, Tennessee 37066
Telephone: 615-888-2453
Owners: Fred and Mike McDonald and Tim Aston
Operating season: June, August, and October
Trips in: Tennessee

IN THEIR OWN WORDS: "Big Buffalo Trail Ride is for families who love horses and enjoy riding together. On our rides, families camp together, eat together, and ride together. The rides are for people who have their own campers and horses."

THE TRIPS: There are three rides scheduled each year—two rides in the summer and one foliage ride in October. The rides are a week long and follow trails that are old logging roads through the Tennessee hills: "sparkling streams, rugged hills, and secluded hollows." Participants stay in their own tents or campers; electrical hookups are available. Meals are provided at the dining hall. All ages are welcome. When you're not riding, you can canoe, fish, tube, or swim in the Buffalo River, which borders the campground. Each night there's live music and entertainment. Custom trips can be arranged, too.

EQUIPMENT: Guests take their own tents, campers, or trailers and horses. There are no horses for rent. Stalls are available for rent, and feed is available.

RATES: Adults pay $125 for the week; children aged 6 to 11 cost $100; kids 3 to 5 cost $75, and for those 2 years and under it is free.

## NATURE EXPLORATION/WILDERNESS TRIPS

**America Wilderness Alliance**
7600 East Arapahoe Road, Suite 114
Englewood, Colorado 80112
Telephone: 303-771-0380

Trip Coordinator: Patsy C. Fleming
Operating Season: May to October
Trips to: Montana, Idaho, Colorado, Alaska, California, Utah,
    Minnesota, Maine, Wyoming, Hawaii, Alaska, Oregon,
    Arizona

IN THEIR OWN WORDS: "Wilderness adventures are un-
matched in memories and friendships. They are full of discovery,
excitement, and surprises. You can enjoy a highly participatory
trip, or one less challenging, whichever suits your inclination and
mood."

THE TRIPS: The Alliance coordinates a number of trips, all
involving adventure and all taking advantage of the great outdoors. They offer backpacking, kayaking, sailing, horseback riding,
canoeing, pack tripping, fishing, rafting, and combination trips of
two or more adventures at a time. Some possibilities: a parent-child
horseback ride adventure in the Bob Marshall Wilderness for eight
days, five-day llama trips in the High Siskiyon Wilderness of
Oregon, or a combination two-day rafting and hot air ballooning
trip in Colorado.

EQUIPMENT: Everything is provided: "All you bring is a
sense of adventure and your toothbrush."

RATES: Costs vary from trip to trip but here are some
samples: the parent-child horseback trip costs $615 per parent and
$550 for kids 6 to 18; the rafting and balloon trip costs $98 per
person for four or more, $89 for a child 12 to 17, and $105 for
children 3 and under.

### Wilderness Threshold Trips
Sierra Club
730 Polk Street
San Francisco, California 94109
Telephone: 415-776-2211
Owners: Nonprofit organization, founded in 1892, to help care for
    the country's wilderness areas and to fight to preserve them.
Operating season: June–August
Trips in: California, Maine

IN THEIR OWN WORDS: "Wilderness Threshold trips have
one specific goal in mind—to make it easy for families to enjoy the

outdoors together. . . . We welcome single parents, grandparents, or aunts and uncles."

THE TRIP: There are five trips offered, all designed to help inexperienced families learn outdoor skills while increasing their awareness of an area's plant and animal life. Camps vary according to location: on wilderness trips, pack stock is used to carry food and equipment; on some trips, motor vehicles are used for equipment, while participants hike; and on lodge-based trips the "camp" may be just a few yards from the road. Groups meet and have breakfast and supper together. Families are free during the day for nature study, hiking, fishing, or swimming. Evenings often involve group activities. Some of the choices for 1987 are a week on Santa Catalina Island for families with kids 6 and over; a week in the John Muir Wilderness with camp at Honey Moore Lake; a Toddler Tramp at the Acadia National Park in Maine; a week at a rustic lodge on the western slope of the Sierra Nevadas for families with kids 4 and older; and a week at Emerald Lake Basin in the John Muir Wilderness.

RATES: The packing trips range from $195 to $435 per adult; $130 to $290 per child.

### Chewonki Foundation
RR 2, Box 1200
Wiscasset, Maine 04578
Telephone: 207-882-7323
Owner: Nonprofit educational institution.
Operating season: Year-round, most family activities between
    mid-August and Labor Day
Trips in: Maine

IN THEIR OWN WORDS: "Chewonki Foundation programs encourage participants to develop their personal potential, gain a sense of community, and heighten their interest in and sensitivity to the natural world. . . ."

THE TRIPS: Family wilderness trips last from six to ten days; there's no official minimum age, but 7 is probably the best cutoff. All participants must know how to swim. Trips are based on canoeing, hiking, kayaking, or sailing, for example, ten days canoeing down the Allagash Wilderness Waterway, seven days sailing along the coast of Maine, and six days of backpacking in Baxter

State Park with camping in the Chimney and Russell Pond areas. Each trip has a maximum of ten participants, and two Chewonki leaders accompany each group. Responsibility for chores is shared so that everyone has a chance to learn camping skills.

For families interested in the natural history of the Maine coast, there's a seven-day workshop that includes daily fieldwork and evening discussions. There's no age minimum for workshops; participants live in simple screened cabins and eat in a central dining room. Wilderness trip participants sleep in tents and help with the preparation of all meals.

Custom-designed trips can also be arranged for groups of ten or more.

EQUIPMENT: Chewonki provides their own sleeping bags and packs.

RATES: The Natural History workshop costs $300, $200 for kids under 12; the wilderness trips range from $305 to $440.

### Canyonlands Field Institute/ED Ventures
Box 68
Moab, Utah 84532
Telephone: 801-259-7750
Owner: Nonprofit organization
Operating Season: February to November
Trips in: Utah

IN THEIR OWN WORDS: "From river canyon to alpine meadow, you explore the ecology, geology, and archaeology of this amazing country through the naturalists' and the artists' perspectives."

THE TRIPS: ED Ventures sponsors field seminars and backcountry trips. The age minimum is 5; participants have to be able to hike and have a "flexible attitude." The seminars use indoor and outdoor classrooms and are one to three days long. Participants arrange their own accommodations. The backcountry trips take participants into the heart of the country by raft, by jeep, or with pack animals for two to four days. A guest naturalist highlights the natural and cultural history of the areas visited. Camping arrangements, meals, transportation, and outfitter fees are included. The territory to be explored is Arches and Canyonland National Parks, the canyons of the Green and Colorado Rivers, and the wilderness of the Colorado plateau—"wind and water have transformed this pastel landscape into a maze of silent passageways and majestic arches sheltering abundant signs of the Anasazi cliffdweller culture." Custom-designed trips are also possible for groups of two or more, and if you're just passing through, you can call ahead to arrange for the services for a day of a private naturalist who knows "how to turn kids and adults on to the natural world."

EQUIPMENT: Meals and outfitter services are provided. Sleeping bags and tents may be rented for $20 to $30 per week.

RATES: Costs vary. A sample: The prehistoric cultures of the San Juan River raft trip, three days long, costs $285 for adults, $265 for children under 18 (less for Institute members).

### National Wildlife Federation
1412 16th Street NW
Washington, D.C. 20036
Telephone: 703-790-4363 or 202-797-6800
Owner: Nonprofit group
Operating season: June–August
Trips in: Colorado, New York

IN THEIR OWN WORDS: "Nature investigations are our primary focus as well as environmental education and conservation. . . . The entire family has a chance to participate in a wide variety of outdoor discovery activities—it's a 'camp' experience for the whole family."

THE TRIPS: The federation operates three scenic vacation spots called "Summits." The site in the Colorado Rockies features cascading waterfalls and snow-capped peaks, bighorn sheep, elk, and muledeer. The Adirondack Summit is on Lake George at Silver Bay, where participants canoe, swim, hike, and bird watch. The third summit is in Maine along the craggy seacoast. Accommodations vary from summit to summit: you can choose from inns and lodges to dormitory-style buildings and "campus townhouses." At each summit the programming is offered for kids aged 3 and over. The adult program includes wildlife photography, bird identification, hikes, folk music, field ecology, and outdoor skills. Activities are all supervised by experts. For teens aged 13 to 17, there are outdoor skill sessions, rope course work, canoeing, and hiking trips; for kids aged 5 to 12, there's a choice of stream studies, wildlife investigations, bird walks, nature hikes, folk tales, outdoor games, and arts and crafts; and for 3- and 4-year-olds there's a program called "Your Big Backyard Preschool Program" that operates from 8:00 A.M. to noon.

RATES: The adult course is $185; the children's programs are $50 for the little ones and $110 for the others. Accommodation costs vary, of course, depending on the type of room you choose. A sample: to stay in a room with a private bath at the Adirondack Summit costs $264 for each adult if there are two to four in a room; children's rate is $132. A less expensive alternative is a room in a dorm at the Maine Summit: $152 for adults four to a room, $119 for each child.

## CANOEING

### Bear Track Outfitting Company
Box 51
Grand Marais, Minnesota 55604
Telephone: 218-387-1162
Owners: David and Cathi Williams
Operating Season: Year-round
Trips in: Minnesota

IN THEIR OWN WORDS: "We are very receptive to families, having five children ourselves, aged 3 weeks to 10 years. We believe our customers become part of our family."

THE TRIPS: The Williamses outfit canoeists, plan trips, and run a canoe camp for kids 11 to 17. Their territory is the Boundary Waters Canoe Area, one million acres of land and water in the northern third of the Superior National Forest, completely forested with hundreds of lakes, wildflowers, birds, wildlife, and game fish.

There's no age limit for the Bear Track trips, and life vests are provided for everyone. A typical canoe trip organized by the Williamses starts with an orientation—an introduction to the North Country, the equipment, and the route. After dinner in town, the group (usually ten people) packs its gear; early the next morning they set out from the canoe base at Seagull Lake. "We usually route families on a trip that has no real hard portages, has smaller lakes and sometimes base camping on a lake with day trips that include fishing, photography, swimming, exploring, bird and moose watching." Evenings are spent around the campfire, roasting marshmallows and watching the Northern Lights. A sailing and canoe package is available, too: four days of sailing charter to Isle Royale National Park followed by a canoe trip into the Boundary Waters Canoe Area for three days.

In the winter, Bear Track offers cross-country skiing tours and winter camping. "We don't recommend these for kids under 10—they can't keep warm." The trip lasts three days. The night before the tour begins, there's an orientation in Grand Marais at a cabin or motel. On the first day, the group travels to the base camp and sets up; winter skills such as firewood cutting are taught. The days are short and the nights are long, so there's a lot of conversation and storytelling inside the wood-heated tents. During the day, group members ski, ice fish, or take photographs. On the third day, camp is broken and the group heads back to the starting point "and hopes that the cars and trucks will start."

EQUIPMENT: Bear Track can outfit a canoeing family completely, with canoes, food, camping equipment, and lodging in their cabins.

RATES: The rates per person per day for canoe trips are $28.50 for two to three days, $26.50 for seven days or more. The more people in the group, the lower the cost. The sailing/canoeing package costs $1,345 for the base price, $175 for each additional person; the winter camping expeditions cost from $265 to $425 (three to five days) for four people.

### Gunflint Lodge
Box 100 GT
Grand Marais, Minnesota 55604
Telephone: 800-328-3325
Owners: Bruce and Susan Kerfoot
Operating season: May 1–October 20 and December 15–April 1
Trips in: Minnesota

IN THEIR OWN WORDS: "With over 50 years outfitting by our family, we have the background and experience to expertly plan your trip with you."

THE TRIPS: The Kerfoots operate the lodge—24 cabins—for family vacations. (See the Camping and Cabins section.) They also outfit canoeists and plan trips along 50 different routes that may last 1 to 14 days. For the younger or less experienced families, they can arrange trips on small lakes with easy portages; for the more experienced, there are more challenging routes. The package includes dinner, lodging, and breakfast before and after the trip; a route briefing; and complete outfitting for six days. The Kerfoots also offer canoeing lessons for anyone 6 years and older at no extra charge.

EQUIPMENT: The Kerfoots supply the canoe, life vests, sleeping bags and pads, cooking kits, duffels, a tent, food, and even the dish towels.

RATES: The "Family Package" costs $220 per adult, $99 for each child.

### North Star Canoe and Bike Rentals
Route 12-A
Ballock's Crossing
Cornish, New Hampshire 03745
Telephone: 603-542-5802
Owners: John and Linda Hammond
Operating season: May through October
Trips in: New Hampshire

IN THEIR OWN WORDS: "Leave your tensions and pressures of daily life at home and become absorbed in the serenity and magnificence of this historic river."

THE TRIP: The Hammonds, who live on a working farm located on the river, will help you plan any length canoe trip along the cool, clear waters of the Connecticut River, which forms the border of Vermont and New Hampshire. For beginners and families, North Star recommends that you start with their day trip. Then, when you're ready for overnight canoe camping, they'll route it for you and outfit you. They'll also help arrange a canoeing/bicycling combination trip—they call it "pedal-and-paddle." If you want a guide, that too is possible.

EQUIPMENT: North Star will rent canoes, paddles, lifejackets, bicycles, and helmets.

RATES: The daily rate for canoe rental is $24; overnights are $18 per canoe for each additional day. Groups of eight or more get a 10 percent discount; ages 12 and under get 25 percent off.

## RAFTING

**Outdoor Adventure River Specialists (OARS)**
P.O. Box 67
Angels Camp, California 95222
Telephone: 209-736-4677, 800-346-6277
Operating dates: April through October
Owner/operator: George Wendt
Trips in: California, Oregon, Arizona, Utah, Wyoming, Idaho

IN THEIR OWN WORDS: "River rafting is the ideal family activity because it appeals to all ages. It's challenging, fun, and healthy."

THE TRIPS: OARS is licensed to operate in California, Arizona, Utah, and Oregon. They recommend three of their trips for families: a five-day trip on the mostly smooth San Juan River in Colorado, the one- or two-day trips in the South Fork of the American River in Utah in April, and the five-day trip on the Rogue River in Oregon. Kids 7 years and over are welcome on these trips.

EQUIPMENT: Food, waterproof duffels, guides, camping gear, and child-size lifejackets are provided. You have to take your own tent, sleeping bags, and eating utensils.

RATES: Prices vary from $77 for the one-day trips to $500 for the five-day trip. Costs vary with the date. There are special rates for children; for instance, the $500 San Juan River trip is $450 for kids.

**Grand Canyon Dories, Inc.**
P.O. Box 7538
Menlo Park, California 94026
Telephone: 415-854-6616
Owner: Martin Litton
Operating Season: April 1–October 31
Trips in: Arizona, Idaho

IN THEIR OWN WORDS: "On an organized wilderness river trip the group is kept together not only by a community of interest but also by the very nature of the experience. There are things to fascinate every member of the family but the main thrust of the outing is always anticipation of what will appear around the next bend."

THE TRIPS: Litton recommends the five-day sampler in the Grand Canyon for children; he thinks the other Grand Canyon trips should be saved for kids 12 and over. This sampler is an introduction to the Canyon. It covers 90 miles of the Colorado River's course and 10 miles on the open, clear water of Lake Mead. Other trips that he recommends for kids as young as 4 years old are Hells Canyon of the Snake River, which includes fishing, exploring, birding, "botanizing and geologizing"; the Grande Ronde River, with time for fishing, hiking, and watching bald eagles and osprey; and all the trips on the Salmon River, once called the River of No Return. All trips are at least 5 days long, some as long as 20.

EQUIPMENT: Included in the price of your trip are meals, waterproof duffels, tents, inflatable kayaks and/or paddle rafts, lifejackets, and transportation from certain points to launch sites and back again. On some trips camping gear is included; on others you can rent a complete set for $4 per day or take your own.

RATES: The trips cost from $396 to $1,924, all-inclusive, with a 10 percent discount for kids under 16 on Grand Canyon trips and 25 percent on all other trips. Early payment means another 5 to 10 percent off. Litton explains that his trips cost an average of $85 to $95 per day.

## Mariah Wilderness Expeditions

P.O. Box 248
Point Richmond, California 94807
Telephone: 415-233-2303
Owners: Donna Hunter and Shelley Barclay Tennyson
Operating season: Year-round
Trips in: California

IN THEIR OWN WORDS: "We provide wilderness tours within a safe and supportive environment which encourages the family to play together and experience new adventures together."

THE TRIPS: The owners are former social service workers who wanted to combine their love of the out-of-doors with the chance to offer personal growth through the challenges of the wilderness. Donna has been rafting for ten years all over the United States, and Shelley is a graduate of Outdoor Leadership Training Seminars in Colorado.

The trips Mariah runs are one and two days long on the South Fork, the Middle Fork, and the North Fork of the American River and on the Merced River. A minimum age of 7 has been set. Of special interest are a set of two-day trips for fathers and sons, mothers and daughters, fathers and daughters, mothers and sons, and single parents and their children.

EQUIPMENT: Participants take their own sleeping bags and tents, cup, plate, and eating utensils.

RATES: The special-interest trips are $135 per person, with a 10 percent discount for kids 15 or under.

### Bill Dvorak's Kayak and Rafting Expeditions
17921 U.S. Highway 285
Nathrop, Colorado 81236
Telephone: 303-539-6851
Owner: Bill and Jaci Dvorak
Operating season: March through September
Trips in: Utah, Colorado, New Mexico

IN THEIR OWN WORDS: "We've had 18 years experience outfitting river trips that focus on child/adult relationship building. Our staff is attracted for that reason and therefore motivated as well as specifically trained to enhance and facilitate that kind of relationship."

THE TRIPS: Dvorak's groups have 8 to 25 people, and his trips last from 1 to 12 days. He's set 5 years old as his minimum age for the following trips, which can be recommended for families: the Upper Colorado–Lower Gore Canyon trip, one to four days, suitable for beginners and old hands as well; the Green River Wilderness trip, four to seven days, through one of the wildest desert wilderness places on the map; Slickrock Canyon trip, two to three days, on the Dolores Canyon, where moderate rapids are good for beginning kayakers; the six- to nine-day Lower Canyons–Ragan Canyon trip on the Rio Grande, warm water and warm weather along the border of Texas and Mexico; the one-half day Salida-to-Cotopaxi trip on the Arkansas River; and the one- to two-day

Gunnison Gorge trip on the Gunnison River, designated a gold medal trout fishery by the Division of Wildlife.

Rafting, kayaking, and canoeing lessons are available as well.

EQUIPMENT: Food, waterproof duffels, and lifejackets are all provided. Take your own tent and sleeping bags and pad or rent them for $25 and $15, respectively.

RATES: Special trips planned with kids in mind lasting from two to six days are free for kids 16 and under. A sample: a trip for a family of four for three days on the Upper Colorado is $590.

### Rocky Mountain River Tours
P.O. Box 2552
Boise, Idaho 83701
Telephone: 208-344-6668
Owners: David and Sheila Mills
Operating season: June through September, but the water is best
for kids in July and August.
Trips in: Idaho

IN THEIR OWN WORDS: "Our crew of river guides is the backbone of our vacation business. . . . They love working as guides and meeting people. Eighty-two percent of our guests are referred by past guests and that says it all. . . ."

THE TRIPS: The Mills have been rafting and running paddle boats on the river for 15 years, "and we still look forward to our next trip!" The owners recommend rafting on the middle fork of the Salmon River for families: "It is a wonderful place for a family to share laughter, adventure, and to meet new friends." The trips last six days, and July and August are the best times for kids. Children must be at least 6 years old to participate; they don't need to know how to swim because lifejackets are always worn on the water. The trip allows for hiking, fishing, bird watching, sunbathing, and swimming. You may spot deer, elk, mountain sheep, or an occasional otter family. Each night a different campsite is set up along the river; the menu is based on fresh fruit and vegetables, and there are no meals repeated in the six days. Sheila Mills has written a Dutch oven cookbook and teaches the guides new recipes every summer. There's an orientation night before the trip begins on the lawn of a lodge in Stanley, Idaho.

EQUIPMENT: Rocky Mountain provides lifejackets, tents,

eating utensils, two waterproof bags per person for sleeping bags and clothing, and a camera container. Participants should take their own sleeping bags, or, if they prefer, they can rent a bag for $10.

RATES: The six-day trip costs $920, with a 10 percent discount for children 12 and under. The same discount applies for groups of ten or more friends or relatives.

### Idaho Afloat
P.O. Box 542
Grangeville, Idaho 83530
Telephone: 208-983-2414
Owner: Scott Fasken
Operating season: June through September
Trips in: Idaho

IN THEIR OWN WORDS: "As the owner and operator, I personally run each trip. I have a low guest to guide ratio of four to one so that, especially for families, the guides have time to spend with the guests leading hikes, organizing volleyball games, etc. . . ."

THE TRIPS: Fasken has logged 14,000 miles of safe rafting since 1969.

He recommends all of his midsummer trips, from late June to late August, for families. Kids should be at least 6 years old and know how to swim. Trips last from three to six days and are along the Salmon River and the Snake River in Hells Canyon. For families who aren't sure they're ready for camping out, Fasken has put together what he calls lodge trips, which offer the thrill of the rapids, great meals, relaxation in the riverside hot springs, plus the comfort of overnight accommodations at dude ranches along the river. At the ranches there's time for hiking, fishing, horseback riding, or just sitting on the porch. For families who want their whitewater trip more mild than wild, he offers three-day trips on the Lower Snake, which has great scenery but calmer rapids than the upper section. And finally, families can choose a horseback riding–river combination that combines three days of riding and three to four days of rafting. Customized trips are also possible.

EQUIPMENT: Food, duffels, lifejackets (minimum weight 35 pounds) are all provided. Participants either take their own sleeping bags and pads and tents or rent the whole set for $40.

RATES: Rafting trip costs range from $225 for a two-day trip to $800 for a six-day trip (the most expensive includes all transportation from Boise and back). The lodge trip is $1,300. Readers of *Great Vacations with Your Kids* are entitled to a special discount of one-third off for children under 12.

### Hughes River Expeditions
P.O. Box 217
Cambridge, Idaho 83610
Telephone: 208-257-3477
Owners: Jerry Hughes and Carole Finley
Operating Dates: Late April through mid-October
Trips in: Idaho, Oregon

IN THEIR OWN WORDS: "A river trip in the wilderness and a white-water river is an ideal and unique vacation opportunity for families. During the summer over half our clients are families with children 5 years and over. Hughes is a small, owner-operator style of business. . . . We have two small children and we truly value family trips as an important segment of our business . . . we can fit a particular family into a style of trip that fits its own interests and needs. . . ."

THE TRIPS: Jerry Hughes has been a professional guide on the rivers of the region for 22 years; he's had his own company for 11. He's outfitted some famous outdoor types, including Peter Ueberroth, Sir Edmund Hillary, and crews from the National Geographic Society.

Hughes's trips last from three to seven days. "We've taken children as young as 3 years but 5 years is a better age." The largest group is 24, but your family, whatever its size, will constitute a group. It's best if the kids can swim, but because lifejackets are worn at all times, it's not absolutely necessary.

Hughes's trips take place in the backcountry and white-water rivers of Idaho. According to Hughes, the ideal rivers for family vacations are the Middle Fork (four-, five-, and six-day trips from June to September), Snake River–Hells Canyon (three- to five-day trips June through September), and Salmon Canyon (four-day trips in September and October).

EQUIPMENT: Hughes will provide you with just about everything—a roomy four-person tent for every two guests, waterproof gear packs, foam-lined camera boxes (you have to supply your own camera), tarps, and comfortable camp chairs. Sleeping bags and pads are available on request at no extra charge. Each expedition carries a "river library" of books and articles about the area. The accompanying staff does all the camp work and cooking, and the menu includes fresh meats and fish, fresh fruits and vegetables, and Dutch oven–baked biscuits, muffins, and cakes. Take your own fishing tackle and clothes for layering.

RATES: Trips cost from $430 to $880 per person, and there's a 10 percent discount for 12 and under.

### Eastern River Expeditions
Box 1173
Greenville, Maine
Telephone: 207-695-2411 or 207-695-2248
Owner/operator: John Connelly
Operating season: April to October
Trips in: Maine

IN THEIR OWN WORDS: "The most frequent (and fervent) comments we have are in appreciation of our staff. We are lucky to have mature staffers, who are experts about safety, knowledgeable about rivers and wildlife, and full of spirit and fun. Our files are filled with glowing letters praising individual guides as well as the company's 'esprit de corps.' "

THE TRIPS: Eastern trains rescue and military groups and offers college courses in boating skills. It has three base camps, in Maine, in West Virginia, and in New York. For kids 5 and over, they suggest a one-day rafting trip on the Kennebec River; for kids 12 and over, an overnight on the Penobscot River. Of special interest to families is the possibility of arranging a custom clinic in canoeing and kayaking. With Mt. Katadin as the backdrop, instructors take small classes on dam-controlled rivers with moderate temperatures.

The people at Eastern are also willing to help families plan a trip to the north woods of Maine. They can tell you about renting canoes, sailboats, motorboats, windsurfers; finding a good local guide for fishing; locating trails that are best for short family hikes; arranging short, family-type canoe trips; going moose watching on logging roads; renting bikes to explore the back roads and trails.

Eastern will also provide a list of nearby accommodations and names of area baby-sitters.

EQUIPMENT: Tents, food, waterproof duffels, cooking gear, and lifejackets are provided; you'll have to take your own sleeping bags for overnight trips.

RATES: A two-day trip costs about $200 per person.

### Wild Water Adventures
P.O. Box 3554
Eugene, Oregon 97403
Telephone: 503-895-4465
Owner: Al Law
Operating season: March 1–November 30
Trips in: Oregon

IN THEIR OWN WORDS: "We are a small outfit catering to families and small groups. We specialize in individual attention. Families often organize their own 'custom tours' with us so that they have their friends along on the trip."

THE TRIPS: Law recommends a number of his trips for families. The minimum age ranges between 4 and 6, depending on the trip. (Children should weigh 40 or 50 pounds to fit the lifejackets.) Trips last from a half day to nine days and longer. Some of the possibilities: the North Fork of the John Day River, a low-water family kayak run plus trout fishing; three to six days on the Deschutes River, which is fine for beginners age 6 and up; Grande Ronde for three or five days, good for age 6 and up; the Klamath River, good for age 6 and up with good swimming and lots of opportunities to take wildlife photos; the one-day trip on the McKenzie River, fine for age 4 and up; and one- or two-day trips on the North Umpqua for age 8 and up.

Some of the activities that would appeal particularly to kids on Wild Water's trips are supervised swimming in river pools; body surfing in rapids; inflatable-kayak lessons; Indian petroglyph tracing; fishing for trout, catfish, and bass; gold panning; hikes on hills out of camp; outdoor cooking lessons; photography lessons; and games such as frisbee and volleyball in camp.

EQUIPMENT: Everything is provided except tents and sleeping bags, but both can be rented for $10 for two people for a two- to three-day trip. Wild Water's menus have been featured in a camping book. Forget about burned hot dogs and canned beans. Wild Water offers pan pizza, lemon-herb chicken, "Guide's Stew," and peach-apricot crisp.

RATES: For adults, trips range from $30 to $395. There's a youth discount for ages 13 to 16 and a child's discount for those under 12.

### Outback Expeditions
P.O. Box 44
Terlingua, Texas 79852
Telephone: 915-371-2490
Summers: P.O. Box 544, Creede, Colorado
Telephone: 303-658-2332
Owner/operator: Larry G. Humphreys
Trips in: Texas, Colorado

IN THEIR OWN WORDS: "We're a small company with personalized service, a highly experienced and professionally trained staff. We have an impeccable safety record."

THE TRIPS: Guides are chosen for their "good humor and professionalism." The company has been organizing wilderness trips since 1971 and offers guided family adventures for kids 4 years and older on river trips, 12 and over on backpacking excursions. The Upper Rio Grande trip can be a day or two long; trips on the Dolores River in Colorado last three to six days. The Dolores slices its way through canyons and sunny valleys: "The scene changes with every bend." Wilderness backpacking or mountaineering trips run by Outback are three to seven days long and explore the western part of the country, passing through fields of tundra flowers or near herds of elk.

EQUIPMENT: All equipment is provided except sleeping gear; rentals are possible.

RATES: The two-day trip on the Upper Rio Grande is $150 per person; the Dolores River trips are $75 per day; children under 12 get a 15 percent discount.

## SAILING

### Adventure Sailing Escape
Royal Palm Tours, Inc.
P.O. Box 06079
Fort Myers, Florida 33906
Telephone: 813-489-0344
Owner: Ron Drake
Season: Year-round
Trips in: Florida

IN THEIR OWN WORDS: "The shared responsibility of sailing, cruising, docking, mooring, anchoring, and navigating brings
families much closer together than a typical hotel stay. Limited to
sailings of no more than five boats, sailing 'in company' for a week
creates a second family, flotillawide, every time out. . . ."

THE TRIP: Royal Palm's sailing program is for people whose
only sailing experience is wearing boat shoes. It gives families the
chance to sail without hiring a captain. The "Escape Package" is
seven days and six nights long and begins with a day-long Skipper
School for novices. After that, it's hands-on skippering, navigating,
crewing, docking, mooring, and anchoring with coaching by radio
as needed: "Rarely does a flotilla look like ducks in a row." The
captain of the flotilla is a 50-year-old Dutchman named Jacques.
Anyone who wants to spend extra time at the end of the flotilla
week with Jacques can qualify for American Sailing Association
certification. The protected Intracoastal Waterway, Pine Island
Sound, Charlotte Harbor, and the Gulf of Mexico are the flotilla's
cruising grounds. Stops along the way include some of the undevel-
oped islands of the Florida coast, Cabbage Key, and South Seas
Plantation.

EQUIPMENT: Sailing yachts are 27 to 41 feet in length.
Participants sleep on board at a different marina or resort each
night. Included in the cost of the package are the yacht charter,
dock rentals, all linens, most meals, sea bags, charts, and the
supervision of the fleetmaster.

RATES: The price of the package varies with the number of

people. A family of four would cost $780 per person for each adult and $680 per child under 12.

NOTE: Royal Palm also rents three-leveled, 38-foot coastal cabin cruisers with four double beds and one single, including a refrigerator, propane range, full galley, shower, and tub—ideal for six people. Captains are available on request. Rental fees range from $225 for an eight-hour day to $1,350 for a week.

### Maine Waterways and Deer Isles Sailing Center
Deer Isle, Maine 04627
Telephone: 207-348-2339 or 800-845-2267
Owners: Carl and Dana Selin
Operating season: January through April
Trips in: Florida

IN THEIR OWN WORDS: "Explore the sandy island beaches, feel the warmth of the clear tropical waters, test your fishing skills, learn to snorkel and sail."

THE TRIP: Although based in Maine, this sailing center has a winter sailing program in the Florida Keys. Participants sail during the day, from 9:00 A.M. to 5:00 P.M. and spend the nights either in a motel or in a guest apartment in the Selins' home. It is also possible to arrange to sleep on board the boat, using the facilities of the Bonefish Yacht Club Marina.

A family group of five or six are often able to have their own boat. The charters are captained and offer an excellent opportunity to learn to sail. Kids as young as 2 years old have been on these charters; flexibility makes it easy to plan around everyone's needs and desires.

EQUIPMENT: Participants sail on a 1986 Gulf-32 motorsailer or a similar boat. They take their own sleeping bags and do their own shopping and food preparation.

RATES: A full-day charter costs $275, a half-day $175.

Accommodations in conjunction with the charter are $35 per day for a group of four, with cooking privileges included.

### Annapolis Sailing School
Box 3334
Annapolis, Maryland 21403

Telephone: 301-267-7205 or 800-638-9192
Owner: Jerry Wood
Season: Year-round
Trips in: Florida, Maryland

IN THEIR OWN WORDS: "We are the first and largest sailing school in the nation. . . . It's hard to imagine a family activity as rewarding as sailing."

THE TRIP: Annapolis offers a seven-day Family Sailing Vacation package at two of its locations, in Annapolis on Chesapeake Bay and in St. Petersburg, Florida, on Tampa Bay. The vacation (for families of two to six people) begins with a Weekend Beginners course. While taking the course, the family spends nights on shore. The optimum minimum age for participants is 12, although special arrangements may be made for younger children. Once the essential skills have been mastered, you and your family take off on a five-day live-aboard cruise in a 26- or 30-foot cruising auxiliary sailboat that sails as part of a fleet accompanied by Annapolis instructors on their own lead boat.

EQUIPMENT: Beginning students learn to sail on a 24-foot Rainbow (built as a teaching boat), and the live-aboard portion of the package is on either an Annapolis 26, designed and built especially for the school, or a Newport 30.

RATES: A beginner's course plus a cruise based in Annapolis is $1,275 for a family of four; in St. Petersburg it's $1,595. Included is the cost of accommodation at a motel with a kitchenette during the course, and the Monday through Friday live-aboard cruise. Participants must provide their own sleeping bags, food, and other equipment; a list is supplied.

### Steve Colgate's Offshore Sailing School
East Schofield Street
City Island, New York 10464
Telephone: 212-885-3200 or 800-221-4326
Owners: Steve and Doris Colgate
Operating season: Year-round
Trips in: Florida, Rhode Island, Maine, New York

IN THEIR OWN WORDS: "There's nothing else like it. No other sailing school offers this opportunity, this unforgettable mix of instruction and vacation."

THE TRIPS: Offshore is the largest sailing school in the world: more than 50,000 students have taken courses there. Offshore's headquarters is City Island, New York, but it has schools in some popular vacation spots—on Captiva Island on Florida's Gulf Coast, Bay Point in Florida's northwest Gulf Coast, Newport on Rhode Island Sound, and Bar Harbor, Maine, in Frenchman's Bay. Offshore runs the school and arranges for the accommodations at resorts at the various sites. A good choice for families is the school on Captiva Island, where guests stay at South Seas Plantation, a 330-acre tropical paradise that offers children's programs for family members who are too young for sailing lessons. (Twelve is the official minimum but exceptions can be made.) "Learn to Sail," "Sailing and Cruising," and "Bareboat Cruising Preparation" are some of the course choices. Family members can sign up for different courses and can sail at the same time, go to class at the same time, and have free time together. Offshore has its own travel agency, Offshore Travel Inc., which can make any and all arrangements.

EQUIPMENT: On Captiva Island you'll learn on 27-foot Olympic class Solings. "Sailing and Cruising" is taught on Laser 28's, and "Bareboat" is taught on 36-foot S2's or Hunter 40's.

RATES: Costs vary from place to place. A sample: "A Learn to Sail" course on Captiva Island with accommodations in a one-bedroom beach villa costs $842 per person from mid-October to mid-December for a full week, Sunday to Sunday.

# 7

## CITY VACATIONS

Cities are great places to go for vacations with kids. There are lots of things to do and lots of resources to count on. Obviously one couldn't cover every city that would be fun for you and your kids so we've chosen six of the most popular. Next time around we'll add more. Just tell us which ones you'd like covered.

In the following chapters we've included information that pertains especially to families. Enough has been written for tourists that needn't be repeated here. We wanted to cover what you won't find in other books—baby-sitting services, hotels with family plans, special tours for kids, and so forth.

Before we begin, we want you to know about a relatively new phenomenon, newspapers published in a number of U.S. cities that are meant especially for parents. We've looked through all of them, and we're impressed by what wonderful resources they are for families. Not only will you find articles of interest, a calendar of events just for kids, and a listing of services available to you, but you can also use the publishers of the paper as contacts for specific information you may need.

Here's a listing of some of the papers we've discovered. The National Parenting Publications Network, P.O. Box 153, Pomfret, Connecticut 06424 (203-974-3566) will be able to tell you about parent publications in the area you're visiting in case there's not one listed here. Check each of our city sections for the rest. Before you set out on your trip, write for the latest issue. (Send $1 to cover postage and handling.) You'll be amazed at how much you'll learn:

*Impact Parenting*
4747 West 22nd Street
Phoenix, Arizona 85016

*Parents' Press*
1454 Sixth Street
Berkeley, California 94710

*Peninsula Parent*
(covering San Francisco)
P.O. Box 89
Millbrae, California 94030

*San Diego Family Press*
P.O. Box 23965
San Diego, California 92123

*Kids, Kids, Kids*
P.O. Box 2277
Saratoga, California 95070

*Colorado Parents*
P.O. Box 985
Boulder, Colorado 80306

*Denver Parent*
818 E. 19th St.
Denver, Colorado 80218

*Connecticut Parent*
P.O. Box 153
Pomfret, Connecticut 06424

*Florida Parent*
309 NE 5th Avenue
Delray Beach, Florida 33444

*Tallahassee's Child*
1635 North Monroe Street
Tallahassee, Florida 32303

*Family Times*
P.O. Box 17481
Tampa, Florida 33682

*Atlanta Parent*
P.O. Box 8506
Atlanta, Georgia 30306

*Youth View*
1401 West Paces Ferry Road
Suite A-217
Atlanta, Georgia 30327

*Louisville's Child*
(serving Louisville, Kentucky)
P.O. Box 2352
Clarksville, Indiana 47131

*Indy's Child*
8900 Keystone Crossing
Suite 538
Indianapolis, Indiana 46240

*KC Parent*
(serving Kansas City)
6400 Glenwood
Suite 300
Overland Park, Kansas 66202

*Baltimore's Child*
P.O. Box 19951
Baltimore, Maryland 21211

*Metro Parent*
518 Paris Avenue SE
Grand Rapids, Michigan 49503

*Minnesota Parent*
300 W. Franklin
Number 212
Minneapolis, Minnesota 55404

*Suburban Parent Magazine*
444 Ryders Lane
East Brunswick, New Jersey 08816

*Delaware Valley Parent*
Bristol Pike & Street Road

Suite 200
Bensalem, Pennsylvania 19020

*The Children's Pages Monthly*
(serving Dallas)
P.O. Box 113149
Carrollton, Texas 75001-3149

*Houston Kid Times*
P.O. Box 272351
Houston, Texas 77277

*San Antonio for Kids*
P.O. Box 40486
San Antonio, Texas 78229

*Parent Express*
(serving Salt Lake City)
P.O. Box 7163
Murray, Utah 84107

*New Family Life*
P.O. Box 5186
Arlington, Virginia 22205

*Seattle's Child*
P.O. Box 22578
Seattle, Washington 98122

*Potomac Children*
Box 39134
Washington, D.C. 20016

## BOSTON

Boston's a great place for families. It's a manageable size, has lots of child-oriented sights and activities, has a good public transportation system, is full of history come-to-life, and is fun.

### For Information

Before you go, call the Greater Boston Convention and Visitors Bureau toll-free number, 800-858-0200. You'll get a recording, but if you leave your name and address they'll send you basic information about sights, events, and accommodations. Send, too, for a copy of *Boston Parents Paper,* Box 1777, Zip: 02130. Once you get to Boston, call the Events Line—267-6446—and/or visit one of the bureau's two offices and be sure to pick up a copy of the Bureau's free *Boston: The Official Guidebook.* The Prudential Visitor Center, 617-536-4100, open 9:00 A.M. to 5:00 P.M. daily, has brochures on many city sites. It's on the west side of Prudential Plaza, near the Copley T and Prudential T subway stations. Parking is available at the Prudential Center Parking Garage.

The Boston Common Visitor Information Center is downtown, on the Tremont Street side of Boston Common, and it's the first step on Boston's historic Freedom Trail. *No* public phone here—visit them in person for information on the city and state.

Use the Park Street T station or park at the Boston Common Underground Parking Garage.

The National Park Service Visitor Center, 15 State Street, Zip: 02109, 617-242-5642, opposite the Old State House, offers information and displays on Boston, restrooms, and phones. It's open 9:00 to 5:00 daily and is near the State Street T stop; the closest parking is in the Government Center Garage.

The Bostix Ticket Booth at Faneuil Hall, near the Government Center T stop and the Government Center Garage, is the city's official entertainment and cultural information center. You'll find information on theater, music, dance, historic sites, and special visitor attractions. They're open 11:00 to 6:00 Monday through Saturday, Sunday noon to 6:00. Half-price tickets are available on the day of performance.

There are a number of Boston guidebooks available. If you wait until you get to the city to buy one, stop in the downtown area at the historical Globe Corner Bookstore, 3 School Street, which once was the center of literary America and now has a large section just for travel books. Some of the ones we recommend: *In and Out of Boston With (or Without) Children* by Bernice Chesler ($10.95), published by Globe Pequot Press. This is a well-researched, well-organized guide to the city with museums, parks, historic sites, nature centers, nearby beaches and ski areas, and all kinds of other helpful information.

*Car-Free in Boston: A User's Guide to Public Transportation in Greater Boston and New England* (Association of Public Transportation, Inc., P.O. Box 192, Cambridge, Massachusetts 02238, $3.95). This book includes everything you need to know about getting around Boston on public transportation, schedules and routes included.

Other books worth a look are *The Greater Boston Parks and Recreation Guide* by Mark Primack, published by Globe Pequot Press ($9.95); *Historic Walks in Boston* by John Harris ($9.95), also from Globe Pequot Press; *Frommer's Guide to Boston* ($5.95), Simon & Schuster; and *The Blue Guide to Boston*, distributed by W. W. Norton ($15.95).

## Tours of the City

Brush Hill's Beantown Trolleys, 109 Norfolk Street, Zip: 02139, 617-287-1900 or 800-647-4776, or 1-800-343-1238 in Massachusetts. You can travel the historic Freedom Trail on a trolley. With a ticket you can ride all day, get off at important landmarks, visit at your own pace, and rejoin the continuously narrated shuttle service at any time. The trolley leaves from the Visitors' Information Booth on Tremont Street at Boston Common, and from Copley Square in the Back Bay, seven days a week, starting at 9:30 A.M. Tickets for children under 12 are $4.50; adults pay $6.

Uncommon Boston, Ltd., 65 Commonwealth Avenue, Boston, Zip: 02116, 617-266-9768, gives visitors an insider's view of Boston Gardens, galleries, clubs, and libraries and plans special events for children.

Daytrippers, Inc., 2 Arden Road, Medford, Zip: 02155, 617-391-6040, are the people to call for personalized tours of metropolitan Boston by car or foot.

The Gray Line of Boston, 367 Dorchester Avenue, South Boston, Zip: 02127, 617-426-8800, offers fully narrated bus tours of Boston.

New England Sights, Inc., 18 Brattle Street, Cambridge, Zip: 02138, 617-492-6689, operates custom car tours for families.

Children will enjoy Make Way for the Ducklings, a walk through Beacon Hill along Mrs. Mallard's route; A Kid's View of the North End; and Waterfront Tours, all run by the Historic Neighborhoods Foundation, 617-426-1898. Call for times and prices.

### The Freedom Trail

Think Boston and you think history. And in fact, a lot has happened here, much of which you can learn about along the Freedom Trail.

The trail isn't a straight path you can take from start to finish. Instead, it's a historical tour of Boston winding in and out of the heart of the city, and most of the stops along the way are free.

The best place to start is at the National Park Service Visitors' Service at 15 State Street, Zip: 02109. You can grab a map and walk on your own, or join one of the free guided walks offered several times a day that give you an earful of history from the Revolution through 1812. Stops along the Freedom Trail include the following:

> The State House
> The Park Street Church
> Granary Burying Ground
> King's Chapel
> Benjamin Franklin Statue
> Old Corner Bookstore
> Old South Meeting House
> Old State House
> Faneuil Hall
> Quincy Market
> Paul Revere House
> Old North Church
> Copp's Hill Burying Ground
> The Charlestown Navy Yard (USS *Constitution,* USS *Constitution* Museum, USS *Cassin Young*)
> Bunker Hill Monument and Museum

A good way for kids to see part of the trail is Boston By Little Feet, an hour-and-a-half tour given on Sundays at 2:00 P.M. from May through October. It is suggested for kids from 8 to 12 with an accompanying adult and is led by an enthusiastic local historian who knows when the kids have had enough. Call 617-367-2345 for details.

Recommended for stops along the trail for kids 5 and over is "The Whites of Their Eyes," a multimedia presentation that recreates the battle of Bunker Hill and the events that led up to it. For kids 6 or over, a stop at the USS *Constitution* Museum is also fun. The museum presents the story of how the famous ship was built and how her crew of 450 men and boys lived while at sea—what they ate, how they slept and worked together, and how they often fought among themselves. Kids can try out an 18-inch hammock, climb to the ceiling on an actual fighting top, or match their decision-making skill with those of the *Constitution*'s captains as they sailed into battle. Strollers are allowed, and there are guided tours (with advance notice) and self-guided tours available. There is a playground next to the museum and another across the street.

## Back Bay

The Back Bay area used to be a shallow mudflat until it was filled in back in the mid-19th century. Today it gleams with elegant townhouses—look up for details on chimneys, gables, and balconies on houses on Commonwealth Avenue and Marlborough Street. Boutiques and outdoor cafés give the area a cosmopolitan flavor.

Copley Square is an architectural delight, with several churches and antique buildings, but kids will have more fun at the Boston Public Library (the oldest free municipal library in the world), where, with an adult in tow, they can look up the newspaper for the day they were born. The children's room has special programs all the time. And you can add a touch of class by stepping over to the Copley Square Hotel for tea and crumpets among the palms between 2:00 and 5:00 P.M.

For a wide-angle view of the city, kids will love the John Hancock Observatory at the John Hancock Tower, Copley Square. Special exhibits and a sound-and-light show describe how Boston has changed from a Revolutionary period town to a modern city; a short film gives you a helicopter peek, and kids will like the telescopes that bring landmarks closer. Admission is $2.75 for adults; kids under 5 are admitted free.

Also fronting on the square is the new glass and chrome shopping mecca, Copley Square Plaza, with high-priced shops, movies, and restaurants. A good snack spot here is Au Bon Pain, best for soup, croissants, and special coffee.

Walk out of the Plaza and over the pedestrian walkway to the Christian Science Center. Children may lose patience with a detailed tour of the center, but they'll be awed by the Mapparium. You enter via a glass catwalk and find yourself encircled in the world as it was politically divided in 1932. It's fashioned from 608 individual sections of colored glass, each a quarter of an inch thick, and brilliantly lit with electric lights. Because the glass doesn't absorb sound, you can hear whispers from every part of the room. Telephone 617-262-2300 for hours.

Boston's landmark for kids—the swan boats—grace the Boston Public Garden from the first Saturday before April 19 until the last Saturday in September. Take bread to feed the ducks during the 12-minute ride. Flowers and meandering paths make this a good spot for a picnic and unwinding.

Nearby is the Gibson House at 137 Beacon Street (Zip: 02116). Four floors of this townhouse are filled with Victoriana just as the last Gibson left them in 1956. It's open May through October, Tuesday through Sunday, 2:00 to 5:00 P.M., and some afternoons in winter. Call 617-236-6338. The Gardner Museum and the Museum of Fine Arts (for older, more sophisticated kids) are also in this area.

Try Legal Seafoods for fresh fish (Boston Park Plaza Hotel, Columbus Avenue and Arlington Street) and children's specials or the Magic Pan, 47 Newbury Street, with crepes geared to kids.

For some modern-day excitement, try The Skywalk at the Prudential Tower, 617-236-3318. A speedy elevator whisks you up 50 floors in seconds for a wonderful view of Boston.

### Beacon Hill

The "Hill" used to be 60 feet higher than it is today, but even though it's flattened some, the area's still the most prestigious spot in town. It's dominated by the Massachusetts State House, a gold-domed building that makes for an interesting tour, and fronts Boston Common and the Public Garden.

The first Bostonian built a house on Beacon Hill in 1622, and the area has held its cachet through the years. The streets are cobblestoned and narrow, and the houses have lots of period architectural detail. Louisburg Square is a lovely, tree-lined spot bound by elegant brick townhouses and is an inviting place to stroll any time of year.

There are a few museums and antique houses to visit here, but they aren't interesting to children. They'll probably be more

thrilled by the Hampshire House at 84 Beacon Street, the proto-
type for the TV show "Cheers." It's oak-paneled and properly
Bostonian and overlooks the Public Garden, a nice spot for a
civilized brunch on Sunday.

On Charles Street, you'll find several reasonably priced
restaurants and delis, with menus posted in the windows. Rebec-
ca's at 21 Charles Street has a fine reputation as a gourmet food
restaurant with an informal setting, where kids can find something
good to eat, too.

In the summer, free concerts at the Hatch Shell on Storrow
Drive are local traditions. It's best to park in the Underground
Garage at Boston Common and walk from Beacon Street over the
Arthur Fiedler Footbridge and plant a blanket on the lawn. Also in
the summer, but not free, are Concerts on the Common, where pop
singers play to thousands on warm nights. Check the *Boston Globe*
for the schedule.

### Downtown and Chinatown

Bostonians say the busiest intersection in New England is at
Washington and Summer Streets: called Downtown Crossing. Six
major department stores, including the famous basement of Fi-
lene's, converge at this pedestrian mall, where street musicians and
mimes entertain in all kinds of weather. Within a few blocks you'll
find lots of stops on the Freedom Trail, such as Ben Franklin's
birthplace marker and the Old South Meeting House. A little of
these goes a long way with kids.

Between Downtown Crossing and Back Bay sits the third
largest Chinatown in the country, which you enter officially
through the Chinese Gate, a gift from Taiwan, at Beach and
Edinboro Streets. The area is rough around the edges, filled with
markets and shops catering to the community, and many restaurants, all run by Chinese. The best time to visit is Sunday mornings, when many of the restaurants offer *dim sum,* the Chinese
brunch that's especially fun for kids. Waiters take trolleys of
nibbles around, and you pick what you want while the waiter keeps
a running tab. The Imperial Tea House, 70 Beach Street, is a local
favorite, so be prepared to wait in line. The festivities during the
Chinese New Year feature a day-long parade with firecrackers and
dancing dragons.

Boston's theater district, which has shrunk in recent years, is squeezed between these two parts of town. Look in the *Boston Globe*'s Thursday calendar section or consult Bostix at Faneuil Hall for what's going on when you're in town. The restaurants here aren't worth a stop.

### North End and Haymarket

The North End, Boston's little Italy, is quickly becoming yuppified, but it's still a colorful place to visit and to eat in. You can walk there from the Faneuil Hall Marketplace, along Haymarket to Blackstone Street; there's no parking at all.

Haymarket, along the way, is a venerable Boston tradition, a colorful produce market open Fridays and Saturdays until early evening. Vendors crowd the streets hawking fruits and vegetables from pushcarts, and bargaining is acceptable behavior. Kids will be amazed at the wholesale meat markets housed in small storefronts along the street. Other stores are crammed with cheese, fish, and specialty foods that are hard to find in other places. Haymarket's appealing because it's still real, not a contemporary version of an upscale market, like Faneuil Hall.

The North End has been home to generations of European immigrants, most recently to Italian families, and although the area is changing, there's still a strong neighborhood flavor in the narrow streets, bakeries, and restaurants, where you'll hear as much Italian as English. The stores are fun for browsing, and there are so many restaurants the best bet is to look at posted menus before you make a choice. The European, at 218 Hanover Street, has a children's menu and offers all Italian dishes, with pizza a favorite. Regina Pizzeria at 11½ Thatcher Street, the original restaurant in what is now a chain, serves pizza only in a plain atmosphere. You'll probably have to wait for a booth.

After lunch or dinner, stop in one of the cafés featuring Italian bakery items and cappuccino and feel like you're in Europe for a while.

Several points on the Freedom Trail are here in the North End, including Rose Fitzgerald Kennedy's birthplace, the Paul Revere House, and the site of Benjamin Franklin's boyhood home.

Italian feast days are still celebrated here with parades, and they draw huge crowds from all over the city.

Kids in need of a rest would enjoy a stop at the North End branch of the Boston Public Library. There are a nice children's area and a diorama of the ducal palace in Venice.

Durgin Park, a Boston eating institution, is in this part of town. The atmosphere's rough and rowdy, you share tables covered with checkered cloths, and the portions, of favorites such as prime ribs and Indian pudding, are huge. Prices are reasonable, but you'll probably have to stand in line for a table.

### The Waterfront and Faneuil Hall Marketplace

You can spend several days in Boston with children and never leave this area, because it's chock full of things to do with kids. The big attractions are all the museums and dozens of eating spots.

First, the museums. On the waterfront, start with Museum Wharf, where you'll find the Children's Museum, the Computer Museum, and the Tea Party Ship and Museum, all accessible via the South Station or Aquarium T stop and within a few blocks of each other.

THE CHILDREN'S MUSEUM (300 Congress Street, Zip: 02210, 617-426-6500). A fabulous place. It is an example of hands-on learning at its very best. Toddlers can jump and slide in Playspace while older kids run up and down the Climbing Sculpture. Our kids loved the do-it-yourself television show and Grandparents' House. There are changing tables, strollers, a restaurant (a McDonald's branch), and small-size drinking fountains. Leave enough time for kids to go back to their favorite exhibits. There will be many.

BOSTON TEA PARTY SHIP AND MUSEUM (Congress Street Bridge, Zip: 02110, 617-338-1773). Where Boston's most notorious protest is re-created. You can explore a replica of the original ship and even toss some tea overboard. Older kids especially like the "Where Do You Stand?" exhibit, which explores the issue of protest. Strollers are allowed.

THE COMPUTER MUSEUM (300 Congress Street, Zip: 02110, 617-426-2800). This is the world's only museum devoted to the past, present, and future of computers. The hands-on exhibits feature everything from vintage keypunch machines to the latest in personal computers. Kids can design a car, alter the computer image of their face, or have a conversation with a talking computer. Strollers are allowed, and there are guided tours every Saturday and Sunday at 1:30 and again at 3:00.

For older children, the John F. Kennedy Library across the bay at Columbia Point is an exciting stop. Walk up to Central Wharf to get to the Aquarium.

NEW ENGLAND AQUARIUM (Central Wharf, Zip: 02110, 617-973-5200). Its center is a 187,000-gallon ocean tank that spirals to the ceiling. As you walk up the ramp alongside the tank, sharks, huge sea turtles, and moray eels watch your progress. In all, there are more than 70 exhibits that feature marine life from as far as India and the Amazon and as near as New England. The "Edge of the Sea" tidepool exhibit, where kids are encouraged to pick up and touch a variety of creatures, is popular with the littlest visitors. The dolphin and sea lion show is another kids' favorite. Facilities include a snack bar, ramps, and small-size drinking fountains; strollers are allowed.

In the summer, you can get to the Boston Harbor Island via ferries from Long Wharf. The free service, run by the Boston Harbor Island State Park, stops at six islands, where you can picnic, camp, swim, and explore historic ruins. Ferries run from May 30 to September 30. For details, call the State Park office, 617-749-0051.

The playground and the view from Waterfront Park (or Christopher Columbus Park) are worth a stop.

After the museums, cross over Atlantic Avenue to get to Faneuil Hall Marketplace, a complex of three 500-foot-long buildings dating back to 1826. The copper-domed central building houses stand-up food spots featuring everything from frozen yogurt to gourmet potato chips to every kind of ethnic food you can imagine.

Let kids pick what they want to eat, and picnic on a bench outside on the cobblestoned, traffic-free mall, where street entertainers and special events keep the place hopping all year long. This is also a good place to let kids go free with a few dollars in their pockets, because pushcarts sell all the little things they like to buy.

## Another Boston Feature

The Boston Museum of Science located in Science Park along the Charles River, is 200 yards away from the MBTA's Science Park Station on the Lechmere Green Line, 617-589-0100.

This is an "interactive, participatory" museum with more than 400 exhibits and live animal shows, demonstrations, and special weekend presentations. One of its newest features is Omnimax, a movie with images that fill a seven-story-high dome. The museum includes a popular dinosaur exhibit, planetarium shows, Computer Place, the Theatre of Electricity, and more. For changing diapers or nursing you can use the first aid room; there are a restaurant with high chairs, a children's gift shop, and a small-size drinking fountain.

### Time Out

For baby-sitting, contact Parents in a Pinch, 45 Bartlett Crescent, Brookline, Massachusetts 02146, 617-739-KIDS. Sitters are trained, screened, Red Cross–certified child-care professionals and available for days, evenings, weekends, and overnights. The co-owners Ronnie Mae Weiss and Davida Manon say that it's best to call at least 48 hours in advance. For same day/next day service, there's a $10 surcharge. The rates are $8/hour for one child with a four-hour minimum, 50 cents extra for each additional sibling. Holiday rates are higher.

### Accommodations

#### Bed and Breakfasts

For a free guide to bed and breakfast accommodations and guest houses in Massachusetts with some in Boston, call 800-343-9072 and ask for *The Spirit of Massachusetts Bed and Breakfast Guide,* or order by mail from the Massachusetts Division of Tourism, 100 Cambridge Street, Boston, Massachusetts 02202.

Two bed and breakfast services that specialize in rooms in the Boston area are New England Bed and Breakfast, Inc., 1045 Centre Street, Newton Centre, Massachusetts 02159, 617-244-2112 or 498-9819; and Greater Boston Hospitality, P.O. Box 1142, Brookline, Massachusetts 02146, 617-277-5430. The latter sent some sample listings: A four-story townhouse on Beacon Hill with rooms with private bath and an English breakfast served in a Queen Anne style dining room for $50 for two; $15 for a child in an adjoining room; a 1940 custom-built home in Brookline with play areas for kids, a sun deck, and free breakfast for $35 to $60 per night, no charge for children under 1 year.

*Hotels*

THE BOSTONIAN HOTEL (Faneuil Hall, 617-523-3600 or 800-343-0922). This hotel is right in the middle of the Faneuil Hall Marketplace. It normally costs $180 to $210 for a room, but weekend and seasonal specials may be half that. Cribs are available for $5 per night, and children can always stay free in their parents' room. Baby-sitting is available for $10 per hour with 24 hours notice required. The Bostonian's rooftop restaurant offers a children's menu; however, it is one of the city's finest restaurants, quite expensive, and often booked weeks ahead of time for weekend nights.

BOSTON MARRIOTT HOTEL/COPLEY PLACE (110 Huntington Avenue, Zip: 02116, 617-236-5800 or 800-228-9290). The hotel is in the heart of the city, a five-minute walk from Boston Common in the Back Bay area. Facilities include an indoor pool; cribs are provided at no charge. Two-bedroom suites are available. There's a children's menu in the dining room, and a children's menu is available through room service. Special supersaver rate on a room sleeping up to five people is $179 on a space-available basis. Children 18 or younger are free if they stay in their parents' room.

EMBASSY SUITES HOTEL (400 Soldiers Field Road, Zip: 02134, 617-783-0090 or 800-EMBASSY). All of the one-bedroom suites include a living room, bedroom, bath, refrigerator, wet bar, two color televisions, and three telephones. All of the suites overlook a skylit atrium. A complimentary full American breakfast is included in the rate, and the hotel has an indoor pool, a whirlpool, and a sauna. Rates are $99 for Friday or Saturday night; $160 on weeknights. The hotel is located on the Charles River, on the Boston/Cambridge line, and there's a free shuttle service to central sites in Cambridge and Boston. A special package called The Family Frolic includes a two-room suite with room for up to four people, full breakfast for everyone, free parking, a welcome bag of balloons, games, a map of Boston, coupons for Steve's Ice Cream, milk and cookies for the kids and liqueurs for the grown-ups at bedtime, and four passes to Boston area attractions. The cost is $139 for the first night, $110 for additional nights.

HOWARD JOHNSON HOTEL (575 Commonwealth Avenue,

Zip: 02215, 617-267-3100 or 800-654-2000). There's a family plan from Thursday through Sunday with a rate of $51 per room including breakfast and parking. Kids under 12 stay free, and right next door are the 28 flavors.

THE MIDTOWN HOTEL (220 Huntington Avenue, Zip: 02115, 617-262-1000 or 800-343-1177). The basic rate is $79 for a double room, and kids under 18 stay free with their parents. Free underground parking is a plus, and in nice weather, the outdoor pool is fun.

THE RITZ-CARLTON (15 Arlington Street, Zip: 02117, 617-536-5700). Right by the Boston Public Garden, this elegant hotel offers "a weekend of social savvy" for kids—"Children should be seen and heard at this refined and recreational weekend designed to practice and polish their social skills." There aren't many other programs like this one; it includes a grand tour of the 60-year-old hotel, and instruction and demonstration in table setting, table manners, food preparation, grooming, and dancing in preparation for a Saturday night dance. Kids stay in twin-bedded rooms; the fee is $200. The suggested ages are 8 to 12. Parents staying at the hotel while their kids participate in the social savvy weekend pay a special rate of $140 for a room. These weekends are held throughout the winter on seven different dates.

SHERATON BOSTON HOTEL AND TOWERS (Prudential Center, Zip: 02199, 617-236-2000 or 800-325-3535). There's usually a family weekend plan, sometimes as low as $69 per room. Kids under 17 always stay free in their parents' room. The hotel has a glass-covered indoor pool and its own health club. Cribs are provided free, and baby-sitting is available through the Housekeeping Department for $4.55 per hour.

## CHICAGO

Chicago is a spectacular-looking city, with its lakefront its most striking feature. Scattered along the shore are playgrounds, picnic sites, and marinas—all wonderful places to stop to rest or play. Lake Michigan is almost always within walking distance of wherever you are. You can visit a museum in the morning, sail on a lake, and take a swim in the afternoon, depending only on your own two feet for transportation.

For anyone with an interest in architecture, Chicago is a dream—you'll find the works of Louis Sullivan, Frank Lloyd Wright, and Mies van der Rohe and two outstanding examples of the architecture of the 1970s, the Sears Tower and the John Hancock Building. To see some spectacular outdoor sculpture, walk from the Archicenter (330 South Dearborn) north on Dearborn to see Calder's "Flamingo" on the Federal Center Plaza; Chagall's "Four Seasons," a mosaic, on the First National Bank Plaza (be there at lunchtime in summer for free entertainment); Miro's "Chicago" and Picasso's "Lady" facing each other on Daley Plaza across from City Hall; and Dubuffet's "Monument with Standing Beast" in front of the State of Illinois Center, where you can wander in, explore the atrium, and ride the glass elevators. Chicago starts to celebrate every year as soon as the weather gets nice. From June to August there are concerts by the Chicago Symphony Orchestra at the Ravinia Festival in Highland Park (easily reached by special train at concert time) and free concerts in Grant Park; take a picnic supper and make yourself comfortable on the lawn. To find out about what festivals are happening where and when, call the Visitor's Event Line, 312-225-2323.

The best guidebook to the city for families is not available at bookstores—it's called *Chicago: A Child's Kind of Town* and is published by the Department of Child Psychiatry, The Children's Memorial Hospital, 2300 Children's Plaza, Chicago, Illinois 60614. It costs $4.50, is available by mail, and is an excellent guide to everything the city has to offer that is of special interest to kids, with good advice on taking excursions with kids, and even some connect-the-dot activity pages to keep the kids busy while on line or in buses.

A more standard source of information on the city is the Chicago Convention and Tourism Bureau's Water Tower Information Center, Michigan and Chicago Avenues, 312-225-5000, or the one at McCormick Place on the Lake, 2300 South Lake Shore Drive, 312-791-7000. The Mayor's Office of Special Events has a hotline number, 312-744-3315, with information on what's happening when you arrive.

For general information on the city, pick up a copy of *Chicago Magazine,* a monthly that you'll find at newsstands all around town. But for more child-oriented information, get a copy of *Chicago Parent News Magazine,* a monthly available free in family-type locations. Call them at 312-508-0973 if you're having trouble finding a copy. (Their address is 7001 North Clark Street, Chicago, Illinois 60626.) Another Chicago-based publication just for parents is called *Mother's Network News* and is designed specifically for kids 4 years old and under. It includes events such as storytelling, classes for kids, and workshops. Copies are $3 each and are available by mail from P.O. Box 11569, Chicago, Illinois 60611, or by phone, 312-642-3022. A year's subscription, six issues and three "Special Reports," costs $20.

## Tours and Overviews

A good starting point for your Chicago adventure is "Here's Chicago," a multiimage show about the city that's located in the Water Tower Pumping Station. The first show starts at 10:00 A.M., and shows run continuously every half-hour. Admission is $3.75 for adults, $2 for kids 12 and under. Call 312-467-7114 for details.

And for kids who like to get a view from the top, we suggest the 39-second elevator ride up to the Observatory of the John Hancock Center. From the observatory you'll be able to see Chicago, Lake Michigan, and the three-state surrounding area, 80 miles on a clear day. By renting an "audio wand" for $1.50 you can hear all about Chicago and the observatory while you're up there. The admission is $2.50 for adults, $1.50 for kids 5 to 15, and free for kids under 5. If you want to combine a trip to the observatory with a viewing of "Here's Chicago" (they're two blocks apart), you can buy a combined ticket and save 20 percent.

Another spectacular view from the top is possible from the 103d floor Skydeck of the Sears Tower. Call 312-875-9696 for details.

If a boat tour on Lake Michigan appeals to you, call Wendella Sightseeing Boats, 312-337-1446. A two-hour tour costs $7.50; one hour is $4.50. Kids under 12 are $3.75 and $2.25. The boats operate from May 30 through Labor Day.

And for those who prefer to remain on dry land, consider the Chicago Transit Authority's Culture Buses. The three routes all start at the Art Institute and stop along the way at all the museums and other points of interest in town. You can hop on and off whenever you want. The culture buses run from Memorial Day to the end of September, and they leave every 20 to 30 minutes. Call 312-836-7000 for information.

## Things to Do and See

We've grouped Chicago's attractions from north to south in walkable clusters. Parks are always nearby. You can get to almost all the places listed here by riding the CTA's Culture Bus.

### Lincoln Park

EXPRESSWAYS CHILDREN'S MUSEUM (2045 North Lincoln Park West, Zip: 60614, 312-281-3222). Located in a park, this is a hands-on museum for kids of preschool age through 12 years. Kids can crawl through the tunnel at "Touchy Business" or perch on a throne or walk through the "Lighted Forest." A "Giant Colorforms Mural" and the "Three Bears' House" are fun for younger kids especially. Older kids like the exhibit on "Chairs"—their function, history, and art—and "Chicago," a minicity that includes a post office, a hospital corner, and other places to play. The "Recycle Arts Center" is where kids can poke through bins full of unusual materials to take home to make into jewelry, puppets, robots, or whatever their imagination allows. Family workshops—on jewelry making, mime, mask making, and so on—are scheduled throughout the year. Suggested admission is $2 for adults and $1 for kids. Strollers must be parked; there are changing tables in the men's and women's restrooms, a gift shop, and kid-size drinking fountains.

LINCOLN PARK ZOO (2200 North Cannon Drive, Zip: 60614, 312-294-4660). Not far from the Children's Museum is the zoo, home to 2,400 animals. Guided tours, films, and talks about animals are scheduled daily. You can watch the elephant workout or check out the nation's largest polar bear pool. The younger kids will like the Farm-in-the-Zoo and the Children's Zoo, which encourage real close-up observation. The zoo is free, and we recommend it. It's compact and easy to navigate with kids.

### Grant Park Area

The following five places of interest are all close to the greenery of the lakefront and Grant Park—perfect for stretching out and having picnics or boat rides.

THE FIELD MUSEUM OF NATURAL HISTORY (Roosevelt Road at Lake Shore Drive, Zip: 60605, 312-922-9410). One of the largest and most famous museums in the world, The Field is a favorite of kids. There are nine acres of exhibits and special displays: dinosaurs, Egyptian mummies, and a "Place for Wonder," a treasure room full of touchable displays for all ages. At the "Pawnee Earth Lodge" you can hear songs and stories of Indian life, and on weekends there are often family programs and tours. The museum is open 9:00 A.M. to 5:00 P.M. Admission is $2 for adults, $1 for kids 6 to 17, free for kids under 6, and $4 for families. Thursdays are free for everyone.

THE ADLER PLANETARIUM (1300 South Lake Shore Drive, Zip: 60605, 312-322-0300). The Sky Show is for kids 6 and over; the younger ones have a special children's version on Saturdays at 10:00 A.M. The planetarium is open every day. Boat rides depart from the planetarium, so when you've finished looking around inside, why not get some fresh air out on the lake? The admission to the planetarium is free; the Sky Show costs $2.50 for adults, $1.50 for kids 6 to17.

JOHN G. SHEDD AQUARIUM (1200 South Lake Shore Drive, Zip: 60605, 312-939-2438). They call this Chicago's "Ocean by the Lake." It contains 7,000 animals of more than 700 species. The six major galleries take the visitor on a journey through six major aquatic areas, and there are more than 160 exhibits in all. Kids especially like the Coral Reef Exhibit, where the diver enters, feeds the animals, and then talks to visitors through a microphone in the dive mask about the sharks, sea turtles, moray eels, and other colorful reef fish in the exhibit. "Tributaries," an area with smaller tanks, and the "Shark Exhibit" are kid pleasers, too.

Workshops are offered all year long for kids 3 to 6 and 7 to 12. Fees range from $4 to $10 for a single session; kids under 4 must be accompanied by an adult. Behind-the-scenes tours for kids 8 and up can be arranged. There are infant changing tables in the men's and women's rooms, and a gift shop, and strollers are allowed at all times.

JUNIOR MUSUEM OF THE ART INSTITUTE (Michigan Avenue at Adams Street, Zip: 60603, 312-443-3600). The Junior Museum of this larger, world-famous museum features a major exhibit designed especially for kids and focusing on works in the museum's permanent collection, a new one every 2 years. Workshops are available throughout the year. Kids 4 to 6 with their parents have their own Early Bird Workshops, and kids 7 and older and their parents have Family Workshops that include a gallery walk and related art activity. Gallery walks are available to kids 9 and older and their parents on Saturdays, and storytelling and drawing in the galleries are all scheduled on weekends. Each month a different artist works in a different medium while people of all ages look on, and every day there are gallery games and self-guides available. Just check at the Little Library for scheduling. Special holiday workshops are held during the week between Christmas and New Year's Day. The museum offers many services to families: There are infant changing tables in the women's restroom. Strollers are generally allowed (a few special exhibits are exceptions). There are a cafeteria complete with booster seats, a children's gift shop, small-size drinking fountains, and self-guided tape tours for special exhibits.

CHICAGO PUBLIC LIBRARY (Cultural Center, Thomas Hughes Children's Library, 78 East Washington Street, Zip: 60611, 312-269-2835). This library schedules programs for kids from preschool age through eighth grade. During the school year, programs generally take place on Saturday mornings at 11:00. Children's programs are listed in the Cultural Center Calendar and are all free of charge. In summer, the library and the Council on Fine Arts combine to present a series of kids' programs, including puppet shows, drama, music, storytelling, book talks, and appearances by authors and illustrators.

A permanent display in the library may interest your kids, too; it's a storybook dollhouse that contains clues to over 60 children's stories, poems, and nursery rhymes. A nice idea!

### Hyde Park Area

MUSEUM OF SCIENCE AND INDUSTRY (57th Street and Lake Shore Drive, Zip: 60637, 312-684-1414). Admission and parking are free for this, the oldest, largest, and according to their staff, most popular contemporary science and technology museum. Every year 4 million people visit! Most of the exhibits are three-dimensional and participatory: visitors push buttons, turn cranks, operate computers, lift levers, and activate recorded messages. There's nothing passive about a visit to this museum. Younger kids like "Curiosity Place," a preschool science exhibit, and they're always fascinated by the hatching chicks in the "Food for Life" exhibit. The older kids seem to like the World War II German U-505 submarine, Colleen Moore's fairy castle, a full-scale replica of an underground coal mine, the Henry Crown Space Center with the actual *Apollo 8* capsule, the Omnimax Theater, and the National Business Hall of Fame.

The museum's brochure called *ABC* (25 cents at the museum store) serves as a guide to the exhibits that are most appropriate for the younger kids.

Throughout the year the museum offers classes for kids 3 to 5 and 5 to 14. The youngest have had classes on "Bridges and Blocks," "Grouping and Sorting," and "Down on the Farm," and the oldest have studied "Autumn Adventures," "Hardware Store Science," and "Building Things." On Sunday afternoons there are usually two-hour classes for families with topics such as "Animal Homes," "Halloween Science," and "Constructions."

The museum offers infant changing tables, a restaurant, and small-size drinking fountains. It allows strollers at all times.

DU SABLE MUSEUM OF AFRICAN AMERICAN HISTORY (740 East 56th Street and Cottage Grove, Zip: 60637, 312-947-0600). Not far from the Museum of Science and Industry, you'll find hands-on demonstrations of African music, film, and art. Guided tours for school-age kids are available, too.

Reflecting the polyglot character of Chicago are a number of ethnic museums scattered throughout the city that may interest you and your kids. We've already mentioned the Du Sable, but there are more: The Balzekas Museum of Lithuanian Culture, 6500 South Pulaski Road, 312-847-2441, includes a children's museum with Lithuanian artifacts, hands-on exhibits, and arts workshops; the Polish Museum of America, 984 North Milwaukee Avenue, 312-384-3352, features folk art and costumes with one-hour tours available; Spertus Museum of Judaica, 618 South Michigan Avenue, 312-922-9012, the Midwest's best and most complete Jewish museum; Swedish-American Museum of Chicago, 5248 North Clark Street, 312-728-8111, features exhibitions demonstrating the contributions of Swedes to American culture (hours vary, so call ahead for details); Ukrainian National Museum, 2453 West Chicago Avenue, 312-276-6565, has exhibits of ceramics, wood and metal carvings, Ukrainian Easter eggs, and costumes. The hours of many of these ethnic museums are erratic, so be sure to call ahead for details.

And one more possibility: The Children's Theatre of Second City performs a show for kids at 1616 North Wells every Sunday at 2:30 P.M. The shows are either original scripts written by the director or created by the cast through improvisation. After the show, kids can go on to the stage with the actors and participate in theatre games. For information, call 312-929-6288.

## Time Out

ART RESOURCE STUDIO (2828 North Clark, Zip: 60657, 312-975-1671). Located on the lower level of the Century Mall, a onetime vaudeville theater. On weekends the studio offers what they call Child-Free Shopping—from 1:30 to 6:30 on Saturdays and 1:30 to 4:30 on Sundays they'll entertain your kids (3 to 10) while you shop. The cost is $4 per hour. During the week the studio offers a variety of one- to two-hour arts and crafts workshops for kids 4 to16. Drop-ins are fine. Call for details.

CREATIVE DEVELOPMENT CENTER (677 West Wrightwood, Zip: 60614, 312-549-3339). In the summer, their August Adventure Club combines a studio art experience and a field trip. Drop-ins are welcome; kids 5 to 9 are okay.

AMERICAN REGISTRY FOR NURSES AND SITTERS (3921 North Lincoln, Zip: 60613, 312-248-8100). A more conventional way of entertaining your kids while you're off doing grown-up things is this service that is open from 9 to 6 Monday through Fridays. It's been operating since 1950 and is bonded. The rate is $4 per hour with a 4-hour minimum plus cab fare after 9:00 P.M. You pay a $2 agency fee per session and 25 cents more each hour for additional children. Advance notice is recommended, but "don't hesitate to call the same day."

## Accommodations
### Bed and Breakfast

BED AND BREAKFAST, CHICAGO, INC. (P.O. Box 14088, Zip: 60614-0088, 312-951-0085). This reservation service offers accommodations in private homes or in what they call "self-catering" apartments. For families, the owner of the service, Mary Shaw, recommends self-contained units. During holiday and vacation times, she often has vacant homes available, many complete with toys, cribs, and so on. Apartments start at $65 per night, and weekly and monthly rates are available. We discovered two tempting possibilities: a self-contained, twin-bedded garden apartment with a sofa sleeper in the living room located in the heart of Old

Town for $65 per night; and a two-bedroom, two-bath apartment with a wood-burning fireplace, a greenhouse, and a backyard with play equipment for $150 per night or $1,500 per month.

## Hotels

DAYS INN (644 North Lake Shore Drive, Zip: 60611, 312-943-9200 or 800-325-2525). Located opposite the Navy Pier, eight blocks from the Water Tower and two blocks from McCormick Place, this urban property of the budget chain offers rates as low as $39 per night double occupancy. The rate is called the Super-Saver and requires a 29-day advance reservation. Other special rates of $59 are available on shorter notice; kids under 18 stay free. There's an outdoor pool.

THE DRAKE (140 East Walton, Zip: 60611, 312-787-2200). The Drake welcomes kids and lets them stay in their parents' room at no extra charge. Across the street from the hotel are a playground and a place to swim. There are a children's menu and 25 booster seats available in the restaurant. Baby-sitting can be arranged through the housekeeping department at $4 to $5 per hour. Weekend rates begin at $110 per night for a twin room.

RITZ-CARLTON (160 East Pearson Street, Zip: 60611-0142, 312-266-1000 or 1-800-621-6906). Kids are treated to special services at the Ritz, and they're all listed on an information card, "Ritz-Carlton Services Especially for Kids." The concierge will tell you what's happening especially for kids while you're in Chicago; strollers are available at no charge to hotel guests, and baby-sitting is available for $4 per hour for a four-hour minimum. The housekeeping staff will supply games, coloring books, and crayons for the kids and some very practical baby supplies such as bathtubs, shampoo, bottle warmers, cribs, cots, diapers, and high chairs. The café has a special menu for kids under 12, and just across the street from the hotel there's a fenced-in playground, and only three blocks away is the Oak Street Beach.

The Ritz "Family Package," which includes two rooms, one with a king-size bed and one with two twins, costs $325 per night. Weekend packages called "Adventure Chicago" cost $139 per night for a queen-size or twin-bedded room and includes use of the hotel's health club. Kids can stay free in the room with parents. This package is available Thursday, Friday, and Saturday nights only.

## LOS ANGELES

Another city that's fun for kids, Los Angeles has a sprawl that needs some getting used to. Good planning is the key to your vacation in L.A. Plan your sightseeing around a car; take your own or rent one. We've arranged the section on things to do and see here by area so that you can avoid the traffic as much as possible.

### For Information

You should most definitely have a copy of *L.A. Parent,* a tabloid-size newspaper published monthly and distributed at places that appeal to families. The day-by-day calendar of events in every issue is invaluable for planning your stay. Reprints from back issues on subjects such as "The Best Baby-sitting Agencies," "Child's View of Chinatown," and "Daytrips for Toddlers" are available from the publisher for $2. Write to Box 3204, Burbank, California 91504 or call 818-846-0400. A guidebook we recommend is *Places to Go with Children in Southern California,* by Stephanie Regan, published by Chronicle Books ($7.95). The book will help you have fun in L.A. and beyond.

And for a good, general guide to L.A., we like Tom and Karen Horton's *Dolphin Guide to Los Angeles,* which also tells you what kids will like to do in that town.

For general tourist information, maps, and advice on what's worth doing and seeing, contact the Greater Los Angeles Visitors and Convention Bureau, 5051 South Flower Street, Los Angeles 90071, 213-239-0204.

An interesting possibility: For those of you whose kids are TV or movie fans, we've come across an interesting possibility that you may want to explore while you're in Los Angeles. A man named Jack Weinberg operates an organization called "Hollywood on Location" and can tell you exactly where and when you can find television and movie personalities filming around Los Angeles. Each weekday at 9:30 A.M. he publishes a new "Location List" telling you what's being filmed where, who is involved, and the address and times of location sites. On a typical day, he says, there's an average of 35 different locations, almost all within a 10-mile radius. For $19 you and anyone who's going along with you in the car gets a Location List and a large map pinpointing locations. For a brochure and a sample list and map, write to him at 8644 Wilshire Boulevard, Suite 204, Beverly Hills, California 90211 or phone 213-659-9165.

## Things to Do and See
### Downtown

LOS ANGELES CHILDREN'S MUSEUM (310 North Main Street, Zip: 90012, 213-687-8800). This relatively new space offers a hands-on environment for kids aged 2 to 12. This is a place full of energy and excitement with a recording studio that kids can use; "Ethnic L.A.," a Mexican-American and a Japanese-American environment; "Zoetrope," the animators' workshop with a neon Mickey Mouse to oversee the activities; "H.E.L.P.," the Health Education Learning Project, which depicts a doctor's office and an emergency room; "City Streets," where kids have a chance to drive a bus, ride a policeman's motorcycle, and pretend to be a fireman; and one of the favorite exhibits of all, a working television studio. Throughout the year there are special workshops and performances, with folk singers, puppet shows, preschool arts and crafts classes, improvisational theater, and a how-to-make-sushi demonstration. During the summer, the museum operates wonderful "Inside L.A." Tours that require advance registration. Last summer the excursions included trips to a drum factory, Dodger Stadium, a toy factory, a shipyard, and a tortilla factory. Costs are $7 to $10, and tours last from one to two hours each. The Children's Museum has infant changing tables, strollers are allowed, and there are small-size drinking fountains.

Right near the Children's Museum is Olvera Street, where Los Angeles began. Now it's a touristy Mexican-American area with lots of shops and restaurants. Little Tokyo's not far from the museum, located between Alameda and Los Angeles Streets and First and Third Streets.

LOS ANGELES PHILHARMONIC SYMPHONIES FOR YOUTH (135 North Grand Avenue, Zip: 90012, 213-972-7300). The Philharmonic presents six specially designed concerts for kids throughout the school year. The fun begins one hour before performance time in the lobby with a workshop presented by the staff of the Children's Museum. Lobby activities begin at 9:00

A.M., concerts last from 10:15 to 11:15 A.M.—just the right amount of time for kids.

In summer the symphony sponsors a six-week multicultural performing arts festival for kids 5 and up. A performing arts or crafts workshop follows an Open House performance of a music, dance, or theater piece. You can also sit in on a rehearsal of the Philharmonic and picnic in one of the Bowl's areas set aside for just that purpose. Call 213-850-2077 for information.

### South Central Los Angeles

NATURAL HISTORY MUSEUM OF LOS ANGELES COUNTY (900 Exposition Boulevard, Zip: 90007, 213-744-DINO or 213-744-3411). This is the third largest museum of its kind in the United States with what you'd expect—collections of fossils, exhibits of earth sciences and life sciences, and areas devoted to archeology, gems and minerals, mammals, marine biology, and, of course, dinosaurs. Younger kids love the dinosaurs, the La Brea fossils, and the Discovery Room best. Older kids like the antique autos, the gems and minerals, and the Discovery Room, too. Children's workshops are scheduled throughout the year. One recent one was called "Dinosaurs and Their Kin: From Allosaurus to Zanclodon." In June, the museum presents its Festival of Folk Art; in December, it holds a Native American Indian Festival; and at Christmas vacation time, Disney films are featured. Strollers are always allowed; it has a restaurant open from 10:00 A.M. to 4:00 P.M. and a Children's Gift Shop.

### Los Feliz and Hollywood

Griffith Park is the largest municipal park in the United States with 4,000 acres of picnic areas, playgrounds, hiking trails, bridle paths, a miniature railroad, pony and stage coach rides, a nature center, and a carousel. Travel Town is an outdoor museum in the park where kids can climb on the transportation.

GRIFFITH OBSERVATORY (2800 East Observatory Road, Zip: 90027, 213-664-1191). The planetarium transports you to times and places way beyond the realm of everyday existence—to all parts of the solar system, to Stonehenge or ancient Egypt or beyond the Milky Way. Shows last an hour and change several times a year. Admission is $2.75 for kids 16 and over and $1.50 for those 5 to 15. Kids under 5 are admitted only to the 1:30 show and other special children's shows.

In the observatory's Hall of Science, exhibits include the Foucault Pendulum, the Solar Telescope, six-foot earth and moon globes, and meteorites; tours are given throughout the day.

LOS ANGELES ZOO (5333 Zoo Drive, Zip: 90027, 213-666-4090). Located in Griffith Park, the zoo costs $4.50 for adults and $1.50 for kids 5 to 15 and is free for kids under 5. Here you can see 2,000 animals in natural settings, ride an elephant or camel, see the "World of Birds" or "Meet the Elephants" shows. There's a Children's Zoo with a baby animal nursery and a barnyard. Strollers may be rented for $1.50. Give yourself two to four hours to "do" the zoo.

### Mid-Wilshire

GEORGE C. PAGE MUSEUM OF LA BREA DISCOVERIES (5801 Wilshire Boulevard, Zip: 90036-4596, 213-936-2230). The Page Museum was built to house a heritage of over 1 million Ice Age mammals, birds, and plant specimens recovered from the world-renowned La Brea asphalt deposits or "tar pits," as they're more commonly called. The museum features more than 30 separate exhibits, including reconstructed skeletons of sabertooth cats, mammoths, wolves, and other animals. The "La Brea Story," a 15-minute multimedia introductory film, is a favorite of kids who visit, and the older ones especially like the glass-walled paleontology lab. Admission is $1.50 for adults, 75 cents for kids 5 to 17. The museum is located right in Hancock Park. Strollers are okay; there are a children's gift shop and small-size drinking fountains. Although there's no restaurant at Page, there's a cafeteria at the nearby L.A. County Museum of Art, and the park is perfect for picnic lunches.

BOB BAKER MARIONETTE THEATER (1345 West First Street, Zip: 90026, 213-250-9995). This theater has been in the same spot for over 25 years. Showtimes are usually Saturdays and Sundays at 2:30; extra performances are scheduled during Easter, summer, and Christmas vacations. Admission is $6 for kids, $7 for adults and includes the performance, a tour of the group's workshop, and refreshments. Reservations are a must.

## Beyond the City

If you have the time to venture beyond city limits, here are some possibilities your kids should like:

NBC STUDIOS (3000 West Alameda Avenue, Burbank, California 91523, 818-840-3537). This is the only network that opens its doors to you. Tours give you a look at the largest TV studios in the world, where the "Tonight Show" and many daytime game shows are filmed. You'll learn how a show is put together and how it goes from an idea all the way to television sets all over the United States. The 75-minute walking tour goes off every half-hour from 9:00 to 4:00 on weekdays, 10:00 to 4:00 on Saturdays, and 10:00 to 2:00 on Sundays. For free tickets to any of the shows, go to the ticket counter, which is open 8:30 to 5:00 weekdays, 9:30 to 4:00 weekends. The minimum age limit is generally 8 years old, but to be in the audience of the "Tonight Show," kids have to be at least 16. You can write in advance of your visit to "Tickets" at the address listed, giving the name of the show you want to see and the number of tickets you need and enclosing a self-addressed stamped envelope.

UNIVERSAL STUDIOS (100 Universal City Plaza, Universal City, California 91608, 818-508-9600). Here you can have a two-hour train tour through sound stages, the back lot, even a glimpse at a star's dressing room. There are animal shows and special effects demonstrations designed to amaze you. The newest is a 30-foot-tall, 6½-ton King Kong. Tours are available daily, 8:00 A.M. to 5:00 P.M., for $12 .50 for adults; $9.50 for kids 3 to 11; free for kids under 3.

MARINELAND (6610 Palos Verdes Drive South, Rancho Palos Verdes, California 90274, 213-377-1571). Located 40 minutes from downtown L.A., Marineland is a 108-acre oceanarium where visitors are encouraged not just to look but to get involved. Visitors can actually snorkel in 70 degree water among 1,000 fish at the Park's "Baha Reef." Bathing suits, wet suits, masks, fins, snorkels, even towels and hair dryers are provided. Scuba divers can make a Shark Dive into the cage at the Center of the Shark Exhibit; nondivers can watch through underwater windows. Throughout the day at Marineland there are shows starring dolphins, sea lions, and killer whales. For a break from sightseeing, there's a playground with swings, slides, and climbing and crawling devices. A day's ticket costs $10.95 for adults, $7.95 for kids 3 to 11; kids under 3 are admitted free. Strollers, wheelchairs, and cameras can be rented.

KNOTTS BERRY FARM (8039 Beach Boulevard, Buena Park, California 90620, 714-827-1776 or 714-220-5200 for recorded information). This, the nation's oldest theme park, really did start off as a berry stand on ten acres of rented land along the dusty roadside of Buena Park. Now it is 150 acres with four theme areas, nonstop entertainment, rides, and 35 eating spots. Only in America! Knott's is 30 minutes south of Los Angeles, and it features a Ghost Town complete with cowboys, can-can girls, and gold panning; Camp Snoopy, six acres of rides and shows, and Fiesta Village and Roaring 20's, a re-creation of a California amusement park in the 1920s. The park is open year-round, and admission, which includes unlimited rides, shows, and attractions, costs $14.95 for adults, and $10.95 for kids 3 to 11 (under 3 is free).

DISNEYLAND (Junction of Santa Ana Freeway and Harbor Boulevard, Anaheim, California 92802, 714-999-4565). The world according to Disney, about 30 miles from Los Angeles. Seven theme lands, heaven for kids. To avoid long lines, visit the most popular attractions (Matterhorn, Bobsled, Space Mountain) when the park opens, and in summer come later and stay into the evening to enjoy the fireworks. For the complete scoop on Disneyland, we recommend *Steve Birnbaum Brings You the Best of Disneyland: The Official Guide*, published by Hearst Professional Magazines, Inc. ($6.95).

## Time Out

Remember Sitters Unlimited? (See Chapter 5.) They got their start in southern California. Through them you can arrange baby-sitting that is never passive; they'll get your kids involved in arts and crafts and music and even take them on trips. The organization has franchises throughout Los Angeles and Orange counties. Contact their headquarters (23046 Avenida de la Carlota 653, Laguna Hills, California 92653, 714-380-8733) for details on the franchise closest to the spot you'll be visiting.

Another source for baby-sitting in the Los Angeles area is the Community Service Agency, 19562 Ventura Boulevard, Suite

204, Tarzana, California 91356, 818-345-2950. In-hotel baby-sitting costs $23.50 for the first four hours plus $3.50 for transportation and a $3.50 agency fee. Give the Fletchers, the people who own the agency, 4 to 6 hours advance notice for an evening sitter, 12 to 24 hours for a daytime sitter.

## Accommodations
### Bed and Breakfasts

EYE OPENERS BED AND BREAKFAST RESERVATIONS (P.O. Box 694, Altadena, California 91001, 213-684-4428 or 213-797-2055). The owners, Ruth Judhis and Betty Cox, tell us that about 30 percent of their hosts accept children. Rates start at $35 and go to $60 for double occupancy.

BED AND BREAKFAST OF LOS ANGELES (32074 Waterside Lane, Westlake Village, California 91361, 818-889-8870 or 818-889-7325). Approximately half the hosts in this network are happy to have families. A particularly tempting one is a guesthouse overlooking the Pacific Ocean; it has two bedrooms and a bath and rents for $100 for the night. Another good bet for families is a guest wing of a private home with its own kitchen, bath, one bedroom opening onto a patio, and another with twin beds. It costs $85 for four people per night.

### Hotels

ANAHEIM HILTON AND TOWERS (777 Convention Way, Anaheim, California 92802, 714-750-4321). Two blocks from Disneyland and 28 miles south of downtown Los Angeles, this hotel offers a "Kids Klub" from June to September for children 5 to 15. It operates from 10:00 A.M. to 3:00 P.M. on the one-acre sun deck near the pool, and it includes whiffle ball, volleyball, arts and crafts, team sports, and board games. The Anaheim Hilton is the largest hotel in southern California, with a staff of 1,300. The concierge keeps a file of activities for families. There are lots of high chairs and booster seats, a Kids Menu, and 50 percent off on items on the room service for kids. Baby-sitting is available for $5 to $6 per hour, and cribs are provided free. Children stay in the same room as their parents free, or, if you prefer two rooms for more privacy, the price is based on two singles, rather than two doubles.

DISNEYLAND HOTEL (1150 West Cerritos Avenue, Anaheim, California 92802, 714-778-6600 or 800-854-6165). Our kids went crazy just looking at the brochures for this, the "official hotel of the Magic Kingdom." It's linked to Disneyland via monorail, has three swimming pools, a white sand beach, ten tennis courts, and "Seaports of the Pacific," a mini–amusement park of its own with a video game center, remote-controlled boats, and two-seat pedal boats for rides on the marina. There's free entertainment day and night and 16 restaurants and bars. There's even a children's program in the summer and during holiday times. Kids 5 to 12 meet with counselors at the Yukon Klem Club from 6 to 10 every evening for dinner and games ($15 per kid). Kids 3 to 12 have a crafts workshop every Sunday for two hours. Baby-sitting is available for $26 for four hours. Rates are $92 to $178 per night for a double, with no charge for kids under 18; roll-away beds are $12 extra; cribs are free.

MARINA PACIFIC HOTEL AND HOTEL SUITES (1697 Pacific Avenue, Venice, California 90291, 213-452-1111). Located 30 minutes from downtown L.A., 15 minutes from the airport, this hotel is only 500 feet from the Venice Beach Boardwalk. Suites with living room, kitchen, and bedroom are available for families. Rates begin at $65 for a double. One- and two-bedroom suites are $185 and up. Cribs are available at no extra charge.

THE WESTIN BONAVENTURE (404 South Figueroa Street, Los Angeles, California 90071, 213-624-1000). Located in the heart of downtown Los Angeles, the hotel's five towers are a city within a city: five-level shopping gallery, a heated pool, tennis next door at the Los Angeles Racquet Club, even a lake right in the atrium lobby. The Bonaventure offers a family weekend special— 50 percent off the normal rate for two rooms and free parking. Kids under 18 stay free of charge in the same room as parents. Regular double occupancy rates range from $119 to $159. Specialty suites are available for $545 to $1,720 per night.

## NEW YORK

We live in New York City and we love it. Forget that old cliché about New York's being a great place to visit but "I wouldn't want to live there." Living here is great; visiting is exciting, too. There's so much to do here that you could easily go on sensory overload, so we've sorted through the possibilities and chosen the places we like best. We've arranged them geographically so that you can digest the Big Apple in small bites. Take time to appreciate our city by not rushing through it. Include a playground, picnic, or sky-high view each day to balance all the concrete and tall buildings. New York is a great city for walking. Every street is another adventure from the mosaic on the side of a building to the people walking behind you speaking a language you've never heard before. Although our public transportation is efficient—our subways and buses take you any place you want to go—walking is the best way to enjoy the city.

To help you get ready for your trip to New York, there is a lot of good information available. Here we include books, information offices, organizations, and even tapes that will help you make your family's trip as good as you want it to be.

## Books

You'll have no problem finding plenty of general guidebooks to New York. *Candy Apple: New York for Kids,* is a new guidebook by Bubbles Fisher, a grandmother who's discovered 600 things to do and written them all down. A Frommer book, published by Prentice Hall, it costs $11.95. We like *Frommer's New York on $45 a Day* (Simon & Schuster, $9.95) and the *I Love New York Guide* by Marilyn Applesberg (Collier/Macmillan, $4.95). But for information on seeing the town with kids, there are three we recommend: *A Kids New York* by Peter Lawrence, published by Avon ($6.95); *The Best Things in New York Are Free* by Marian Hamilton, published by Harvard Common Press ($10.95), with a chapter especially for kids; and *Kids Love New York!* by Lynn Schurnberger, published by Contemporary Books ($9.95). And for more up-to-the-minute information on what's going on in town for kids, you should know about five magazines/newsletters that are published here especially for parents. Each one is a gold mine of ideas for what to do with the kids and where to go for help if you need it.

- *PARENTGUIDE Magazine* is available from Parent-guide Inc., 2 Park Avenue, New York, New York 10016, 212-213-8843 ($9.90 for a year's subscription; $19 for two years), or on newsstands for $1.50 per copy.

The "What's Happening" section is jam-packed with possibilities.

- *New York Family Magazine* is a relatively new addition to the parent publication scene. Published by Susan Ross and Felice Shapiro, it is available on newsstands for $2, but there are free copies to be had in some schools, the offices of some children's dentists, and so on. It, too, has a calendar of family events. For information, contact the publisher, 420 East 79th Street, Suite 9E, New York, New York 10021.

- *New York City Family Entertainment Guide* is a seasonal listing of entertainment, party services, museums, theater, and other activities for kids that's available in child-oriented shops. If you'd like to order one before your trip, send $1 and a stamped, self-addressed envelope to Family Publishing, 37 West 72nd Street, New York, New York 10023.

- *The Big Apple Parents' Paper* is a monthly paper published by Buffalo-Bunyip, Inc., One World Trade Center, Suite 8817, New York, New York 10048. It costs $7.50 for six issues and can be picked up all over town. This paper, too, has a calendar of events for the month as well as regular features.

- *Parents and Kids Directory,* published by Marquee Communications, P.O. Box 1257, Peter Cooper Station, New York, New York 10276, also lists special events. It is published four times a year and is free.

- *Children's Focus: A Cultural Newsletter* is a monthly publication that focuses on arts and cultural events geared to children between the ages of 5 and 12. A recent issue included a notice about a rock musical for kids, workshops at the Bronx Zoo, a puppet festival, and free films at libraries. Single copies are available for $1 from Myra Henry, Children's Focus, P.O. Box 7196, Flushing, New York 11355. A year's subscription is $7.

And one more recommended resource is a poster-map of the city especially for kids, called *New York City Illustrated for Kids*. It's available around town, or by mail from Topographics, Inc., 315 Church Street, New York, New York 10013. It's priced at $4.95

plus $1.50 postage (add sales tax if you're writing from New York State).

The most obvious but sometimes overlooked source of information on New York is the City's Convention and Visitors Bureau, 2 Columbus Circle, New York, New York 10019, and 207 West 43d Street 212-397-8222. Everything's free—from maps to calendars of events to tickets for television shows. And for information on what's happening in the parks of New York—and there's always something—simply dial 212-755-4100.

## Tours

If you prefer to have someone else arrange your tour of the city, or at least a part of it, consider these possibilities.

### Joyce Gold Tours

Joyce Gold is a historian and teacher who has given walking tours of New York for 12 years. She's also described her tour in a book she calls *From Windmills to the World Trade Center: A Walking Guide to Lower Manhattan* (available by mail from Ms. Gold for $3.75 at 141 West 17th Street, New York, New York 10011, 212-242-5762). Her tours begin in the spring and run through the fall. There are four different tours in all, always on Sundays. She walks her groups through the Financial District, Greenwich Village, Chelsea, and Ladies' Mile and condenses what she's learned from the 700 books she's read on the subject of New York. Tours last two to three hours and cost $8 per person. Kids should probably be at least 10 years old to be able to appreciate the tour.

### The Museum of the City of New York

The museum offers a season of walking tours from April to October, exploring various parts of Manhattan and Brooklyn. The cost is $10 per person. Call 212-534-1672 for information.

### Theater Tours of New York, Inc.

Kids 12 or over will enjoy a behind-the-scenes look at Broadway (unfortunately, for insurance purposes, there are no more actual backstage visits) with this group. The same people produce a historical review plus a cruise each summer on the South Street

Seaport's boat *The DeWitt Clinton*. The cruise and show lasts two hours and costs approximately $30. For information, call 212-947-5370.

### Circle Line Cruise

The Circle Line Cruise is a classic great for kids, especially on a nice day. The cruise takes three hours and is a great way to orient yourself and the kids to what New York looks like. Boats sail from March to November. The first boat leaves at 9:30 A.M., and there's a sailing every 45 minutes. The ride costs $12 for adults, $6 for kids under 12. Call 212-563-3200.

### Staten Island Ferry/Statue of Liberty

For 25 cents, round-trip, you can take a cruise across New York Harbor. You'll pass the Statue of Liberty en route, but for a visit to the Statue you'll have to take the Statue of Liberty Ferry from South Ferry. The round-trip costs $3.25 for adults, $1.50 for kids 11 and under, and there's a $1 charge for anyone over 12 who visits the Statue. Call 212-269-5755 for ferry information.

### Pioneer

The schooner *Pioneer* is a part of the South Street Seaport, which also offers cruises of the harbor for two or three hours at a time. The two-hour cruise is $16 for adults, $11 for kids; add $5 for the three-hour cruise. The *Pioneer* is docked at Pier 16 and cruises from early May to mid-September. Call 212-699-9416 for information.

### I See New York by Helicopter

I See New York is a sightseeing option run by Island Helicopter, based at 34th Street and the East River. Tours run every day, 9:00 to 5:00, and there are five itineraries to choose from. The shortest is a 16-mile flight over the river that costs $30 per person (children must pay full fare because safety regulations require that they occupy their own seat). Call 212-683-4575 for information.

### Talk-a-Walk

For do-it-yourself walking tours of lower Manhattan, consider the four cassettes created by Sound Publishers, Inc.: World Trade Center to Bowling Green, Customs House to Seaport Museum, Seaport Museum to World Trade Center, and across the Brooklyn Bridge. All are suitable for interested kids 6 years old and over and cover history, culture, architecture, and legend. Tapes are $9.95 each and are available from Sound Publishers, 30 Waterside Plaza, Number 10D, New York, New York 10010, 212-686-0356.

## Things to See and Do

Before we begin, here's a quick geography lesson. Fifth Avenue divides Manhattan into the East and West sides. Cross streets are numbered from 8th Street north. The lower the address on the cross streets, the closer it is to Fifth Avenue. Between 60th Street and 110th Street, Central Park intervenes and the distance between East and West widens substantially but is still walkable.

To help you cluster your sightseeing, we've listed places in geographical groups. Each day, pick a neighborhood and go exploring. Don't try to cover everything we list. It's taken us 20 years! Walk whenever you can. If you want to ride, get a subway or bus map (supposedly available free at token booths, definitely available at the Visitors Bureau). Don't be afraid to ask New Yorkers how to get around: they really are very helpful as a rule. Kids under 6 ride free, and exact change is always necessary. Stock up on tokens at a subway booth at non–rush hour. Let us begin:

### Museum Mile

Museum Mile is a wonderful stretch of Fifth Avenue from 104th Street south to 81st Street. When planning, remember that most museums are closed Mondays.

THE MUSEUM OF THE CITY OF NEW YORK (Fifth Avenue at 104th Street, Zip: 10029, 212-534-1672). Start by watching "The Big Apple," a multimedia history of New York City that kids love. Then go on up to the Toy Gallery and Dolls' House Gallery; then on to the Dutch Gallery, complete with a fort that kids can explore; and the Fire Gallery, full of antique fire engines and firefighting equipment. Older kids like the six period rooms, peopled with mannequins portraying New Yorkers from the 17th to the 20th century. Every Saturday from early November to April at 1:30 the museum hosts a puppet festival for kids of all ages (those under 5 must be with an adult), followed by a "Please Touch" demonstration during which kids can handle authentic antiques from 17th-century New York. On Sundays at 2:30 there are concerts featuring up-and-coming performance artists followed by an informal gathering with the artist from 3:30 to 4:00. Right across from the museum, at 105th Street, is the extraordinarily beautiful Conservatory Garden in Central Park. We spent an hour at the museum, went out for 30 minutes in the park, and back for another hour and one-half. It made a perfect break. The Museum of the City of New York has changing tables, allows strollers, has an excellent gift shop and small-size drinking fountains, and charges no admission fee.

THE JEWISH MUSEUM (5th Avenue at 92nd Street, Zip: 10128, 212-860-1889). This is a lovely, small museum, located in the former Warburg Mansion. There are always special exhibitions geared to kids. When we were last there "In the Picture" allowed kids to wander in and out of a life-size re-creation of one of the museum's paintings. Our kids loved it. Often the exhibits have special activity sheets for children. The museum is closed Fridays and Saturdays. On Sundays there are often special workshops or performances for kids and parents; call for information. No strollers are allowed.

THE COOPER-HEWITT MUSEUM (2 East 91st Street, Zip: 10128, 212-860-6898). This is another gem of a museum—nice and small and manageable. It's a part of the Smithsonian, actually, and is devoted to historical and contemporary design. On Saturdays, there are often workshops for kids. Call for details. No strollers are allowed, but free backpacks are available.

THE GUGGENHEIM MUSEUM (1071 Fifth Avenue, Zip: 10128, 212-360-3513). The giant snail up ahead is the Guggenheim. The design is great for kids, who like to spiral down the ramps. On Tuesday evenings from 5 to 8 admission is free.

METROPOLITAN MUSEUM OF ART (82nd Street and Fifth Avenue, Zip: 10028, 212-879-5500). You already know all about this one. The kids will love the sculpture gallery, the armor, the mummies, and, depending on the theme, the exhibit in the Costume Gallery. Every weekend there are programs for kids 5 to 12 years old and their parents that include gallery talks and sketching, slide talks, and gallery hunts. On Sundays from 1:30 to 3:00 there are drawing classes in the galleries; for those who prefer do-it-yourself, there are written gallery hunts available at the Great Hall Information Desk.

### Playgrounds Along the Way

Along Fifth Avenue, at 100th, 95th, 84th, and 79th and below at 77th, 71st, and 67th Streets there are playgrounds in Central Park that make perfect diversions for the kids. The Children's Zoo in the Park is further south at 64th, and the Carousel, a wonderful treat for kids at 50 cents a ride, is in midpark at 64th Street.

If you're still going strong, you can walk east to Madison and visit the Whitney Museum (at 75th Street)—kids like the Calder Circus in the lobby—or just window shop for as long as the kids can stand it.

### Toys and Other Good Things

F.A.O. SCHWARZ (767 Fifth Avenue at 58th Street in the General Motors Building, 212-644-9400). Spend some time in this kids' paradise. They're good about letting kids play with display toys and from time to time have special events for kids.

TRUMP TOWER (Fifth Avenue and 56th Street). For a look at affluence on parade and for a place to rest your feet, this is a convenient stopping point.

IBM GALLERY (56th Street and Madison Avenue, 212-407-6100 for a recorded announcement; 212-407-6209 for a conversation with a real person). Exhibits vary, but often they're great for kids and participatory. No admission fee; call ahead for details.

MUSEUM OF BROADCASTING (1 East 53rd Street, Zip: 10022, 212-752-4690). This unique institution is like a library of television and radio programs. Its collection spans 60 years of broadcasting: in all, 25,000 radio and television programs. Visitors may come by and watch or listen to their favorite program from the past for an hour at a time. Possibilities include "Howdy Doody," inaugurations of presidents since Truman, Watergate hearings, *The Nutcracker* with Baryshnikov, and on and on. Admission is $3 for adults, $2 for students, and $1.50 for kids under 13.

MUSEUM OF MODERN ART (MOMA) (11 West 53d Street, 212-708-9400; program information, 212-708-9781). You decide whether your kids are going to enjoy the art. Children under 16 are free. Every once in a while there are parent-child workshops. Call the program number for details.

MUSEUM OF AMERICAN FOLK ART. While they're waiting for their new building to be built, this museum is having exhibits in other people's spaces, usually in Manhattan, often in midtown. Kids like their shows because the work is so much like their own. Call 212-481-3080 to ask where they are at the moment and make a stop at their gift shop at 62 West 50th Street.

ROCKEFELLER CENTER (from Fifth to Sixth Avenue, 48th to 51st Street). This favorite for tourists has great appeal in both summer and winter. In the warm weather, admire the Channel Gardens; in winter watch (or join) the ice skaters. Right in the midst of Rockefeller Center at Sixth Avenue and 49th Street you'll find "The New York Experience," a multiscreen show that tells the story of New York from past to present with lots of flash and special effects. It's fun and is shown every hour on the hour from 11:00 Monday to Saturday and from noon on Sundays. Admission is $4.75 for adults, $2.90 for kids under 12. Call 212-619-1000 for information.

THE CHILDREN'S MUSEUM OF MANHATTAN (314 West 54th Street, Zip: 10019, 212-765-5904). Everything here is designed for kids, primarily for ages 3 to 12. The exhibits change regularly, and some permanent exhibits include "Color and Light," which has a dress-up area, and a "Nature Area" with its own collection of small animals to hold and touch. Special events— Halloween parties, puppet performances, mapmaking, clay workshops—are often scheduled for weekends and vacation times. Strollers are okay.

## Midtown—On the West Side

EMPIRE STATE BUILDING (34th Street and Fifth Avenue). Has a great view from the 102nd floor. It costs $3 for adults, $1.75 for kids under 12. Call 212-736-3100 for hours. In the lobby of the building is the Guinness World Records Exhibit Hall, for people who like to find out about the "best," the "greatest," and the "largest."

*INTREPID* SEA-AIR-SPACE MUSEUM (46th Street and 12th Avenue on the Hudson River). This was a great surprise to us. We resisted going at first but actually liked it as much as the kids did. The museum is actually in and on an aircraft carrier built in 1943 and decommissioned in 1974. The kids are free to climb and explore. Open Wednesday through Sunday, $4.75 for adults, $2.50 for kids under 12.

### Midtown—On the East Side

CITICORP CENTER (153 East 53rd Street, 559-2330). This city version of a shopping mall has tables for picnics and a Saturday Kids Corner at 11:00, where you may find magicians, puppets, or musicians.

THE UNITED NATIONS (First Avenue and 45th Street, Zip: 10017, 212-754-7713). Children 6 or over may like the tours of the UN given every 15 minutes from 9:15 A.M. to 4:55 P.M. every day of the week. Free tickets to open sessions of the General Assembly are also available on a first-come, first-served basis. The tour costs $2.50 for students in grade 10 and above, $2 for students in grades 1–9, and $4.50 for adults. Be sure to visit the gift shop with a large selection of pretty things from all over the world. The UN, situated along the East River, is a nice, cool spot in the summer. You can stroll along the river's edge and enjoy the breeze; unfortunately, no picnics are allowed in this inviting space.

### Way, Way Downtown

Start off this tour at the World Trade Center. On the 107th floor of Tower 2 you can take a look at a view you won't soon forget. It costs $2.95 for adults, $1.50 for kids 6 to 12, and is free for 6 and under. Call 212-466-7377 for information. If you walk north of the Trade Center, there's a lovely park on Charles Street between Independence Plaza and Manhattan Community College. A good lunch spot is Hamburger Harry's at 157 Chambers Street, 212-267-4446, with booster seats, a children's menu, and all. As you go downtown after lunch, decide whether you want to head for the Financial District and Wall Street—for the older kids, a look at tours of the American Stock Exchange, 212-623-3000, may be fun—or go crosstown to South Street Seaport.

SOUTH STREET SEAPORT (212-608-7888). This is a mix of restored seaport buildings reminiscent of the area's 19th-century glory and chic restaurants, boutiques, malls, and public terraces. There's always something going on down here; often free performances on weekends out in the open. We've seen some great magicians and jugglers, some carolers at holiday time, and two comedians who were very, very funny. A multiscreen film presentation, "The Seaport Experience," made by the same people who put the "New York Experience" together, is shown every day. It's $4.25 for grown-ups, $2.75 for kids under 12.

THE SEAPORT MUSEUM (207 Front Street, Zip: 10038, 212-669-9400), is not one building but actually an 11-block landmark district that includes daily tours, films, and special programs; galleries; a children's center with hands-on programs; a re-creation of a 19th-century printer's shop; the lightship *Ambrose*; and the great four-masted bark *Peking*. Admission of $4 for adults, $2 for kids 7 to 11 allows you to see it all.

### More Downtown

New York is a conglomeration of ethnic neighborhoods, and two that are especially fun to explore are Chinatown (Canal Street going west from the Manhattan Bridge to Centre Street, south to Chatham Square and some blocks north of Canal to Grand Street) and nearby Little Italy. We suggest walking around Chinatown— there are lots of little stores where you can buy inexpensive gifts to take back home with you—having lunch or dinner in Chinatown, and then going on to Mulberry or Grand Street for an Italian ice or pastry.

Not far away are Greenwich Village and Soho, filled with boutiques, galleries, and lots of food treats. In this area, too, you'll find:

MUSEUM OF HOLOGRAPHY (11 Mercer Street, Zip: 10013, 212-925-0526). It's in the middle of Soho and has two floors of exhibits on holography, three-dimensional images created with laser light. Strollers are allowed; admission is $3 for adults, $1.75 for kids 12 and under. (Not recommended for the littlest—the exhibits are too high for them to see, and no stools are provided.)

FORBES MAGAZINE GALLERIES (62 Fifth Avenue, at the corner of 12th Street, Zip: 10011, 212-206-5548). Known as "the best museum" to one of our kids who's been visiting it and loving it since he was 3 years old. Kids will like the collection of toy boats in an oceanlike environment, the Fabergé eggs, and the 12,000 toy soldiers.

While you're in the area, there are lots of parks for you and the kids: Washington Square Park at the downtown end of Fifth Avenue has playgrounds and impromptu entertainment in all seasons; the Mercer Street Park north of Houston Street next to the New York University Cole Sports Center with a fountain to cool you off on those hot, steamy New York days; and Abingdon Square Park, good for all ages, with a big sandbox.

And for kids 4 years and over in search of entertainment in this same neighborhood on Saturdays and Sundays there are performances of musical adaptations of fairy tales at the 13th Street Theater, 50 West 13th Street, 212-675-6677. Tickets are a real bargain at $3.

### Upper West Side

The Upper West Side is the area that begins at Central Park South, heads west to the Hudson River and Riverside Park, and up beyond Columbia University at 117th Street and Broadway. Its eastern border is Central Park, and wherever you are on the Upper West Side you're never far from the glorious park and all it has to offer you and your kids. If you're going to picnic in this neighborhood—and we think you should if the weather is nice enough—stop first at Zabar's, a food emporium that defies description. It's at Broadway and 80th Street, just a short walk from Central Park or even shorter walk to Riverside Park. Also in the park, on the west side, are the Swedish Cottage Marionette Theater at 79th Street (call 212-988-9093 for schedule), Heckscher Puppet House and Playground at 62nd Street (same phone number above), and playgrounds at 93d Street, 91st Street, and two particularly exciting ones at 85th and 67th Streets just off Central Park West. Lincoln Center is in this part of town; there, depending on the season, you'll find dance, opera, symphony, or theater. The Lincoln Center Library has a children's section with special exhibits from time to time.

THE AMERICAN MUSEUM OF NATURAL HISTORY AND THE HAYDEN PLANETARIUM (79th–81st Streets and Central Park West, 212-873-4225 for museum, 212-873-8828 for planetarium). These two need no introduction. Favorites at the museum include the diving whale; the dinosaurs, of course; the 94-foot dioramas with mammals of three continents; the Minerals and Gems Hall; and the Discovery Room for ages 5 to 10 on Saturdays and Sundays from 12 to 4:30 P.M. You won't want to leave without seeing the Nature Max Theater, a four-story screen presentation that's thrilling. Kids of all ages like the museum. The planetarium is best for school-age kids, with its sky show using the world's largest computer automation system and over 100 special effects projectors plus two floors of exhibits, including one of the world's largest meteorites, the Hall of the Sun, and "Your Weight on Other Worlds." Strollers are allowed; there are a nice children's gift shop and small-size drinking fountains.

Right next door to the planetarium and museum is the New York Historical Society, 170 Central Park West, 212-873-3400. From time to time they have an exhibit of interest to kids and programs especially for them. Call to check.

### Harlem

For a brochure about the area with information on tours and special events, contact the Harlem Visitor and Convention Association, 310 Lenox Avenue, New York, New York 10027, 212-427-3317. Some of the highlights of a visit to this area follow.

THE MUSEUM OF THE AMERICAN INDIAN (Broadway at 158th Street, Zip: 10032, 212-283-2420). This museum is devoted to collecting, preserving, studying, and exhibiting everything connected with the anthropology of the aboriginal peoples of the Americas. Demonstrations by visiting Native American artists and artisans—in the past they have included basketry, bead work, doll making, and silver work—take place in the first-floor exhibit area. Call for details.

THE STUDIO MUSEUM (144 West 125th Street, Zip: 10027, 212-864-4500). This museum celebrates contemporary and historical African, Caribbean, and American art. Special events include puppet shows, storytelling, and concerts.

AUNT LEN'S DOLL AND TOY MUSEUM (6 Hamilton Terrace, on 141st Street between Convent and Saint Nicholas Avenues, Zip: 10031, 212-281-4143). Call ahead to make an appointment to see Aunt Len's collection of over 3,000 dolls, dollhouses, and antique toys.

As long as you're uptown, go all the way up to the Cloisters, a branch of the Metropolitan Museum of Art dedicated to medieval art, located in Fort Tryon Park, overlooking the Hudson. Call 212-923-3700 for information on special children's programs.

## The Other Boroughs

If you have a day to spare, why not spend it in one of the other boroughs—Queens, Brooklyn, Staten Island, or the Bronx? There are lots of special things to do in each, and most are easy enough to reach by public transportation. Just call the numbers listed here for directions.

### Staten Island

Start off your day with a ride on the Staten Island Ferry. You'll see Governor's Island, the Statue of Liberty, Brooklyn, New Jersey, the Verrazano Bridge, and the Manhattan skyline. The ferry runs seven days a week, 24 hours a day. Call 212-806-6940 for information. When you get off the ferry, you can take a number 1 bus or taxi (a taxi is less than $3 and is recommended) to Snug Harbor Cultural Center, 26 landmark buildings overlooking New York Bay. On Sundays there are free guided tours; call 718-448-6166. The highlight of a visit to this area will be a stop at the Staten Island Children's Museum. The museum is full of hands-on environmental exhibitions, really creative offerings that kids love. For the price of museum admission ($2 for adults and kids) you may catch a special performance—music, dance, theater, or puppetry—usually on Saturday mornings. Every spring the museum sponsors Meadowfair, an outdoor arts festival for the whole family. The Children's Gift Shop is a nice place to buy souvenirs or presents for friends back home. Call 718-273-2060 for information. From here you can take a cab to the comfortably sized Staten Island Zoo, where the kids can have a pony ride and feed the animals. Call 718-442-3100 for details. Admission is $1 for everyone over 3; children under 3 are admitted free, and Wednesdays are free for everyone.

Richmondtown Restoration, a re-creation of life in Staten Island over the past 300 years, is another good destination for adventurous families. There are 26 historic buildings on 20 acres, and 12 are open to the public. Your kids will want to see the 17th-century school, the antique doll and toy exhibit, and the old fire engines. Outdoor demonstrations of gardening, domestic chores, woodworking, harness making, and so forth, take place during the summer season. Tours for kids 3 and up and their parents are available. Call 718-351-1611 for information on daily events.

For an idea of what's happening on Staten Island on the day you decide to go, call the Staten Island Council on the Arts hotline, 718-720-1800.

### Brooklyn

If you begin your visit in the historic landmark section of Brooklyn Heights, you'll enjoy the most spectacular view of lower Manhattan from the Promenade. One of our favorite playgrounds is at the end of Pierrepont Street at the Promenade. Prospect Park—large and lovely with wooded hills, lakes, and open meadows—has a zoo and a Children's Farm (open from spring through the fall). Call 718-788-0055 for events in the park, 718-965-6560 for zoo information, and 718-965-6586 for the Children's Farm. A short walk from the park is the Brooklyn Museum (Eastern Parkway at Washington Avenue, Brooklyn, 11225), an imposing building where special programs for kids are often scheduled. The gift shop here is excellent and there's a separate one just for kids. Call 718-638-5000 for information.

THE BROOKLYN BOTANICAL GARDEN (1000 Washington Avenue, Zip: 11225, 718-622-4433). Fifty acres of everything from a replica of a Japanese stone garden to a children's garden planted and harvested by New York's school kids is right next door to the museum. Information is available by calling.

BROOKLYN CHILDREN'S MUSEUM (145 Brooklyn Avenue at Saint Mark's Avenue, Brooklyn, New York 11213, 718-735-4432). The museum is a wonderful stop in Brooklyn. This is the world's first children's museum. There's always something exciting happening, from the permanent exhibits that include a plastic model of a diamond crystal that kids can climb all over to a three-foot-wide river that flows by the entrance, to lots of other things to be manipulated, played with, and enjoyed. On weekdays after school, and on weekends there are all kinds of great workshops and activities: helping to make a mural, listening to stories, and so on. The kids' gift shop has inexpensive souvenirs, and the whole experience is one we recommend.

THE NEW YORK AQUARIUM (on Coney Island at West 8th Street off Surf Avenue, Brooklyn, New York 11224, 718-266-8500). This is another Brooklyn offering for kids. Indoor and outdoor exhibits are fun, and in nice weather there are performing sea lions and dolphins in the outdoor aquatheater. Our kids loved the show. The aquarium sponsors many weekend programs for kids and their parents throughout the year.

### The Bronx

THE BRONX ZOO (185th Street and Southern Boulevard, Bronx, New York 10460, 212-220-5100). Everyone's heard of this zoo. This is a full day's excursion and fun for all ages. Pack a picnic (the lines can be long at the snack bars) and take your time seeing all there is to see—the new Jungle World, the World of Darkness, the World of Birds, Wild Asia, and best of all, for kids, the Children's Zoo. Here the little ones can explore a prairie dog tunnel, try on a turtle shell, or climb on a rope model of a spider's web. Our kids—from the 3-year-old all the way up—love it. The zoo is a lovely place with all kinds of special events at different times of the year.

THE BRONX CONSERVATORY AND BOTANICAL GARDENS (Southern Boulevard and 200th Street, Bronx, Zip: 10458, 212-220-8700). These are right across from the zoo and are very beautiful, but it's doubtful that you'll have energy left over after the zoo trip. Perhaps another day.

### Queens

One of the most neglected boroughs, Queens has this wonderful new offering for families.

THE NEW YORK HALL OF SCIENCE (47-01 111th Street, Corona, New York 11368, 718-699-0005). Here's a hands-on science museum, a place where the worlds of science and technology are close enough to touch. Exhibits dealing with color and illusion, investigation of atoms, and self-sensing feedback are all staffed with "explainers"—college students, majoring in sciences and communications, who explain, demonstrate, and discuss. These "explainers" also lead on-floor demonstrations and workshops. On weekends there are family workshops for kids 5 years and up. We saw a laser demonstration, watched the dissection of a cow's eye, and spent some time at a color and light workshop. The museum provides backpacks for small children and has an area for changing and nursing babies, small-size drinking fountains, and a "snack-a-mat" for sandwiches, drinks, and snacks. We recommend this welcome new addition to New York wholeheartedly.

THE ALLEY POND ENVIRONMENTAL CENTER (228-06 Northern Boulevard, Douglaston, New York 11363, 718-229-4000). If the crowds and quick pace of New York get to you, consider a retreat here. Alley Pond is a nature center located on the northern fringe of a park. It is home to rabbits, snakes, turtles, fish, frogs, and a dove and includes exhibits of taxidermied animals and a please-touch display. The center's backyard consists of woodlands, a meadow, wetlands, and Alley Creek, a tidal waterway that attracts migrating birds in the fall and spring. On any day of the year you're likely to find an educational program in progress that you can attach yourself to. The center also schedules walks with their naturalists, stargazing, macramé snowflake workshops, and lots of other activities. Call for schedules. The gift shop has treats for as little as 25 cents, picnic benches are available, and admission is free.

## Time Out

For the times you want to do grown-up things here are some people who can help with the kids:

MOM'S AMAZING, LTD. (Suite 4B, 144 West 86th Street, Zip: 10024, 212-580-1495). Marcia Cantarella set up this company as a support and resource system for working mothers. For people who live here she tracks down after-school activities, plans parties, and shops; for visitors she can plan outings, find baby-sitters, and suggest activities. To use her service, you'll need to become a member for $35 per year.

BARNARD COLLEGE (212-280-2035). Barnard students are available to baby-sit for $4.50 per hour. You'll have to provide transportation for your sitter in the evening; remember that the students are unavailable during vacation times.

GILBERT CHILD CARE AGENCY, INC. (115 West 57th Street, Suite 3R, Zip: 10019, 212-757-7900). This agency charges according to the age of the child—newborn to 2 months is $6.50 per hour, 2 to 9 months is $5.60, 9 months and over is $4.75. There are a four-hour minimum and a $2.50 transportation charge during the day and $5 after 8:00 P.M. Arrange sessions by 3:00 P.M. the day before you want a sitter. For the same charge, sitters will take kids to any events the parents request—the Circle Line, Radio

City, and so forth. The agency is licensed and bonded and has been operating since 1980.

PART TIME CHILD CARE, INC. (19 East 69th Street, Zip: 10021, 212-879-4343). This agency has been providing sitters since 1944. Call before 4:00 P.M. of the day you want an evening sitter; a day before for daytime service. Hourly rates range from $5 to $7 per hour plus a commission of 12 percent. There's a four-hour minimum, clients pay the bus fare during the day and a $5 transportation fee for evening assignments. At holiday time, rates go up slightly.

## Accommodations
### Bed and Breakfasts

Although New York may not be the kind of place that suggests "bed and breakfast," there are two bed and breakfast agencies just waiting to find you a room in an apartment or private house, or, better still for families, an entire unhosted apartment.

URBAN VENTURES, INC. (P.O. Box 426, New York, New York 10024, 212-594-5650). Mary McAulay and Frances Tesser have been placing visitors in New York homes since 1979. Possibilities range from penthouses to walk-ups, entire apartments with no host, or bed and breakfast with a host who can "offer advice and an umbrella." Prices range from $25 to $85 per night, and for entire apartments, $60 per night or up. One apartment that they have listed is a one-bedroom on Columbus Avenue, in a new building. The owner uses it on weekends and rents it during the week for $400 for five nights or $100 for one night.

CITY LIGHTS B AND B, LTD. (P.O. Box 20355, Cherokee Station, New York, New York 10028, 212-737-7049). According to the owner, 65 percent of this agency's hosts are happy to take families. Most have a spare room, cots are provided for kids, and cribs are available at a small additional cost. Unhosted apartments are available as well. Rates range from $35 to $75 per night with a minimum three-night stay; unhosted apartments range from $65 to $180 per night. Accommodations are primarily in Manhattan, but there are some spacious townhouses in Brooklyn Heights and Park Slope that welcome guests.

## Hotels

HOWARD JOHNSON (851 Eighth Avenue, Zip: 10019, 212-581-4100). You can walk to many of the city's sightseeing attractions from this hotel. There's no charge for kids 18 or under in the same room as their parents, and cribs are free. Baby-sitting is available for $5.50 per hour with two hours advance notice. Rates range from $107 to $137.

LOEW'S SUMMIT HOTEL (Lexington Avenue at 51st Street, Zip: 10022, 212-752-7000). All rooms have refrigerators; cribs are available at no extra charge. Children 14 and under stay free with parents, and baby-sitting is available for $8 per hour. The hotel has a health club with Nautilus equipment, exercise cycles, jacuzzi, and sauna, too, but it's for adults only. Regular rates range from $125 to $155 per night for double rooms.

MANHATTAN EAST SIDE HOTELS (505 East 75th Street, Zip: 10021-3103, 212-772-2900, 800-ME-SUITE). This all-suite group manages nine properties in all—the Beekman Towers, Dumont Plaza, Eastgate Tower, Lyden Gardens, Lyden House, Plaza Fifty, Shelburne Murray Hill, Southgate Tower, and Surrey Hotel—and all but one of these are on the East Side. There are studios, one- and two-bedroom suites, and at the Plaza Fifty, even a three-bedroom. All have kitchens. Regular rates average just under $200 per night for a one-bedroom suite, but special promotional deals are offered from time to time. For instance, at this writing, there was a three-nights-for-the-price-of-two arrangement available. Weekend rates are usually much lower, too, as low as $97 per night for a one-bedroom suite, $75 for a studio suite.

RAMADA INN (790 Eighth Avenue, Zip: 10019, 212-581-7000). An outdoor rooftop swimming pool and free parking are available for guests. There is no charge for children 18 or under in the same room as their parents, and cribs are free. The housekeeping department will help arrange baby-sitting for $5.50 per hour. Rates range from $107 to $127.

SHERATON CITY SQUIRE HOTEL (790 Seventh Avenue at 52nd Street, Zip: 10019, 212-581-3300, 800-325-3535). Within walking distance of Radio City Music Hall, Fifth Avenue, and the theater district, this West Side hotel has an indoor pool. Cribs are free, and children under 17 may stay free in their parents' room. A children's menu is available from room service, and baby-sitting at a cost of $6 per hour during the day and $10 at night is offered through the housekeeping department. Rates normally range from $130 to $190 for a double, but on Friday, Saturday, and Sunday a $95 special is available.

## SAN FRANCISCO

A lovely city, San Francisco. Somerset Maugham called it "the most civilized city in America," and it just may be. Two advantages that San Francisco has for visiting families are that it's scenic and at the same time, compact. It's an easy place to visit. The public transportation makes getting around a cinch.

San Francisco is a city where the setting is as important as streets and museums. Nature plays a significant role in the goings-on and activities of the people who live and work here. The westernmost boundary of the city, extending from the ocean to the bay, is part of the Golden Gate National Recreation Area; under its management are museums, islands (including Alcatraz), beaches, and even a working pier with theaters and restaurants. Taking a walk in this city affords continually changing vistas of bridges, coastal ranges, bays, and the ocean in endless variations. The best way to enjoy San Francisco with children is to take them out into this urban wilderness where nature and civilization come together in a unique way, almost unknown to the rest of the United States.

### For Information

The San Francisco Convention and Visitors Bureau at the Powell Street BART Station has a Dial-an-Event phone line (415-391-2000) with tapes in several languages. The staff is helpful and hands out maps and other information on the city.

Three periodicals especially for kids and parents that are available free at children's stores and other child-oriented spots are *Parents' Press* (1454 Sixth Street, Berkeley, California 94710); *The Children's News* (3896 24th Street, San Francisco, California 94114); and *Peninsula Parent* with a special San Francisco supplement (P.O. Box 89, Millbrae, California 94030, $1 for a sample copy). Check the pink entertainment pages of the *San Francisco Examiner* for a special kids' section every Sunday, and when you're looking for a guidebook, consider these:

*Places to Go with Children in Northern California* by Elizabeth Pomada, published by Chronicle Books ($7.95)

*Eating Out with Kids in San Francisco and the Bay Area* by Carole Terwilliger Meyers, published by Carousel Press ($5.95)

*Weekend Adventures for City Weary People: Overnight Trips in Northern California* by Carole Terwilliger Meyers, published by Carousel Press ($7.95)

*San Francisco at Your Feet: The Great Walks in a Walker's Town* by Margot Patterson, published by Grove Press ($5.95) is useful, though not written specifically for families.

If you've arrived in San Francisco and forgot some important piece of equipment, or if you just decide not to drag your portable crib across country, you can rent whatever you need at Baby Boom, 221 Clement Street, 415-386-4150. Cribs and playpens are $15 per week; strollers, high chairs, and car seats, $8; Such a Business, One Rhode Island Street, 415-431-1703, or 5533 College Avenue, Oakland, 415-655-6641, also rents these items.

## Things to Do and See
### Getting Around
As we said before, San Francisco's public transportation system should be the envy of most of our major cities. MUNI runs the buses, the electric cars, the cable cars, and the underground trains or MUNI metro. Bus maps are available for $1.50 at stores, at some ticket booths of the underground, and at the Convention and Visitors Bureau. Wall maps in the MUNI Metro Stations are a big help, and if you're ever lost, just call 415-673-MUNI for directions. MUNI fares are reduced for kids ages 5 to 12; kids under 5 ride free. There are two cable car lines: from Union Square to Fisherman's Wharf and from Embarcadero to Van Ness Avenue.

If you travel with your kids on MUNI, be sure to have a collapsible stroller. Be prepared for lots of escalators and architectural impediments. Try to travel in the off-hours, after the morning rush and before the evening commute. The other underground system running in the Bay area is Bay Area Rapid Transit (BART). BART takes commuters between San Francisco and the East Bay; each station has easy-to-read wall maps and fares listed prominently. Elevators that take you to the train platforms may be summoned via a white courtesy phone; meant primarily for the handicapped, these elevators can be used for people with strollers. The BART information number is 415-788-2278.

Sam Trans connects San Francisco with the South Bay, 415-872-6748; to the North Bay it's the Golden Gate Transit System, 415-332-6600. A great way to go to Sausalito and the Larkspur terminal is by ferry from the Ferry Building at the foot of Market Street and Embarcadero. There's food service on board, and you can sit inside or outside. The trip takes one-half hour; for information call Golden Gate Transit, 415-332-6600. (There's a limit of two children per adult for the ferry; kids under 5 ride free.)

Now, let's start our exploration of San Francisco. Our listing is geographical, starting with Union Square, the downtown magnet shopping area.

If you can convince your kids to do some shopping with you, you can hit Macy's, Neiman Marcus, and Saks Fifth Avenue, and when they get tired and cranky, head out to Union Square to feed the pigeons. (We like to save our shopping for the North Beach and Fisherman's Wharf area.) Within walking distance of the Square is the Old Mint, Fifth and Mission Streets, where the admission is free and you get a glimpse into the Victorian past of the city and a look at a famous gold collection.

### Chinatown

Still within walking distance of the Square is the city's Chinatown. The entrance gates stand out prominently at the intersection of Bush and Grant streets; for blocks proceeding toward the bay and in several directions are restaurants, stores, and markets. Some advice for parents: the sidewalks are always congested, so manuevering a stroller is difficult. The best time to visit Chinatown is early morning, when fresh produce and fish are being delivered. When all the crowds and noise become too much, stop at St. Mary's Square on Pine Street between Grant and Kearny. It is a restful park with large shade trees and offers a pleasant break from the congestion.

THE CHINESE CULTURE FOUNDATION (750 Kearny Street, Zip: 94108, 415-986-1822). A visit here provides an alternative to Chinatown shopping. The changing exhibits feature Chinese culture and art. The foundation offers two walks through

Chinatown that take you to the less well known parts of the area:
"The Culinary Walk" includes a *dim sum* lunch, which costs $18
for adults and $9 for kids, and the "Heritage Walk," which lasts
about two hours and covers the history of the area, for $9 and $2,
respectively.

To see how fortune cookies are made, stop on Ross Avenue at
the Golden Gate Fortune Cookie Company.

### North Beach

If you continue toward the Bay from Chinatown, you will
arrive at Washington Square, the heart of North Beach. Along the
way, you will pass the Wells Fargo History Museum at 420
Montgomery Street (415-396-2619). The surrounding area is the
traditional Italian neighborhood of the city. Although Chinatown
continues to encroach on its boundaries, plenty of Italian bakeries
and restaurants can still be found. Dominating the square are the
spires of the church of Saints Peter and Paul, bringing a European
feeling to the whole scene. For kids, there's a good playground on
the square where they can unwind from all the walking and
shopping. Overlooking Washington Square, off to the east, is Coit
Tower, on Telegraph Hill between Lombard and Greenwich
streets. Coit Tower was built by Lillian Coit to commemorate the
heroics of the San Francisco Firemen; take a number 41 Union
MUNI bus, as the climb is quite steep. Inside the tower are
frescoes painted by WPA artists, but it's the almost 180 degree
view of the bay from the East Bay to the Golden Gate Bridge that
makes the visit worthwhile.

It's a logical jump from North Beach to Fisherman's Wharf,
Pier 39, Ghirardelli Square, and the Cannery. Here again is
endless shopping. You'll find anything and everything.

PIER 39. Pier 39 is a large and often controversial shopping
complex that juts out into the bay. For children, there is a two-
tiered carousel. Another thing kids like to do in this area is visit the
Maritime Museum and the Hyde Street Pier, where vintage ships
are moored for the public to visit.

THE MARITIME MUSEUM (at the foot of Polk Street across
from Ghirardelli Square, 415-673-0797). The museum has exhibits centering around the Gold Rush days at sea. Parts of
seafaring vessels are on view with other artifacts. Six ships are on
view at the pier and within walking distance of the Museum.
Admission is free for some of these; others cost $1 to $3.

*The Balclutha,* Pier 43, a Cape Horn sailing ship dating from 1886

*C. A. Thayer,* Hyde Street Pier, one of two survivors of a fleet of 900 that carried lumber from the Pacific Northwest to California cities

*The Eureka,* Hyde Street Pier, a sidewheel ferry that carried passengers and cars daily across the bay during the years from 1921 to 1941

*The Hercules,* Hyde Street Pier, one of a few tugs that made the journey through the Straits of Magellan

*Pampanito,* Pier 45, a fleet submarine of the Balao class designed for long-range cruises in the Pacific during the war with Japan

*Jeremiah O'Brien,* located at the Fort Mason pier, the last unaltered survivor of 2,751 Liberty Ships built during World War II

West of Fisherman's Wharf are the Fort Mason Center and the Marina Green. Fort Mason Center at Laguna and Marina Boulevards is composed of renovated piers that house theaters, galleries, and restaurants.

THE MEXICAN MUSEUM (Fort Mason Center, Building D, Zip: 94123, 415-441-0404). While you're at Fort Mason Center, you may want to visit this museum. Admission is $1, and children under 6 enter free at this excellent, small museum with a folk art collection inherited from Nelson Rockefeller. There are also changing exhibits centered on Mexican artists and themes. Children delight in all the fanciful colors associated with the arts of this region, and the atmosphere is casual. It's just large enough to keep you interested, but not big enough to give you a case of "museum feet." There's a museum store that has some very affordable and interesting pieces for sale.

THE MUSEO ITALO AMERICANO (Fort Mason Center, Building C, Zip: 94123, 415-673-2200). This small museum has a changing exhibition program devoted to Italian-American artists. Admission is free.

### Beyond the Marina Green

THE EXPLORATORIUM (3601 Lyons Street, Zip: 94123, 415-563-3200). The museum costs $4 for adults and is free for kids 17 and under. It's a must-see for all families visiting San Francisco:

the country's first hands-on scientific museum. Housed in a turn-of-the-century warehouse building erected for the San Francisco Exposition, it's filled with experiments to keep you busy. Older children will benefit most from this experience, but younger ones won't be bored. "Explainers," teenagers trained to assist you with the experiments, are helpful and interested in the needs of the children. The Tactile Dome is a by-reservation-only experience that will have you and the kids groping by your wits and senses through a maze constructed by museum experts.

### Golden Gate Park

This is the place in San Francisco where there really is something for everybody. To start with, on the Music Concourse, off Eighth Avenue and Kennedy Drive, there are three museums and the Japanese Tea Garden.

THE DE YOUNG FINE ARTS MUSEUM (415-750-3659). The museum is open Wednesdays through Sundays. Adult admission is $3; for kids 5 to 17, $1; younger kids pay no admission fee. The highlights for children here are the Primitive Arts Galleries and on Saturdays at 1:00 P.M. docent-led tours that introduce children to this collection. The tours are geared to children 6 and older and incorporate the Art for Touching Gallery, where children are allowed to touch art pieces.

THE ASIAN ART MUSEUM (housed in the same complex as the De Young Fine Arts Museum). This museum houses a collection devoted to the arts of Asia, including India, China, Tibet, Nepal, Japan, and Iran. The sculpture seems to captivate children, especially the statue of Ganesha, the Indian elephant god.

THE JAPANESE TEA GARDEN. The Japanese garden is adjacent to the De Young Fine Arts Museum on the Concourse. It's fun to walk with children (accessible with strollers) through an authentic Japanese garden with temples and bridges. There is a teahouse in the garden where you can drink green tea and eat cookies, even when it rains. The garden is at its best in the spring when the cherry blossoms are in bloom.

THE STRYBING ARBORETUM (9th Avenue at Lincoln Way, Zip: 94122, 415-661-1316). The arboretum is free and is several gardens all mapped into one, including a duck pond and roaming geese. There's a scent garden where children can smell their way through the flowers, and tours for children are scheduled from time to time. Call for information.

THE CALIFORNIA ACADEMY OF SCIENCES, including STEINHART AQUARIUM, THE MORRISON PLANETARIUM, and the LASERIUM (on the Music Concourse across from the De Young Fine Arts Museum, 415-750-7145). The Morrison Planetarium (415-750-7141) features sky shows organized around the time of year and the location of the stars. The Laserium (415-750-7138) is a show of lasers coordinated with music. Admission to the planetarium is adults $2, children $1, with shows daily at 2:00 P.M. and, on weekends, hourly shows between 1:00 and 4:00 P.M. Laserium admission is between $4 and $5, depending on the show, $3 for juniors. The laserium is not recommended for little ones; the music is of the Pink Floyd to Springsteen variety.

THE NATURAL HISTORY MUSEUM. Another part of the Academy of Sciences, this museum delights kids with walk-through dioramas of the African veldt, an earthquake exhibit that simulates the feel of a tremor underfoot, and a solar system hung from the ceiling. The aquarium has every kind of fish, plus penguins, dolphins, and a special gallery where the fish swim around you in a circular room. There is a cafeteria downstairs with hamburgers, and so forth, but the prices are a little high. Take sandwiches and eat them in the open courtyard with central fountain.

THE BUFFALO PADDOCK (just off Kennedy Drive on the way to the ocean). The paddock is where the buffalo roam, over several acres.

THE MARY B. CONNOLLY PLAYGROUND (at the east end of the park off Lincoln Way). This is the oldest park/playground in the country and the finest playground in the city. A turn-of-the-century carousel and a barnyard of petting animals are just some of the highlights.

### The Ocean Side of San Francisco
The perimeter of San Francisco is almost all a part of the Golden Gate National Recreation Area, and under its aegis these lands are well kept and overseen by park rangers.

### Ocean Beach
The long expanse of beach from the San Francisco County line to the renowned Cliff House is a windy but impressive beach.

It can sometimes get a little dirty from its city patrons and is not a very good swimming beach, even if the San Francisco weather cooperates.

THE SAN FRANCISCO ZOO (45th Avenue and Sloat Boulevard, Zip: 94176, 415-661-4844). Admission is $3.50 for adults; children under 15 enter free if they are accompanied by an adult with $1 extra admission at the Children's Zoo. This facility has recently been upgraded, and the animals look a lot happier than ever before. Outstanding exhibits are the Primate Discovery Center with a small hands-on gallery and large airy cages that give the effect of the animals' watching you, instead of the other way around. There are also "Gorilla World" and the "Koala Crossing." A beautiful carousel is located outside the Children's Zoo. There are plenty of different food cafés and even a large playground area at the entrance to the park. Strollers are available for rent at the Sloat Boulevard entrance.

If you're looking for San Francisco's best beach, we think it's the one at 25th Avenue and Lincoln Boulevard, part of the Recreation Area that sits just inside the entrance to the bay. It's a lovely beach with picnic facilities, views of the Golden Gate Bridge, and the Marin Headlands. Few if any beaches in San Francisco are warm enough for swimming, but if the weather happens to cooperate, this is the place to be.

### All Around the Town

Here are some museums, performances, and playgrounds in other parts of town that are worth a look.

The Cable Car Museum (1201 Mason Street, Zip: 94108, 415-474-1887) is free and full of memorabilia and cable car lore.

The Fire Department Museum (665 Presidio between Pine and Bush, Zip: 94115) is also free and features vintage fire trucks and other firefighting equipment.

Fort Point National Historic Site (Presidio, beneath the Golden Gate Bridge) is a 19th-century fort built on the site of a Spanish fort and finished in 1861.

Josephine D. Randall Museum (199 Museum Way off Roosevelt, Zip: 94114) is free, is hidden away in a quiet corner of the city, and features a live animal exhibit.

Julius Kahn Playground (West Pacific Avenue and the Presidio) is nestled in the Presidio near the army base of the same name. It's warm when the fog rolls in, protected by the grove of trees that surrounds the park area.

Mountain Lake Park (at Ninth Avenue and Lake) has imaginative play equipment and is almost always filled with kids; there's also a lake with ducks, just right for a quiet walk.

Pickle Family Circus: this vaudevillian circus is the best. With its troupe of performers, there is no need for animals; they are all the entertainment you could need. Sometimes you can catch their performances free in the city parks, but recently they have begun a series of paid events. Watch the pink section of the Sunday *San Francisco Examiner* for dates.

Make-A-Circus: another group troupe of performers, whose emphasis here is on juggling and acrobatics. After the performance, children are invited to meet the performers and learn a few tricks for themselves. Usually they perform free in the city parks; again, check the pink entertainment section of the *San Francisco Examiner.*

Stern Grove Concerts (19th Avenue and Sloat Boulevard) are a Sunday summer concert series that runs the gamut from ballet to jazz. The Ethnic Dance Festival segments are colorful and fun for everyone. Surrounded by a grove of eucalyptus trees, children are happy to be outdoors, and the feeling is casual. If the concert becomes a bit boring for the kids, there's a playground right off Sloat Boulevard to revive tired spirits.

### Beyond San Francisco's City Limits

Two easy journeys, filled with excitement, especially the getting there part, are to Alcatraz and Angel Island. There's also a short cruise departing from Pier 39 or Fisherman's Wharf for those who don't want to take the longer trips.

ALCATRAZ. Ferries leave Pier 41 daily from 8:45 A.M. to 2:45 P.M. for the trip to Alcatraz. In all, it's about a half-hour journey. Food service is available on the ferry, but there is no food on Alcatraz. On Alcatraz, park rangers from the Golden Gate National Recreation Area lead informative tours of the famous prisons. Tickets must be purchased in advance because tours fill up quickly. Call 415-556-0560 for information. Admission includes the ferry ride and is $4 adults, $2.50 for ages 5 to 11. Everyone knows Alcatraz as the famous prison, but few are aware that from 1853 until 1933 this was also an army post. Older children will delight in the tales of the notorious, and they like experiencing the feeling of confinement in the cells. Trails on the island are steep, so this is an excursion set aside for those who are sturdy. Always take warm jackets for bay excursions.

ANGEL ISLAND STATE PARK. You can get there by ferry (call 415-435-2131 or 415-546-2815) from Pier 43½. This is San Francisco's Ellis Island. The original barracks remain and can be visited. The other attractions include plenty of hiking trails and several lovely beaches. The ferry docks at Ayala cove; there are picnic tables and a wading beach. This was an army base, as well, and you can visit these historic buildings while you're on the island.

For information on bay cruises that leave from Fisherman's Wharf or from Pier 43½ and last just over an hour, call 415-546-2810 or 415-781-7877. The cost is $8.95 for adults, $5.95 for children 11 to 17, children $3.95 for ages 5 to 11, and free for kids under age 5.

## The North Bay

Just off Highway One, across the Golden Gate Bridge, is Muir Woods, a pristine grove of redwoods with a gentle trail that is easy for toddlers and grown-ups alike. Mount Tamalpais is another popular hiking spot for families, with trails of varied lengths and steepness.

POINT REYES NATIONAL SEASHORE (30 miles north of San Francisco on Highway 1, 415-669-1539). This beautiful national park is almost in San Francisco's backyard, with many beaches and lots of wilderness.

BEAR VALLEY VISITORS CENTER AND MUSEUM (415-663-1092). You can whale watch from the historic lighthouse set out on the promontory. Some trails are easy enough for young children, for instance, the self-guided trails to the reconstructed Miwok Indian Village and the Earthquake Trail, where you can see the effects of the San Andreas fault. As always, be prepared for cool weather.

*The East Bay*

THE LAWRENCE HALL OF SCIENCE (Centennial Drive at the University of California at Berkeley, Zip: 94720, 415-642-5132). After visiting the University of California at Berkeley campus, take the kids here. Planetarium shows run here until 9:00 P.M. on Thursdays. With a biology lab and exhibit hall, this is the East Bay's answer to a hands-on science museum.

THE OAKLAND MUSEUM (9th and Oak Streets, Zip: 94607). Accessible by BART at Lake Merritt Station, here's a fun museum devoted to the arts, science, and history of California. Housed in an award-winning building, the sculpture garden is a series of platforms stacked one on top of the other, a great place for a children's picnic.

CHILDREN'S FAIRYLAND (Lakeside Park near Lake Merritt, Oakland). Open weekends and holidays 10:00 A.M. to 4:30 P.M., Fairyland offers storybook rides, park, and puppet shows at 11:00 A.M., 2:00 P.M., and 4:00 P.M.

## Where to Eat

Here are five of our favorites.

MING PALACE (933 Clement Street, at 10th Avenue, 415-668-3988). This is a large Chinese restaurant where spilled rice won't make any difference. Plenty of families and lots of kids make for a noisy but comfortable atmosphere. From 9:00 A.M. on, *dim sum* (Cantonese goodies) are served. You choose the selections from a roving cart and pay by the plate. Children enjoy the bite-size proportions and all the variations. It's located close to Golden Gate Park on a street with lots of interesting shops. High chairs and booth seats are available.

GREEN'S AT FORT MASON (Bay at Laguna, Building A, 415-771-6222). Best for family brunch, this vegetarian restaurant is one place where meat eaters are rarely disappointed. Run by the Zen Center, this restaurant serves up only the freshest of foods. The interior abounds with modern art, and the views of the bay from the large windows are a great source of pleasure. The menu includes choices just right for the small eater such as muffins and yogurt. Dinners tend to be a bit expensive, so keep to the early hours for family meals.

HIPPOS HAMBURGERS (2025 Van Ness Avenue/Pacific Avenue, 415-771-3939). A longtime San Francisco hangout, this place delights children. There are 57 varieties of hamburgers, some admittedly bordering on the ridiculous. Also there are kids' menus, a real plus in San Francisco. High chairs and booster seats are available.

ENRICO'S SIDE (504 Broadway/Montgomery, 415-392-6220). Enrico's has booster seats, booths, and outdoor seating as well. It's a snack place in the North Beach neighborhood, a real San Francisco tradition. It's fun to sit at the outdoor tables and watch the passing parade.

YET WAH (Clement and 23rd Avenue, 415-387-8040). Yet Wah also has other locations in the Bay Area, including Pier 39. It is a large bustling restaurant with plenty of choices on the menu. There is something to please everyone, and they're not intimidated by large family groups. High chairs and booster seats are available.

## Time Out

For baby-sitting help in the San Francisco area, contact the following.

CHILDCARE SWITCHBOARD. Call 415-282-7858; phone hours are Monday through Thursday 9:00 A.M. to 4:30 P.M. and Friday 9:00 A.M. to noon. This agency can give you names of baby-sitters from their listings. You'll have to do the interviewing yourself. This is a very reputable nonprofit organization that can also field other child-related questions and refer you to someone who can help.

TOURS FOR TOTS THROUGH TEENS (P.O. Box 504, Corte Madera, California 94295, 415-924-1795). Tours are scheduled weekly or may be custom-designed. Kids of all ages are welcome and the owner, Carol Dodds, will also arrange baby-sitting and overnight care.

SAN FRANCISCO JEWISH COMMUNITY CENTER, TEENS IN EMPLOYMENT PROGRAM (3200 California, Zip: 94118, 415-346-6040). This is a training and employment program for teenagers who have been trained to baby-sit responsibly. Call for a referral.

BRISTOL-HARAN AGENCY (1724 Sacramento, Zip: 94109, 415-775-9100). This agency is bonded. Rates start around $4 an hour, depending on the age and number of children, with a four-hour minimum. Rates increase after 9:00 P.M., and you must be responsible for the sitter's transportation.

## Accommodations
### Bed and Breakfast

BED AND BREAKFAST INTERNATIONAL (151 Ardmore Road, Kensington, California 94707, 415-525-4569). This bed and breakfast network was the first set up in the United States. It's run by Jean Brown, a former nursery school teacher, who explains that the best kind of facility for a family is an "in-law" apartment: "The advantage to these apartments is the ability to keep snacks in the refrigerator or even have a pizza in the dining room. And families can have breakfast without going outside to a restaurant." Ms. Brown is careful to put families with people who are warm to the idea. Ms. Brown warns her clients with kids, though, that virtually every home in San Francisco has one or two flights of stairs so kids must be able to navigate.

BED AND BREAKFAST SAN FRANCISCO (P.O. Box 349, Zip: 94101-0349, 415-931-3083). This bed and breakfast service has a limited number of accommodations for families. One example is a family room for three for $75, which includes a full breakfast and a crib if you need it.

### Hotels

BERESFORD HOTEL (635 Sutter near Union Square, Zip: 94102, 415-673-9900). This is an aging but friendly hotel, centrally located. A room for four (two double beds) costs $65, roll-away beds are $10 extra, and cribs are available. The first floor of the hotel has a lovely bar restaurant complete with fireplace and European chairs; it's called the White Horse Tavern.

THE FOUR SEASONS CLIFT HOTEL (495 Geary Street, Zip: 94102, 415-775-4700 or 1-800-268-6282). This one's a bit pricey, but they go out of their way for kids. There are puzzles, games, bedtime milk and cookies, and a send-off with popcorn, soda, and balloons. Cribs and roll-away beds are available, and all rooms have wet bars. Diapers, bottles, baby bathtubs, and strollers are available on request. The French Room restaurant gives kids a toy and a snack just as soon as they're seated. Baby-sitters are available through the concierge. The hotel is located 1½ blocks west of

Union Square and offers families two adjoining rooms at the single rate, for example, $145 per room per night.

PACIFIC HEIGHTS INN (1555 Union Street, Zip: 94123, 415-776-3310). Their two bedrooms with bath and a Continental breakfast included costs $74.50. A room with two queen-size beds and a kitchenette is $68.50; without kitchenettes it's a few dollars less. All rooms have refrigerators, even if they don't have a kitchenette, and coffee and tea are always available. The inn can arrange baby-sitting for you.

RANCHO LOMBARD HOTEL (1501 Lombard at Franklin, Zip: 94123, 415-747-3030). A family suite that's large enough to sleep six is $125. Room rates range from $50 to $65.

SEAL ROCK INN (545 Point Lobos Avenue at Ocean Beach, Zip: 94121, 415-752-8000). A room big enough for a family of four costs $62 to $80 per night. Badminton, tennis, and Ping-Pong are available.

THE SHERATON AT FISHERMAN'S WHARF (2500 Mason, Zip: 94133, 415-362-5500). Rates vary from $94 to $160 per night normally; seasonal packages are as low as $80. There are an outdoor swimming pool and a special breakfast room.

## WASHINGTON, D.C.

You can visit Washington with your family now or wait until your kids' civics teacher takes them on a school trip. We suggest the former because Washington is fun and full of family-type activities.

Before you plan your trip, we suggest first writing to the Washington, D.C., Convention and Visitors Association, 1575 Eye Street, N.W., Washington, D.C. 20005, 202-789-7000 and asking for a packet of their excellent materials, including *Washington, D.C., a Capital City, Washington Attractions, Calendar of Events, Washington Dining/Shopping, Washington's Accommodations,* and their *Visitor Map.*

The second place to contact is an independent school just outside Washington that publishes a book called *Going Places with Children in Washington.* It began in mimeographed form and has grown to a full-fledged book, still written and edited by parent volunteers. The book is available for $5.95 from Green Acres School, 11701 Danville Drive, Rockville, Maryland 20852. Every sight listed in the book has been visited by Green Acres' parents. In the book, you'll find sightseeing attractions, historic sites, parks, sports, entertainment, restaurants—all geared to kids. In the beginning of the book, the Green Acres people outline a three-day tour that includes the top tourist attractions but promises not to exhaust the family. It includes on the first day a trip to the Washington Monument, a walk to the National Museum of American History, lunch at the Post Office Pavilion, and back to the National Museum of American History. After dinner they recommend a visit to the Lincoln and Jefferson memorials, so beautifully illuminated at night. On the second day, they suggest an FBI tour, a walk to the National Archives, and then a visit to the National Air and Space Museum. For families with younger kids, they recommend a morning at the zoo instead, with the Air and Space Museum on the third day. The second day can wind up at Arlington National Cemetery. For the third day they recommend a tour of the Bureau of Engraving and Printing (weekdays only), the White House (a tour is not even necessary, just seeing the familiar façade is fun for kids), on to Capitol Hill, lunch in the Supreme Court cafeteria, followed by a tour of the Capitol. For younger kids, skip the Capitol, buy lunch from a vendor on the Mall, and spend the afternoon at the Air and Space Museum or at the Capitol Children's Museum. Or, for little ones, consider a boat ride on the Tidal Basin (pedal boats for rent, 202-484-3475).

A third source of information on interesting programs for kids in the Washington area is the National Park Service. For up-to-the-minute information on park activities—such as hikes through Fort Washington Park looking for signs of whitetail deer, holiday storytelling, or a harvest celebration—call 202-426-6975. Or write to the Editorial Office of Public Affairs, National Capitol Region, 1100 Ohio Drive, S.W., Washington, D.C. 20242, and ask for a copy of *Kiosk*, a monthly guide to events.

And, before your trip, be sure to get a copy of *Potomac Children* from Box 39134, Washington, D.C. 20016.

### Getting Around

Washington is an easy town to get around. Public transportation is excellent; don't bother to take your car touring downtown: parking is too expensive and hard to find. Metrobus and Metrorail routes link all parts of the city, and riding the Metro is a real adventure for kids. Children under 5 ride free. For Metrorail/ Metrobus information, call 202-637-2437. Another great boon to tourists is the Tourmobile, 202-554-7950, that operates tours to 18 historic sites aboard shuttle trains. Guides on board give background information, and one ticket (adults, $7, kids 3 to 11, $3.50) allows you to get on and off whenever you'd like.

## What to See and Do

Some of the things we like best about Washington follow. The first two listings are part of the Smithsonian Institution Museum group, the world's largest museum complex, where admission is always free. For recorded information on Smithsonian daily events, call 202-357-2020; for general information, 202-357-2700. For information on presentations given in the Smithsonian's Discovery Theatre by the Institution's Resident Associate Program, call 202-357-1500. Performances are held from October to June, either at the Arts and Industries Building or at the National Museum of Natural History during the week and/or on weekends. Performances all relate to a specific museum or exhibition, and tickets are $2 to $3 per person. Some recent offerings included "Music and the Underground Railroad," with music, story and songs, and a marionette production of "Jack and the Beanstalk" set in the mountains of Appalachia.

NATIONAL AIR AND SPACE MUSEUM (7th and Independence Avenues, S.W., Washington, D.C. 20560, 202-357-1300). The grown-ups among us resisted this one at first, but we ended up loving it. Go early in the day if you can. Take a highlight tour at 10:15 A.M. or at 1:00 P.M. See the "Milestones of Flight" gallery, from the Wright brothers to the command module of the *Apollo* 11 moon-landing mission. And the films presented in the TMAX theater are truly spectacular. Don't leave without seeing them. The museum includes lots of conveniences for families—infant changing tables, strollers allowed, an area for nursing mothers, self-guided tape tours, and an on-site fast food service.

ANACOSTIA NEIGHBORHOOD MUSEUM (1901 Fort Place, S.E., Zip: 20020, 202-287-3369). This is one of the smaller branches of the Smithsonian, and it is devoted to presenting programs and exhibits that relate to black history and culture. The museum offers free, self-guided audiocassette tours and once a month features special demonstrations. Much of the Anacostia is hands-on. There's no restaurant, but a picnic area is available and there's a park not too far away.

CAPITAL CHILDREN'S MUSEUM (800 Third Street, N.E., Zip: 20002, 202-543-8600). Here your kids (most of the exhibits are geared to ages 5 to 12) can paint with a computer, bake a tortilla, launch a satellite, crawl through a manhole, print a poster, or read an electronic newspaper. The four major exhibit areas are Communications, Mexico, Future Center, and Changing Environments. From time to time, the museum also presents musical plays, such as a puppet version of "Rapunzel" or an audience participation presentation of "Snow White." Every weekend, there is a special workshop on mask making or string painting or thumb pottery or some other craft. Admission is $3.

KENNEDY CENTER FOR THE PERFORMING ARTS/PROGRAMS FOR CHILDREN AND YOUTH (Washington, D.C. 20566, 202-254-7190). The Kennedy Center presents free programs for young people during their fall session of performances, which includes contemporary adaptations of well-known tales from September to December; a Cultural Diversity Festival in February featuring poetry, African folktales, and international folk dance; and their Imagination Celebration in April, which involves drama, music, and puppetry at a children's art festival. All of these are held in the Theatre Lab of the center. Every once in a while there are special admission events for kids in other theaters at the center. Call for details.

EXPLORERS HALL, NATIONAL GEOGRAPHIC SOCIETY (17th and M Streets, N.W., Zip: 20036, 202-857-7588). This small museum is nice for kids. It is just four blocks north of the White House. The big feature here is the world's largest unmounted globe: 11 feet from pole to pole and 34 feet around its equator. It usually rotates on its axis, just like the earth. Globe demonstrations can be arranged in advance by calling 202-857-7689.

Kids also like to get a look at the permanent exhibits: "Discovering Prehistoric People," "Cliff Dwellers in the Southwest" (the reproduction of the cliff dwellers' "Kiva" is a big favorite), the "Great Olmec Head," and an under-the-sea exhibit featuring the work of Jacques-Yves Cousteau. Strollers are okay.

NATIONAL ARCHIVES AND RECORDS SERVICE (Constitution Avenue between 7th and 9th Streets, N.W., Zip: 20408, 202-523-3000). Older kids who have studied the beginnings of American government may want to take a look at the Declaration of Independence, the Constitution, and the Bill of Rights. If you and your kids are really interested, you can arrange a behind-the-scenes tour given by docents at 10:15 A.M. and 1:15 P.M. each day. Call 202-523-3183 to make a reservation.

FBI BUILDING (E Street between 9th and 10th Streets, N.W., Zip: 20535, 202-324-3447). The FBI tour is one of the most popular shows in town for kids. They love all the exhibits on crime detection, fingerprinting, blood typing, reminders of some of our more notorious law breakers, and, at the end of the tour, the firearms demonstration. Tours run Monday to Friday from 9:00 A.M. to 4:15 P.M., every 20 minutes or so. Up to 5,000 people per day take this tour!

THE WASHINGTON POST (1150 15th Street, N.W., Zip: 20071, 202-334-6000). If you have kids 10 or older, you can arrange for a private tour of the *Post's* facilities. The news department and all of the production facilities are included, so if your kids are interested in a behind-the-scenes look at a newspaper, call 202-334-7969.

BUREAU OF ENGRAVING AND PRINTING (14th and C Streets, S.W., Zip: 20228, 202-447-9709). Here's where our money and our postage stamps are printed. Continuous free self-guided tours, about 20 minutes long, run Monday through Friday from 9:00 to 2:00. (They're closed the week between Christmas and New Year's, though.) Get on line early—the wait averages 1½ hours during high season. At the end of the tour you'll stop at the Visitor Center, where you can see uncut sheets of currency and engraved prints. Kids love to buy little bags of shredded currency to take home with them.

NAVY MUSEUM (Washington Navy Yard, 9th and M Streets, S.E., Zip: 20003, 202-433-4882). We chose this because it's a little like an indoor-outdoor playground. The point of the museum is to present a chronological and thematic overview of the Navy's history in the United States from the Revolution to the 1980s. What the kids love is the chance to climb on cannons, turn periscopes, and jump all over tanks and missiles. Going on board the decommissioned destroyer USS *Baring* is fun, too. For kids, the museum has put together a *Scavenger Hunt* booklet and an activity sheet that would be good even for the smallest children. There are strollers allowed always, free guided tours, tape tours geared for kids 5 to 7 and 8 to 14, and a park with picnic tables right across the street. Admission is free.

NATIONAL ZOOLOGICAL PARK (3000 Block of Connecticut Avenue, N.W., Zip: 20008, 202-673-4817). This is yet another section of the Smithsonian. Admission is free, but parking costs $3. What a manageable zoo! We spent three hours there recently with kids aged 3 to 16 and we all had a good time. Don't miss the white tigers, the pandas, the giraffes, the hippos, and the reptiles. We picnicked on a bench and avoided the long, long lines at the snack bars. Strollers are available for rent on weekends except in the summer, when they're available every day.

## Time Out

Sitters Unlimited (Chapter 5) has a franchise in the Washington, D.C., area. It's run by Nancy Richards and is located in Virginia at 205 Yoakum Parkway, 1505, Alexandria, Virginia 22304, 703-823-0888. Sitters Unlimited people can take care of your kids in your hotel room or take them out for some sightseeing. Prices begin at $6 per hour with a four-hour minimum and 75 cents extra for each additional child, plus a $4 transportation charge or parking fee at the hotel if it's more than $4.

## Accommodations

A bed and breakfast venture that specializes in accommodations in the city's historic districts is Bed Breakfasts of Washington, D.C., P.O. Box 12011, Washington, D.C. 20005, 202-328-3510. Rates vary from $40 to $75 for doubles, with $10 for each additional person. Unhosted apartments are available and great for families.

### Hotels

Many Washington hotels have special family plans or, even more likely, special weekend rates. Often weekend rates are available every day during the summer. Send for the Hotel Association of Washington's *Weekend Guide*. It's free from P.O. Box 33578, Washington, D.C. 20033.

For a free, one-stop reservation service offering discounts for families, just call 800-VISIT-DC. The system represents 70 hotels in downtown Washington and nearby Virginia and Maryland. It's operated by Capitol Reservations, 1201 K Street, N.W., Washington, D.C. 20005. The following hotels assured us they "warmly welcome" families with kids under 12.

HYATT REGENCY (400 New Jersey Avenue, N.W., Washington, D.C. 20001, 202-737-1234). On Capitol Hill, this hotel features "The Children's Suite," a child-care facility for 4 to 12-year-olds, staffed by Y.M.C.A. specialists. Open from 8 A.M. to midnight, reservations are required 2 hours in advance. Fees are $15 for 4 hours or less; $25 for 5 to 12 hours. Special summer weekend rates are appealing, too—$69 for a double-room.

KEY BRIDGE MARRIOTT (1401 Lee Highway, Arlington, Virginia 22209, 703-524-6400 or 800-228-9290). You can walk across a bridge to Georgetown or go two blocks to the Metro station. The Marriott has an indoor-outdoor pool, and a special children's menu that is also available through room service. The hotel offers special discounted rates for families. One recent promotion offered a $69 per room per night rate and included discounts on sightseeing possibilities, a free fun book, and a free metro subway card. Offers vary with the season; check what's going on when you plan to visit. Cribs are always free, and baby-sitting is available for $5 per hour for one child, $2.50 more for each additional child.

LOEWS' L'ENFANT PLAZA HOTEL (480 L'Enfant Plaza, S.W., Washington, D.C. 20024, 202-484-1000 or 800-223-0888). This one is within walking distance of the Air and Space Museum, the Washington Monument, and the Capitol, and there's a Metro station right under the hotel. The hotel has an open air swimming pool, and there's a playground one block away at the Mall. Rooms all have refrigerators, televisions, minibars, and individual climate controls. Regular room rates are $135 to $165 for a double, but special weekend rates are much lower, for instance, $44.44 per person per night for their "Star Spangled Special." Kids 14 and under stay free in the same room with parents. Cribs are free. Baby-sitting can be arranged through the concierge for $6 per hour.

STOUFFER CONCOURSE HOTEL (2399 Jefferson Davis Highway, Arlington, Virginia 22202, 703-979-6800 or 800-468-3571). Don't let the address put you off. This hotel is adjacent to the Washington National Airport and 10 minutes from D.C. There's a Metro station two blocks from the hotel, and a shuttle van will take you there. There are a rooftop swimming pool, an exercise room, and saunas (the health club is reserved for people 16 and over), a video and pinball game room. Family suites are available. A special family weekend rate of $69 per night includes one free meal per day for kids under 12, complimentary coffee and newspaper with a wake-up call, and in-room movies. For $10 more, your family can stay on the Club Floor. The rooms are larger and include a complimentary breakfast. Cribs are free. Baby-sitting is available with four hours advance notice and costs $4 per hour during the day, $5 at night.

WASHINGTON-PLAZA HOTEL (Vermont and Massachusetts Avenues, N.W., Washington, D.C. 20005, 202-842-1300 or 800-424-1140). Five blocks from the White House and not far from the Vietnam Veterans' Memorial, the National Gallery, and the Lincoln Memorial, the Washington-Plaza has an outdoor pool. Special winter and summer "weekend all week" rates for rooms for one to four range from $49 to $59 per room. Baby-sitting is available for $6 per hour.

## ABOUT OUR LISTINGS:

The properties we list in this book all welcome kids and all willingly responded to our many, many questions. We're relying on you, our readers, to let us know about your own experiences with our choices—good and bad—and to tell us about any new places we can list in the next edition.

## ONE MORE REMINDER:

If you're looking for a place to play tennis, check the tennis and golf chapter but don't overlook Chapter 8 on resorts, Chapter 10 on skiing (many ski resorts turn into tennis and golf spots once the snow melts), and Chapter 11 on farms and dude ranches.

And don't forget the None of the Above listings beginning on page 289.

NOTE: Rates quoted here were accurate at press time but are subject to change.

NOTE: Be sure to check pages 297–99 for a list of publishers' addresses. Some books published by smaller publishers may not be readily available in bookstores but can be ordered directly from the publisher.

Send us your cards and letters. We want to hear from you about your great vacation choices so that we can include them in the next edition.

# 8

---

# Resorts

Some people like to go to one spot and stay there until their vacation is over. They like their meals, their sports, their entertainment all within walking distance. For these people we offer this chapter: resorts with activities galore and free children's programs besides. Remember, too, that there are other resorts throughout the book, in the ski, golf and tennis, and dude ranch chapters. Check them out, too. A book on the subject we recommend is *What to Do with the Kids This Year* by Jane Wilford with Janet Tice, published by East Woods Press ($8.95). The book lists 100 places to stay, all with activities for kids.

Our listings are alphabetical by state; as in everything else in the book, the emphasis here is on the facilities for kids.

**Grand Hotel**
Scenic Highway 98
Point Clear, Alabama 36564
Telephone: 205-928-9201 or 800-228-9290
General Manager: John Irvin

IN THEIR OWN WORDS: "an exciting yet relaxed atmosphere for all age groups, . . . strolling by the lagoon, you can stop to feed the ducks or savor the breathtaking landscaping and gardens. . . . The hotel is located in a residential community, away from busy traffic. All activities are available on property, and parents can feel safe letting their children roam around the grounds. . . ."

DESCRIPTION: The hotel's 550 acres of moss-draped oaks, lagoons, and gardens are located right on Mobile Bay. Since 1847, this resort has been seducing guests with the pleasures of tennis, golf, badminton, croquet, jogging, horseback riding (Point Clear Stables is a picture-book thoroughbred breeding and training farm right next to the golf course), boating, fishing from a charter boat or the Grand Pavilion Wharf, and swimming at the beach or in the enormous 750,000-gallon Grand Hotel pool.

FOR KIDS: Grand Little Ones is the name they've given to the program for 3- and 4-year-olds that runs Monday through Saturday, 10:00 A.M. to 2:00 P.M. Participants splash and swim at the pool and have storytime, follow-the-leader beach hikes, sing-alongs, and more. Parents can register for a full day or for the part of the schedule they prefer. Lunch is available.

The older kids 5 to 12 can join the Grand Juniors Program, which operates from 10:00 A.M. all the way to 10:00 P.M., Monday through Saturday in summer and during vacation periods. Every day is different for the Grand Juniors—beach fun, biking, pool play, fishing contests, after-dinner movies, dance contests, and more. Saturday Supper at the stables is a popular event with a cookout, pony rides, hayrides, and square dancing. Kids can register for a full day of Grand Juniors or for any part of the day; there's no charge for the program. Lunch and dinner can be included.

Baby-sitting for the littlest kids is available by contacting housekeeping. Expect to pay about $3.35 per hour with a three-hour minimum.

ACCOMMODATIONS: All of the 308 rooms have views of the bay, marina, or lagoon; most have balconies. A typical room has two double beds and a sofa bed. Cribs are available at no extra charge.

RATES: Winter rates average $119 per room; in summer, kids under 18 stay free. Various packages are also available, so be sure to ask.

**The Broadmoor Hotel**
P.O. Box 1439
Colorado Springs, Colorado 80901
Telephone: 303-634-7711
General Manager: Douglas C. Cogswell

IN THEIR OWN WORDS: "Each year tens of thousands of people from across the United States and scores of foreign countries converge on the Colorado Rockies. To the Broadmoor. Because the Broadmoor has never changed what it started out to be— a grand resort hotel reminiscent of the finest European traditions."

DESCRIPTION: The Broadmoor has been called the "Riviera of the Rockies" because of its pale pink buildings with red-tiled roofs set on the rim of a large lake. The theme is Mediterranean, and many of the adornments of the hotel were imported from the art centers of Europe and other parts of the world. In June 1918 the Broadmoor opened with a glittering, gala event that had all of Colorado Springs excited. Over the years, the hotel has expanded, built more golf courses and tennis courts, and won 26 years worth of Mobil Five Star awards. A day at Broadmoor can include golf (54 holes in all), tennis (16 plexipave courts), skiing, year-round ice-skating, swimming, and biking. The surrounding Colorado Rockies are a major attraction. Sightseeing in the Pikes Peak region, visiting the Cheyenne Mountain Zoo, making a trip to the Pikes Peak Cog Railway and the Will Rogers monument are all easy excursions from the hotel. Scenic tours can be arranged easily through the hotel.

FOR KIDS: Kids 6 to 12 have their own program during July and August from Monday through Saturday. Hours are 9:30 to 1:00 P.M. and again 6:00 to 9:00 P.M. Mornings offer games, paddleboating, trips to the zoo, and skating and end with a swim and lunch at the pool. At night, the kids have dinner together and afterward play games. On some summer Tuesday nights there's a steak fry for the whole family at Rotten Log Hollow. The children's program is free except for zoo trips and other excursions.

Baby-sitting is available for younger kids for $4 per hour with a three-hour minimum. Contact Guest Services.

ACCOMMODATIONS: There are 560 rooms in all, divided among three facilities—Broadmoor Main, Broadmoor West, and Broadmoor South. The first was built in 1918, the second in 1975, and the third in 1961. There are 60 suites available.

RATES: Rate for a family of four with one room and two double beds in high season (beginning May 1) is $155 to $195; in low season (beginning November 1) it's $105 to $155.

**Club Med**
Sandpiper
Port Lucie, Florida
Mailing Address: Club Med, 40 West 57th Street,
New York, New York 10019
Telephone: 800-CLUB-MED

IN THEIR OWN WORDS: "This is the old, unspoiled Florida
. . . a beautiful place . . . warm, friendly and hassle free, the most
luxurious Club Med ever."

DESCRIPTION: Located 45 minutes north of Palm Beach,
this resort was recently taken over by the Club Med people, who
invested $10 million in changes. The result is a luxurious resort
with 45 holes of golf, 19 tennis courts, and 5 swimming pools, all
along the banks of the milewide St. Lucie River. Although the golf
is a major attraction, the Club Med folks want to be sure that
people understand that it's only one attraction. Others are sailing,
waterskiing, pedal boating, a fitness center, basketball, volleyball,
and the use of a Beach Club on the Atlantic that is accessible via a
free shuttle bus.

FOR KIDS: The Sandpiper has a baby club and a miniclub,
and the services are outstanding. The Baby Club is for kids 4
months to 2 years who are cared for by GOs (the Club Med name
for counselors) from 9:00 A.M. to 6:00 P.M., six days a week. Kids
can stay the entire time or part of the time or go in and out of the
program, whatever best suits the parents.

A specialist on baby food is on staff to plan and make meals
for the little ones, and babies can be fed lunch by the GOs. Parents
are expected to feed them dinner. Bottle warmers, bassinets, potty
seats—all the equipment you might need for a baby—are available.

Kids 2 to 12 are eligible for the miniclub, which meets from
9:00 A.M. to 9:00 P.M. and is open six days a week. Miniclub
members over 8 can come and go as they please; learn archery,
tennis, golf; or just enjoy the minipool outside the air-conditioned
miniclub house. Miniclub members put on shows for guests, go on
picnics, and take excursions.

Miniclub members have early lunch and dinner (special

menus designed to appeal to kids along with the GOs and their fellow club members) or they may eat with their parents. All of this is free. Baby-sitters are available at an additional charge for after 6:00 P.M. for the babies and after 9:00 P.M. for the older kids. Families may join organized excursions to Disney World or the Kennedy Space Center. (These excursions cost extra.)

ACCOMMODATIONS: Guests stay in small clusters of buildings with three stories, built around a courtyard and along the riverfront. Each room has two oversize beds, a sitting area with a couch and two easy chairs, full carpeting, terrace or balcony, bathtubs, and small refrigerators. All rooms are air-conditioned.

RATES: From September to mid-November, kids 2 to 7 stay free. In the same period adults pay $670 for a week, babies 4 months to 2 years, $268; and kids 8 to 11, $469. Prices include accommodations, meals, and all activities: "no hidden costs, no tipping." Call for rates for other times of the year.

### Casa Ybel Resort
2255 West Gulf Drive
P.O. Box 167
Sanibel Island, Florida 33957
Telephone: 813-472-3145 or 800-237-8906
General Manager: Hal Williams

IN THEIR OWN WORDS: "This is a lovely resort, nestled in a lush, tropical setting on Sanibel Island. The island is two-thirds wildlife refuge. . . . The light sea breeze off the Gulf stirs the pelicans, herons, and ibis from their roosts while contented guests watch them take flight."

DESCRIPTION: On the Gulf side of Sanibel Island, this resort offers lots of possibilities. You can follow their Sun-Day schedule activities for guided beach walks, tennis clinics, exercise classes, and so on, or go off on your own to play tennis, swim in the pool, sail a Hobie Cat, bicycle, or just relax. There's golf nearby with discounts for resort guests.

FOR KIDS: "Tiny Tots" is for kids 3 to 6 years old, who have an activity scheduled for them two to three times per week for 1½ or 2 hours at a time. Arts and crafts, beach walks, games, and a snack are all possibilities. Once a week this same age group has a puppet workshop.

"Casa Kids" is a Monday through Thursday program for 7- to 12-year-old kids, which operates during the summer and during school holidays. Games, arts and crafts, beach hikes, swimming, and biking are included.

"Craft Kids" is scheduled two to three times per week for kids 6 to 12.

"Looney Tunes" is an evening combination of a cookout, games, and cartoons for 3- to 8-year-olds, offered once a week. For teens there are special cookouts, beach parties, pizza nights, and so on.

There's a fee for all these programs. All through the week, too, are activities that are meant for kids and adults together—shell crafts, kite making and flying, and poolside bingo.

ACCOMMODATIONS: One- and two-bedroom condos are clustered along the beach. All have a living/dining room area with a fully equipped kitchen, bedrooms, and a screened-in balcony overlooking the Gulf of Mexico. Cribs—portable and full-size—are available for $5 and $10 per night.

RATES: A variety of packages are available. A midweek "Casa Ventura" package, five days and four nights, costs $500 in a two-bedroom villa. This includes a welcome cocktail, lodging, a discount coupon book for dining and entertainment on the Island, and unlimited tennis from April through December.

### South Seas Plantation Resort and Yacht Harbour
P.O. Box 194
Captiva Island, Florida 33924
Telephone: 813-472-5111; for reservations, 800-237-3102
General Manager: Austin L. Mott III

IN THEIR OWN WORDS: "an enclave of tropical tranquility . . . 330 acres of barefoot elegance where not a single tree or shrub was unnecessarily disturbed. . . ."

DESCRIPTION: As you'd expect, all kinds of water sports are possible—sailing, cruising, racing (this is one of the sites of Steve Colgate's Offshore Sailing School; see Chapter 6), jet skiing, kayaking, wind surfing, snorkeling, and charter boat fishing. The resort's two-mile stretch of private white beach is where you'll find some of the best shelling in the world. When you want to get away from the shore, there are 9 holes of golf at the resort, 18 more on neighboring Sanibel Island, 22 tennis courts, and 17 swimming pools.

FOR KIDS: From Memorial Day to Labor Day and during school vacations, South Seas offers children's programs, usually five days per week. Kids 3 to 18 are eligible.

"Fun Bunch" is a program for kids 3 to 6 (no diapers) held from 9:00 A.M. to noon. Activities include swimming, sing-alongs, nature crafts, and sometimes, in the evening, a cookout followed by an evening of cartoons, games, and stories. The program cost is $11 per day with a T-shirt, $7 without; the evening cookout costs $6.

"Kid Tracks" is for kids 7 to 11, from 9:00 A.M. to 2:00 P.M., which includes games, crafts, picnics, and swimming. It costs $14 per day with a T-shirt, $10 without, or $45 per week. "Kid Tracks" has an evening cookout and a beach party each week at $6 and $7, respectively.

"Club Captiva" is especially for teens: it offers sailing and wind surfing lessons, biking, jet skiing, and cookouts. The rate is $20 per day, which includes lunch. At night, special teen-oriented activities are also planned, all at additional cost.

Baby-sitting can be arranged through Guest Services for $5 per hour with 24 hours advance notice.

ACCOMMODATIONS: You can choose anything from hotel rooms to four-bedroom beachfront homes. Portable and full-size cribs are available for $5 per night. Many of the accommodations have kitchenettes.

RATES: There's a great variety of rates, depending on the accommodations you choose. For a sample, a beach villa with two bedrooms for two people would cost $180 to $260 per night depending on season. Kids 12 and under stay free when sharing with parents from mid-April to mid-December. Lower package rates are available; ask about them.

### The Breakers
One South County Road
Palm Beach, Florida 33480
Telephone: 305-655-6611 or 800-323-7500
President: Stayton Addison

IN THEIR OWN WORDS: "A very Palm Beach tradition . . . architecturally, The Breakers is quite literally a design masterpiece—fashioned from the era of Italian Renaissance, inspired by the most notable villa in all of Italy. And artistically, it is perhaps a hotel without equal. Built by over 1,000 artisans, its ceilings were painstakingly hand-painted by 75 artists who were imported from all over Europe. . . ."

DESCRIPTION: The preceding may not sound like the kind of place that would encourage little ones to visit, but that would not be correct. The management of The Breakers assures us that they "warmly welcome" families with children under 12 at their "palace by the sea." The Breakers has its own private beach, an oceanfront pool, two 18-hole golf courses, 14 tennis courts—both hard and clay—and a health club.

FOR KIDS: Organized programs are available for kids 6 and over. They operate all summer long and at Christmas and Easter-time, too, from 10:00 A.M. to 5:00 P.M., seven days a week. The program is free of charge to guests. Some of the activities are bike riding, swimming events, sand castle building, trips to the zoo, and arts and crafts. Each night there's a "family" activity scheduled— movies, bingo, game night, and so on. Swimming and tennis lessons are available for $10 per hour. For children under 6, baby-sitting can be arranged for $5.00 per hour, or $7.50 during peak season.

ACCOMMODATIONS: Rooms and one-bedroom suites are available. Typically a room has two double beds, with a view of either the gardens or the ocean.

RATES: In the peak season (mid-December to mid-April) a double room, on the Modified American Plan, including breakfast and dinner, ranges from $245 to $355 per person per night. Children 12 or under in the same room cost $55 plus $10 extra service charge. In the summertime, rates are one-third to one-half lower, and children 17 and under stay free. There are additional charges for golf and tennis.

### Kona Village Resort
P.O. Box 1299
Kaupulehu-Kona, Hawaii 96745
Telephone: 808-325-5555 or 800-367-5290
General Manager: Fred Duerr

IN THEIR OWN WORDS: "Very few maps show Kaupulehu. Like all Edens it's elusive, difficult to find. . . . Being remote . . .

Kona Village has some rare qualities. Actually, its charm lies in what it does not have. Like shopping arcades, tour groups, or even sidewalks. . . . Other civilized blessings it does without include juke boxes, swinging discotheques, TV sets or radios or telephones in cottages . . . after arrival . . . folks take off their wristwatches."

DESCRIPTION: Kona Village, on the secluded west coast of the island of Hawaii, is a re-creation of the legendary Kaupulehu, where in 1801 an erupting volcano chased natives from the coast. One small area around an emerald bay with coco palms and white sand beaches was spared, and over 150 years later, the location was rediscovered and Kona Village established. The specialty of the house, according to the management, is leaving guests alone. The village, they say, is dedicated to laziness. But, if you want activities, there's no lack of things to do: snorkeling, a motor launch ride to a far cove, volleyball, tennis, fishing, sailing charters, and scuba diving. Guides are available to show guests the slopes of Hualalai and Mauna Kea volcanoes. One of the favorite activities of all is a hike over the nearby lava flows, among house sites, shrines, and shelter caves of centuries ago. There are five golf courses and horseback riding facilities nearby. Throughout the week, there are a variety of activities for grown-ups—botanical walks, lei-making lessons, floral corsage classes, and other island-related crafts.

FOR KIDS: Organized activities for kids are available four to six hours each day. Children 5 and under, accompanied by an adult, can take hula lessons, enter fishing contests, do finger painting, or watch net throwing, poi pounding, and coconut husking. Kids 6 to 12 learn about local marine life or learn to play the ukulele, hunt seashells, go fishing, fly kites, or stargaze. For teenagers, there are snorkeling tours, volleyball games, scuba and sailing lessons.

Baby-sitting is available for $4.50 per hour with 24 hours notice. The cost of most of the children's activities is included in the resort's American Plan rates.

ACCOMMODATIONS: One hundred thatched-roof "hales" (bungalows), spaced for privacy, stand on stilts beside the ocean and lagoon and in gardens. They're meant to look like a Polynesian village of huts, like those of old Hawaii. Sandy paths lead from the cottages right to the beach. Inside the hales are king-size or extra long twin beds, a dressing room, and a bath. There are coffee makers and small refrigerators in every room. Most hales sleep four people.

RATES: The cost of a hale, based on double occupancy and full American plan, ranges from $295 to $480 per day, depending on the setting and size. Kids 6 to 12 cost $70; 5 and under, $25.

### Samoset Resort
Rockport, Maine 04856
Telephone: 207-594-2511
General Manager: James H. Ash

IN THEIR OWN WORDS: "A contemporary architectural masterpiece amidst the unspoiled, natural environment of the Maine coast."

DESCRIPTION: There was a time when *the* grand hotel of the coast of Maine stood on this spot, and the rich and famous came to stay. By 1972, the good old days were long past, and weeds had begun to overtake the hotel before it was completely destroyed by fire. In its place, in 1978, a new resort was built, and a few years later, one- and two-bedroom condos were added. There's nothing old-fashioned about the resort now; its facilities are up-to-date, its architecture angular and sleek. Some of the activities at Samoset are golf, swimming, tennis, cross-country skiing, boating, fishing, and hiking. The resort's fitness center offers racquetball, Nautilus, and coed exercise classes.

FOR KIDS: From Memorial Day to Labor Day and during school vacations, activities are scheduled for kids of all ages from 9:00 A.M. to 5:00 P.M. Kids play outdoors, take advantage of the playground area, walk on the beach, and swim in the outdoor or indoor pool. Some days the group goes to a nearby miniature golf spot. The cost is $5 per day.

ACCOMMODATIONS: Large rooms overlook Penobscot Bay, and all have a patio or terrace. Families may request a bedroom—living area combination with two double beds in the bedroom and a sleeping sofa in the living area. One- and two-bedroom condos are also available for rent.

RATES: Rates during high season—July 1 through October 18—are about $100 for a double, $140 for a suite. Rates with meals can also be arranged. Children 16 and under sharing a room with parents are not charged.

### Tara Dunfey Hyannis Hotel
West End Circle
Hyannis, Massachusetts 02601
Telephone: 617-775-7775
General Manager: Ralph Swartz

IN THEIR OWN WORDS: "We know that a great vacation offers a chance for every family member to relax and have fun doing the things each one of you enjoys. That's why we have children's programs."

DESCRIPTION: The resort is located at the hub of the Cape and offers swimming in outdoor and indoor pools, tennis, and golf. Not far are cross-country skiing, horseback riding, sailing, and biking. A Leisure Activities Department schedules daily events and is available to provide suggestions for a variety of Cape Cod excursions—deep-sea fishing, whale watching, antiquing, and so forth.

FOR KIDS: Children 5 years and older may participate in the full-day program, which operates during the summer, during school vacations, and on some long weekends. The program does not go all day; activities are for 2 or 2½ hours at a time, morning and afternoon. Some activities during the summer are bowling, beach walks, crafts and games, kite flying, miniature golf, and roller skating. During the school year there are face painting, mini-carnivals, and Trivial Pursuit contests. Kids 16 and over may use the health club and take aerobics classes. Most of the children's activities require a separate fee.

Baby-sitting for kids 5 and under costs $5 per hour for a minimum of four hours.

ACCOMMODATIONS: Rooms have two double beds, and all have sliding glass doors that lead out to the balcony. Cribs are available at no extra charge.

RATES: A weekend package in summer costs $404 for two nights and three days; kids under 16 stay free.

### The Mount Washington Hotel and Resort
Route 302
Bretton Woods, New Hampshire 03575

Telephone: 603-278-1000
General Manager: Manfred Boll

IN THEIR OWN WORDS: "We're a classic grand resort with an ambiance hard to find in today's brass and glass resorts. The building itself is magnificent and the service and life-style of the resort hark back to the golden age of White Mountain grand resorts."

DESCRIPTION: The setting is spectacular, right at the foot of Mount Washington and the Presidential Range, the highest mountains in the Northeast. The resort is on the National Register of Historic Places and has been named a National Historic Landmark by the National Park Service. In winter the focus is downhill skiing at Bretton Woods Ski Area (20 trails and 4 lifts) and the Bretton Woods Touring Center, 100 kilometers of trails headquartered in the riding stables. In summer, there's everything you'd expect from a grand hotel—golf, tennis, riding, indoor and outdoor pools, jogging paths, fishing, and miles of beautiful hiking trails. Music is an important part of life at the resort—chamber music, jazz concerts, and big band performances are scheduled throughout the year, and the Mount Washington Orchestra plays for dinner and dancing each night.

FOR KIDS: During July and August kids 5 to 12 have a supervised program of activities Monday through Saturday. The daily schedule includes arts and crafts, treasure hunts, swimming, hikes, movies, tennis and golf clinics, and day trips to local attractions. There's no charge except for lunch, horseback riding, and admission to outside attractions. Kids 2 months to 4 years may spend from 7:30 A.M. to 5:00 P.M. in the year-round nursery. Rates are $3.50 per hour with a three-hour minimum.

In winter, the 3- and 4-year-olds and 5- to 12-year-olds enjoy their own Ski School, called The Hobbits for the older, The Pippins for the younger. Once enrolled, the kids are introduced to the winter environment and the sport of skiing through games and the use of characters from J. R. R. Tolkien's books. The costs are $20 to $30 per day (8:30 to 4:30), depending on day of week and age. Lunch is included.

Baby-sitting is available for $3.50 per hour with a three-hour minimum.

ACCOMMODATIONS: There are 235 rooms in the hotel,

which is open May through October. The Lodge at Bretton Woods, a contemporary motor inn with 50 rooms, each with its own balcony, is open year-round. Two other lodging possibilities are the one- to four-bedroom condominiums, Rosebrook Townhouses and Forest Cottages. Family suites, two rooms with adjoining bath, are available at the hotel.

RATES: Double per-person rates range from $85 to $140; a family suite costs $45 extra per child. Kids in a double room with adults cost $30, for ages 13 to 17; $20 for ages 6 to 12; those 5 and under stay free. A variety of packages are available, as are discounts for extended stays at certain times of the year. Rates include breakfast and dinner. Rooms at the lodge are less expensive. There's no charge for tennis, but there are greens fees and an hourly charge for horseback riding and carriage rides. In the summer, the children's programs are free.

### The Balsam Grand Resort Hotel
Route 26
Lake Gloriette
Dixville Notch, New Hampshire 03576
Telephone: 603-255-3400 or 800-255-0600
Managers: Warren Pearson and Stephen Barba

IN THEIR OWN WORDS: "This is a grand hotel in the New England tradition—1,500 acres on a private estate that's been operating since 1873 . . . high in the White Mountains . . . operating completely within the American plan tradition . . . under any analysis this resort would rate within the top 10 for completeness of facility, quality, service, style, and openness of hospitality."

DESCRIPTION: Travel writers have showered praise upon this grand old resort for years. In winter or summer, fall or spring, the resort offers lots of treats: when there's snow, skating, skiing, snowshoeing, and snowmobiling; when it's warmer, biking, hiking, boating, canoeing, fishing, golfing, swimming (lake or pool), tennis, or trapshooting. During the summer the resort hosts visiting craftspeople—a basketmaker one week, a weaver the next, a water colorist the third. Evenings offer nightclub entertainment, films and dancing in the lounges, chamber music, and guest lectures on topics as diverse as life in Northern Ireland to the story of glaciers.

FOR KIDS: During ski season, there's a Wilderness nursery for kids "out of diapers" on up to 6-year-olds. It operates from 9:00 A.M. to noon and 1:00 to 4:00 P.M. Parents are asked to pick up their kids for lunch. For the diaper set, baby-sitting can be arranged at about $3.50 per hour. For the older kids, 5 and over, there's a fully supervised program from 9:00 A.M. to 4:00 P.M. that operates June 30 to September 1 and again December 20 through April 1. Counselors all have elementary education teaching certificates. Activities depend on the season, of course, and include arts and crafts, hikes, games, drama, swimming, and sports. Kids can eat with or without their parents; the choice is yours. Right off the main lobby is The Cave, a nonalcoholic "Club" especially for teenagers, with videos, movies, games, music, and half-price refreshments.

ACCOMMODATIONS: All rooms are in traditional New England style. In all there are 232 rooms with space for 425 guests at a time. Family suites are available at no extra charge. Cribs, too, are available.

RATES: A double room with a private bath ranges from $90 to $120 per person including all meals and unlimited use of the facilities plus the children's program. The rate for kids in the same room as their parents is $5 times their age with a minimum of $20 per night.

### The Pines Resort Hotel
Lavral Avenue
South Fallsburg, New York 12779
Telephone: 914-434-6000,
800-431-3124, or 800-36-PINES (in New York)
General Manager: Steven Ehrlich

IN THEIR OWN WORDS: "Every season is 'in season' at The Pines, where pleasing you means everything to us."

DESCRIPTION: This is a classic Catskills resort with lots to do, lots to eat, and lots of activities planned for kids and adults alike. In summer there are tennis, paddleball, golf, and an outdoor pool; in cooler weather, ice and roller skating, an indoor pool, indoor tennis, a sauna and health club, and, in winter, skiing is offered. The nightly entertainment is an attraction for many would-be guests, and the resort offers a night patrol service for parents who want to participate: they simply fill out a card, place it on the doorknob of their room, and a counselor checks the room every half-hour from 9:00 until midnight.

FOR KIDS: Any child 2 years old or younger gets his or her own mother's helper at no extra charge. These private counselors are available from 8:30 A.M. until 4:00 P.M. and 6:10 P.M. to 8:15 P.M., while parents have dinner. The counselors supervise the little ones closely: if you give permission for your child to go into the pool, counselors either sit on the steps with the child or hold him or her. Take your stroller to breakfast with you, packed with bottles, diapers, and some familiar toys.

Once children are 3 years old, they can join the Day Camp, which operates throughout the year. The camp begins at 8:30 and lasts until 4:00. The kids get together again at 6:00 P.M. for dinner in their own dining room and are dismissed at 8:15 P.M. Some of the day camp activities are pony rides, arts and crafts, movies, and magic shows. The camp is free, but some activities such as the pony rides and ice-skating require an additional $3 or $4 fee.

Teenagers are offered a flexible program that wisely includes both group and individual activities. Teens go ice-skating, horseback riding, hiking, golfing, or hayriding. They have their own section of the Main Dining Room, their own Daytime Lounge and Evening Dance Club.

Baby-sitters are available each evening starting at 9:00 P.M. Sign up for sitters between 6:00 and 6:30 P.M. the same evening. Baby-sitters cannot be guaranteed; infants and younger children have priority. One child is $3.50 per hour, two are $4.00, and there is a three-hour minimum charge. Remember, there's a night patrol service (described earlier) for the older kids who may not require an individual sitter.

ACCOMMODATIONS: Rooms have two double beds, and cribs are available at no extra charge. All rooms have refrigerators.

RATES: All kinds of packages are available, but as a sample, consider the Washington's Birthday three-night, four-day package, which costs $250 per adult and $80 for children under 9. This fee includes lodging, all meals, and facilities.

**The Grove Park Inn and Country Club**
290 Macon Avenue
Asheville, North Carolina 28804
Telephone: 704-252-2711 or 800-438-5800
General Manager: Herman Rivon Treskow

IN THEIR OWN WORDS: "Our inn was built in 1913 out of native boulders and set in the splendor of the Blue Ridge Mountains. It has a charming turn-of-the-century atmosphere and is listed in the National Register of Historic Places. During the early years Thomas Edison, Harvey Firestone, Henry Ford, the Rockefellers, and F. Scott Fitzgerald were our guests. After a major renovation and expansion in 1984, we became a year-round resort."

DESCRIPTION: Grove Park combines the grace and romance of the beginning of the century with up-to-the-minute amenities. You can take a horse and carriage ride through the pines or work out at the Sports Complex. Offered are swimming in one indoor pool and one outdoor pool; tennis on indoor and outdoor courts; a playroom adjacent to the indoor pool with video games, books, toys, and so on; a nature trail; an 18-hole golf course; exercise/aerobics rooms; and the latest Nautilus equipment.

FOR KIDS: There's an enclosed playground area adjacent to the Sports Center with seven decks, a corkscrew slide, horizontal ladder, swing, and bubble window. For the family together there are horse-drawn carriage rides, a practice putting green, and a Thursday night barbecue. From May 23 to September 1 (and on winter weekends) the Inn offers a Monday through Saturday supervised kids' program from 9:00 A.M. to 5:00 P.M for ages 5 to 12. Activities include crafts, movies, swimming, water games, visits to the Carriage House and Antique Car Museum, and fun in the playground. On Saturday night—Parents' Night Out—the kids see a movie and have a pizza party from 6:00 P.M. to 10:30 P.M. A full day's program is $16, half is $8, and the Saturday Night Program is $14. Baby-sitting for younger kids is available for $3.50 per hour, $4 per hour for three or more children, and $5 per hour after midnight.

ACCOMMODATIONS: There are 389 rooms in all, each decorated in turn-of-the-century style. Cribs are available at no extra charge, but advance notice is requested.

RATES: Regular room rates from November to April are $95 for a double, $200 for a suite; the other months are $30 to $50 more. Kids under 12 stay free in their parents' room; those over 12 cost $15 per child. Special tennis and golf packages and packages that include meals are available year-round.

### The Tyler Place
Box AA
Highgate Springs, Vermont 05460
Telephone: 802-868-3301
General Manager: Freya Chaffee

IN THEIR OWN WORDS: "Here, at The Tyler Place on Lake Champlain, we care for 50 families each week. We've specialized in family vacations for over 40 years."

DESCRIPTION: The mood is informal, the atmosphere low-key. Located on 165 lakeshore acres, The Tyler Place offers tennis, fishing, golf, sailing, wind surfing, canoeing, or just plain sun worshipping. There are daily activities for adults, such as cookouts, staff-versus-guest softball games, water volleyball, and sing-alongs.

FOR KIDS: Every age group is taken care of. For the smallest, you can arrange for a parents' helper who can sit by the hour or even on a live-in basis. The sitters are chosen from a list of local high school girls, most of whom the staff at the resort knows personally. The cost is usually $2.00 per hour. The same girls are available to sit on an hourly basis during the day and at night; the minimum is $5.00. If you take your own parents' helper, you will be charged $10.50 for linen per week, with no extra charge for the sitter.

"Pre-Midgets" is a program for kids 1 month to 3 years old and can include live-in help. Helpers often get together with other helpers and their charges for picnics, playground fun, or indoor play in the carriage house.

"Part Time Midgets" is a low-key variation of the Midget program (described next) for kids 2 and 3 years old who want to participate in some group activities but still want time alone with a parents' helper.

"Midgets" is a full-day—8:30 to 1:30 and 5:30 to 8:30—program, but kids can be picked up earlier. Activities include nature walks, motorboat rides, hayrides, arts and crafts, singing, and games. If you'd like, the older kids can spend time at the pool with swimming lessons. Evening entertainment involves parties, peanut hunts, and storytelling.

"The Juniors," kids 6 to 8 years old, have college-age counselors who supervise them from 8:30 A.M. until 1:30 and 5:30 to 9:00 P.M. The group decides on what it wants to do—canoe, hike, play volleyball, make arts and crafts, among the choices.

"Pre-Teens," 9- to 11-year-olds, have lots of pool and waterfront time. They play volleyball, softball, and soccer; go canoeing; have ice cream–making parties, and at night see movies, dance, play bingo, and go on hayrides. The program runs from breakfast until after lunch and from before dinner to 8:30 or 9:00 P.M.

Junior and Senior Teens are groups 12 to 14 years old and 15 to 18 years old. They have lots of sports activities, a mix of independent and group activities (some free waterskiing) and evening events such as pool parties and video dances. Teens are encouraged to structure their own day with the help of an entertainment director.

ACCOMMODATIONS: Cottages are located on or near the lake. Each has a wood-burning fireplace in the living room and from one to four bedrooms. The inn is a hospitable sprawl of fireplaced lounges, screened porches, outdoor dining areas, and recreation rooms with sleeping accommodations in a separate wing. There's no charge for cribs.

Children usually eat with their peers, but if you'd like your school-age child to eat with you in the main dining room on a weekday, you may make a reservation and pay extra.

RATES: Package rates include lodging, all meals, many free sports, children's programs, daytime activities for adults, and the resort's "low-key" evening entertainment. From mid-June to the end of August, two-room apartments large enough for four people cost $58 to $76 per person for the first two people and $28.50 to $47 for children under 18, depending on age. More specifically, two adults in a three-room apartment with an 8-year-old and a 5-year-old would pay a total of $182 per day, $1,274 per week. During special-rate weeks (five weeks scattered throughout the summer) prices are 15 to 25 percent lower.

**Basin Harbor Club**
Basin Harbor Road
Vergennes, Vermont 05491
Telephone: 802-475-2311 or 800-622-4000
General Manager: Robert H. Beach

IN THEIR OWN WORDS: "With the 1987 season we entered our second century of Beach family ownership and management. Throughout this time, children have always been warmly welcomed. There are families who have been vacationing here for four generations . . . we provide a beautiful site where families can relax together . . . parents don't have to spend their entire vacation time being chauffeurs either, because all facilities are right here, not a couple of miles down the road."

DESCRIPTION: On the eastern shore of Lake Champlain with a view of the Adirondacks, the Basin Harbor Club is known for its "active tranquility." During the day it offers fishing, boating, waterskiing, swimming in the lake or pool, tennis, golf, jogging, or biking. After 6:00 gentlemen and young men over 12 are required to wear a coat and tie in the public areas of the resort; the guests seem to like this bit of formality and voted to return to the custom a few years ago.

FOR KIDS: Children between 3 and 10 are welcome to participate in the activities at the Playground, from 9:00 A.M. to noon. The Playground is a bit like a day camp with swings, slide, sandbox, jungle gym, and a playhouse filled with games, books, and toys. Specific activities are arranged each week, according to the interests and ages of the kids at the Harbor at any given time. Some possibilities are nature walks, outdoor sports, cookouts, treasure hunts, fishing and boating, and arts and crafts. At dinner time, kids eat together with an adult to supervise. Kids gather at 6:45 P.M. and stay together until 9:00 P.M.

For the older children, the schedule is somewhat less structured—golf, tennis clinics, volleyball, softball, pool races, and all kinds of water sports are all available. Evening entertainment includes movies, bingo, teen parties, and trips to local events.

A list of baby-sitters is available at the front desk. Sitters are either staff members or local young people, and rates are approximately $2 per hour.

ACCOMMODATIONS: Cottages, each one different from the other in design, or rooms in the main lodge are available to guests. All accommodations are within walking distance of the dining room and other resort facilities. Some have a lake view; others overlook the golf course and tennis courts. Some cottages have screened porches, and about half of the total 77 have fireplaces; most have a pantry with a refrigerator and wet bar. Some cottages are equipped for handicapped access.

RATES: A typical cottage for four, with living room, two bedrooms and two baths, is $340 daily for two parents and two children. If there were three children and two parents, however, the charge for the third child would depend on age—$5 per day for 2 years and under, up to $55 for 15 and over. All rates include breakfast, lunch, and dinner as well as lodging and children's programs; most facilities are extra.

### Wintergreen Resort
Wintergreen, Virginia 22958
Telephone: 804-325-2200 or 800-325-2200
General Manager: Gunter L. Mueler

IN THEIR OWN WORDS: "We're a four-season resort high in Virginia's Blue Ridge Mountains. In summer . . . our weather is frequently 10 to 15 degrees cooler than most metropolitan areas. Built on the mountain, there are breathtaking 50-mile views of the surrounding countryside. . . . Wintergreen is one of only 5 ski resorts south of New York with a vertical drop over 1,000 feet."

DESCRIPTION: Located 43 miles from Charlottesville, Wintergreen offers a mountaintop golf course and 18 tennis courts, 20 miles of hiking trails, and a complete equestrian center for trail rides and lessons. For swimming, your choice is Lake Monocan or one of five pools.

FOR KIDS: Children 2 to 12 years old have their own program. In winter it operates from 8:30 A.M. to 5:00 P.M. and in summer from 10:00 A.M. to 4:00 P.M. In winter, the 2- to 5-year-olds combine playing and ski instruction. In summer, crafts, playground fun, and butterfly walks are scheduled. Kids 6 and older ski in winter and in summer have swimming lessons and participate in a water rodeo; "hands-on" nature activities; "kids in the kitchen" sessions; "horse sense," a program based at the stables; fishing; and canoeing.

Baby-sitting is available for approximately $5 per hour by contacting the Activities Office 48 hours in advance.

ACCOMMODATIONS: All accommodations are either condominiums or homes. Studios and one-bedrooms include kitchens or kitchenettes; larger condos have full kitchens and separate living rooms. Some have fireplaces.

RATES: A sample of a peak season ski package for three nights, four days for four in a two-bedroom condo is $243. This includes lodging, children's programs, unlimited skiing day and night, and use of Wintergarden (their health club facility).

### The Greenbrier
White Sulphur Springs, West Virginia 24986
Telephone: 304-536-1110
General Manager: Charles F. Ingalsbee, Jr.

IN THEIR OWN WORDS: "For more than two centuries, The Greenbrier has meant ladies and gentlemen being served by ladies and gentlemen . . . it still does."

DESCRIPTION: Another massive, in-the-old-style resort with 6,500 acres in the midst of the Allegheny Mountains. What's to do during the day? Choose from jogging, horseback riding on woodland mountain trails, cross-country skiing, fishing, trap and skeet shooting, garden walks, horse and carriage rides, golf on one of three courses, and tennis on one of 20 courts (5 indoors, 15 outdoors). There are two heated and lighted platform tennis courts for year-round use, too; swimming in an outdoor or indoor pool; bowling; and working out on the par course fitness trail or at the Fitness Center. At tea time there's chamber music, and at night dinner and dancing, if you're not too tired.

FOR KIDS: From mid-June to Labor Day and during school vacation breaks, kids 6 to 12 (5 during holiday time) have their own program from 9:45 A.M. to 4:00 P.M. and 6:45 to 10:00 P.M. every day. The cost is $10 per day, $8 for the evening. Some activities require additional fees. College-trained counselors give the kids a choice of sport they want to pursue with group lessons, and the kids help plan the day's activities. Possibilities include mountain hikes, movies, arts and crafts, carriage rides, and swimming. Kids eat together at 6:45—they have to be registered by 4:00 P.M., though.

For younger kids you may want a baby-sitter. Expect to pay just under $4 per hour and make arrangements with the household department at least two hours in advance.

ACCOMMODATIONS: This enormous hotel has 700 rooms, each individually decorated. Some suites are available, and there are also a variety of free-standing guest houses, cottages, and two estate houses. One, the Valley View, is big enough to entertain 200 people. It has four bedrooms and includes the use of a Cadillac Seville; rental is $200 per person per day based on occupancy by eight people.

RATES: A double-bedded room in winter season costs $98 to $123 per person, including breakfast and dinner as well as lodging. Kids 10 and up are $65; 5 to 9, $35; 1 to 4, $20; and under 1 year, no charge. There's no extra charge for the use of a crib. All sports facilities are extra. Golf and tennis packages are available.

## LEARNING VACATIONS

Although the two places listed next are not, strictly speaking, resorts, both are excellent places for the family to spend time together. They are both organized by universities and are open to graduates and the general public as well. One is on the East Coast and the other on the West.

### Cornell University
Adult University
626 Thurston Avenue
Ithaca, New York 14850
Telephone: 607-255-6260
Director: Ralph Janis

IN THEIR OWN WORDS: "The young people come along with adults and all take courses. The children's program provides an exciting, safe growing experience for each child."

DESCRIPTION: Cornell Adult University (CAU) offers three possibilities: from June 29 to July 26 they have week-long sessions on the Ithaca campus, where adults can choose from six seminars and workshops, with topics such as "South Africa: Crisis and

Challenge" and "Who's on First? Baseball and America." While the adults are in class, the kids have their own very special programming. For the ones who are under 3 years old, CAU arranges babysitting; the 3- to 5-year-olds have a full nursery school program from 8:00 A.M. to 4:30 P.M. that includes field trips and science projects; 5- to 7-year-olds take an ecology course from 9:00 to 11:00 A.M. each morning and in the afternoon swim and have cookouts, and participate in drama and music. Kids 8 to 12 choose morning courses such as horseback riding, computers, producing a weekly newsletter, veterinary anatomy, or wilderness adventures, including a ropes course, canoeing, outdoor survival, backpacking at local sites. Afternoons and evenings are spent visiting the science center, roller-skating, swimming, and playing games. Teens choose from courses such as "Basic Rock Climbing," "Media and You," "Architectural Drawing and Modeling," and "Tennis Workshop." They live in their own dorm with counselors and participate in sports, roller-skating, movies, and other extracurricular activities.

CAU also organizes an educational vacation in Colorado at the five-star Tamarron Resort in the foothills of the San Juan Mountains. A professor of geological science and a professor of Western and Indian history are in charge of the educational component. Kids 4 to 10 join the resort's children's program; those 11 and older are welcome to participate along with the adults. Several afternoons are set aside for hiking, horseback riding, tennis, golf, and swimming.

Another option is CAU at the Shoals, a marine laboratory on an island in Maine. Teenagers accompanied by adults are welcome; there are no special programs for the younger kids, and this one requires "roughing it a bit. . . ."

ACCOMMODATIONS: At Cornell, participants stay in dorms; in Colorado they stay in resort accommodations.

RATES: The Ithaca program costs $260 for tuition for adults; housing and meals range from $195 to $220 (off-campus housing with no meal plan is also possible). For kids, the prices range from $145 for the prekindergarteners to $235 for the teen program. (A special workshop in college admissions, test taking, and so on, is given one week per summer. It costs $50 extra.) The CAU program in Colorado costs $995 for 14 and over; $695, 11 to 13; and $325, 4 to 10. CAU at the Shoals costs $475 to $495.

## University of California at Santa Barbara
Alumni Vacation Center
Santa Barbara, California 93106
Telephone: 805-961-3123
Director: Jim McNamara

IN THEIR OWN WORDS: "You're on a bluff overlooking the Pacific Ocean. Nearby are downtown Santa Barbara, Lake Cachuma, the Santa Ynez Valley horse and wine country, and the quaint Danish village of Solvang. No wonder families return year after year. Probably the Vacation Center's most important charm is the staff. Time and again, vacationers let us know what a pleasure it is to have such wonderful role models for their children during their stay at the Center. . . ."

DESCRIPTION: One of our friends wrote: "My husband and two daughters (ages one and five) spent one week at the Center last summer and found it a perfect vacation for us . . . given the ages of our kids, our life-style, and our budget. . . . There were about 40 families there when we were—plenty of kids of all ages. . . . Vacationers can participate in any activity they choose or just relax, enjoy the beach and bike trails or roam around Santa Barbara. The Center isn't for people looking for a sophisticated time—the atmosphere is camp-like, family-oriented and generally wholesome. . . ."

The Center is tucked into its own corner of the campus, and it offers use of all the facilities of the school including the dining commons, 10 tennis courts, a swimming pool, an outdoor patio for dining, a playground, a fitness program, and education and entertainment programs for all ages.

Family activities include square dancing, carnivals, and campfires. For adults there are wine tasting, seminars by U.C. faculty, and tours of Santa Barbara. Tennis and swimming lessons are included in the cost of the Center's package. Ten week-long sessions are held each summer.

FOR KIDS: The children's programs are set up to be flexible, to allow parents to spend as much time as they'd like with their kids but to be able to do some things on their own as well. Kids are divided into age groups. "Small World" is for 2- and 3-year-olds with activities such as tumbling, making sand castles, music, and making ceramic star necklaces. Kids 4 to 8, 9 to 10, and 11 to 12 are grouped together, and for teens there's a program that includes local excursions and an overnight campout. Children's programs generally run from 9:00 A.M. to 9:00 P.M., excluding meal times. For kids too young for the organized children's programs, baby-sitting is available at $3 per hour (our friends "traded off" baby-sitting with other parents they had met).

ACCOMMODATIONS: Each family lives in a fully furnished suite including a living room, bath, and two to four bedrooms. Daily maid service is provided, and there's a refrigerator for snacks. Cribs are available for $20 per stay.

RATES: Adults (12 and over) pay $390, which includes all meals, lodging, children's programs, tennis and swimming lessons, and use of all campus facilities. The rate for kids 6 to 11 is $270; for 2 to 5, $255; for 1 to 2, $55; and for under 1 year there is no charge. Members of a U.C. alumni association and their immediate family are entitled to a slightly lower rate, but the Center is open to nonalumni as well.

# 9

---

# TENNIS AND GOLF

Lots of you are tennis or golf aficionados. You remember with pleasure the tennis- or golf-centered vacations you took B.C. (before children). In this chapter we want to show you how you can bring back those "good old days"—spend time mastering your sport and just plain enjoying it—while your children are off on their own, involved in supervised activities with kids their own age. It is likely, too, that any of you who love tennis or golf will want your kids to love it as well and that you're eager to get your kids involved. At some of the resorts we list here, kids as young as 4 years old can start lessons.

To get the scoop on introducing kids to tennis and/or golf we spoke to two experts. First, we had a conversation with Roy Barth, the director of tennis at Kiawah Island since 1976. Barth thinks that kids should start being exposed to tennis as a fun experience—and he emphasized the fun part—at 4, 5, or 6. At Kiawah, he explained that the kids in this age group never keep score; instead they practice hitting balls at hand-painted animated targets: an alligator, a pelican, or a raccoon. They are given small racquets, are taught to make contact with the ball, and then are let loose to have fun for a half-hour. Anything longer might seem too much like work. "Kids get hooked by themselves," Barth explained. "Don't force them!"

"I'm a tennis pro and a parent of two kids 9 and 11. When I gave them instructions, they weren't interested. 'We want to have fun!' they told me. Now they come to me for help, and now they play in tournaments, but I laid low for two to three years and let it happen by itself."

We asked Barth what to look for when choosing a resort with a tennis program for kids. He gave us a lot of hints. For kids 10 to 18 he suggested you check to see whether there are possibilities for round-robin doubles. This is good not only for the kids to get practice but also so they meet other kids their age. Find out how often instructional programs are offered and what the ratio is of pro to student—1:4 to 1:6 is best. Ask whether there are ball machines for practice and try to find out something about the reputation of the pro and the program. Barth says it's important to check on the time of the clinics for the youngest kids. "I've experimented," he said, "and when we started late in the afternoon we had cranky, tired kids. Early morning is the best time." He also emphasized the importance of safety—once you're at the resort be sure to take a look and see how well supervised the group lessons are. Barth himself tells about getting hit by a racquet when he was 5 and being afraid to touch one again until he was 7.

After we spoke to Barth about tennis, we turned to the subject of golf and talked to Mike Cook, head teaching pro at Sea Palms Resort in Georgia. Cook likes teaching kids. "When kids listen and pay attention you can teach them so much and you know that the basics will stick with them all through life.

"I started at 4," he went on, "but that's too young. I think that 7 or 8 is better. It is too hard for kids much younger than 7 to really listen." We asked Cook what to look for when choosing a kids' golf program at a resort. He suggested checking on the reputation of the teachers and making sure that kids actually get a chance to play golf, not just hit balls around. "At Sea Palms, the kids have use of one of our courses every afternoon after 3:30. We like to play with kids." The golf clinics that kids attend should emphasize the fun of the game, not just the discipline. And, just as every expert has said before, whatever his or her sport, Cook warns parents against pushing kids. "Let them play other sports besides golf; let them get their feet wet, but don't force them into just one thing."

Many of the resorts listed here offer good tennis and golf. Here we give you only some possibilities; check Chapter 8 for other ideas and don't forget, too, that lots of the ski resorts metamorphose into tennis and/or golf resorts in summer, so also look at Chapter 10.

### Wickenburg Inn
P.O. Box P
Wickenburg, Arizona 85358
Telephone: 602-684-7811 or 800-528-4227
General Manager: Charles "Lefty" Brinkman

IN THEIR OWN WORDS: "Our Inn is in a very relaxed and beautiful setting—most of which is natural. The dress is casual, and the staff is very helpful and understanding. We offer programs in riding and tennis which enable guests to improve their skills and have a good time doing it."

DESCRIPTION: This resort could as easily have been listed under ranches, but we flipped a coin and decided to put it under "tennis" instead. If you like tennis and horseback riding, consider it carefully. The tennis is good—11 acrylic courts with a complete pro shop, instruction center, rebound walls, and ball machines. Clinics and private lessons are available; clinics are three hours of group instruction daily with a 3:1 ratio whenever possible. When you're not playing tennis, try horseback riding (instruction and clinics available) or swimming at the hilltop spa. Two particularly interesting features of Wickenburg are its nature study program and its arts and crafts center. Adults, as well as children, can spend time with the resident naturalist learning about Wickenburg's desert setting or sketching, painting, making pottery, or doing leatherwork, macramé, or weaving at the inn's art studio. There's golf not far away, at the Wickenburg Country Club.

FOR KIDS: During school vacation periods, December 19 to January 3, November 26 to 29, and February 15 to April 18, there are special children's programs organized for kids 4 to 12. Kids 4 to 6 and their counselor do arts and crafts, go on horseback rides, visit the Nature Center, take nature walks, and play games together. The program lasts from 8:45 A.M. to 4:00 P.M., with an hour break for lunch with parents.

Older kids 7 to 12 participate in trail rides, tennis clinics, square dances, and special trips. A special dinner hour for this age group begins at 5:30 (kids can eat later with their parents if they'd rather). At 6:30 P.M. the evening program begins; it runs until 8:30

P.M. The cost is $30 for the 7- to 12-year-olds, $20 for those 4 to 6.

Baby-sitting for younger children is available with 24- to 48-hour notice at $4 per hour with a four-hour minimum.

ACCOMMODATIONS: Spanish-style adobe "casitas" including fireplaces and wet bars are set apart from the Main Lodge so that families can enjoy some privacy and quiet. All have one bedroom, a porch, double sleep sofas in the living room, a powder room, and a bath. Cribs are available at no extra cost.

RATES: Rates are based on a full American plan. All meals, swimming, whirlpool, wildlife study, use of the art studio, tennis court privileges, horseback riding, and other "standard" ranch activities are included. A deluxe casita suite ranges from $160 to $250 double occupancy. Children 2 to 12 sharing the casita cost $25; those 13 and over are $40. Tennis clinics cost $100 extra per person for three days and $150 for five.

### Sonesta Beach Hotel and Tennis Club
350 Ocean Drive
Key Biscayne, Florida 33149
Telephone: 305-361-2021 or 800-343-7170
General Manager: Felix Madera

IN THEIR OWN WORDS: "We're tucked away on our own tropical island but we're still just twenty minutes from Miami's International Airport. Everything you could possibly want for the full life in the sun is right here on Key Biscayne. You can do as little or as much as you please."

DESCRIPTION: Golf is at the Key Biscayne Golf Course, less than two miles from the hotel, which is ranked number one in the state of Florida. The tennis is played on ten layhold courts, three of which are lighted for night play. There are two full-time pros to help with your game, and clinics for six or more include video playback. Besides tennis and golf Sonesta offers deep-sea fishing, sailing, scuba diving or snorkeling, biking, jewelry-making, and a fitness center with all sorts of "feel-good" possibilities such as massages, steambaths, and whirlpools.

FOR KIDS: The "Just Us Kids" program is for children 5 to 13 and runs seven days a week from 10:00 A.M. to 10:00 P.M. year-round. The program is counselor-supervised and free to guests. It includes many field trips—visits to the zoo, bowling, or the Parrot

Jungle. The afternoon is free for the beach, pool, tennis clinics, and more. (There are fees for some of the excursions.) Younger kids can have their own baby-sitters with 24 hours advance notice.

ACCOMMODATIONS: You can choose from a room, a suite in the hotel, or a one-, two-, three-, or four-bedroom villa adjacent to the hotel, complete with a fully equipped kitchen and a private heated pool. Cribs are available for $15 per night.

RATES: Kids under 12 stay free in rooms with their parents. In high season (December to April), a room ranges from $180 (for an island view) to $220 (for an ocean view) per night. Rooms have two queen-size beds.

### Bluewater Bay Resort
P.O. Box 247
Niceville, Florida 32578
Telephone: 904-897-3613 or 800-874-2128
Manager: Richard A. Lumsden

IN THEIR OWN WORDS: "This is a place for getting away from the hectic sights and sounds of the city . . . ideally suited for those who love the great outdoors."

DESCRIPTION: This is a combined residential/resort community on the shores of Choctawhatchee Bay. Besides the golf—a 6,850-yard layout designed by PGA pro Jerry Pate and architect Tom Fazio—there are tennis night and day on 21 courts, three swimming pools, sailing and fishing expeditions to the bay and Gulf of Mexico, and a 2,000-foot island beach.

FOR KIDS: During the summer (beginning of June to the end of August) and during school vacation periods, there's a program for kids 3 to 14 that's free for families who participate in a family package. Kids 3, 4, and 5 have a program from 9:00 A.M. to noon Monday through Saturday. Activities include arts and crafts, nature hikes, treasure hunts, fingerpainting, and sand castle building. Kids 6 to 11 are kept busy from 9:00 A.M. to 4:00 P.M. with movies, sailing, golf and tennis clinics, arts and crafts, and picnics.

Teens have their own activities scheduled throughout the week—volleyball, beach parties, sailing clinics, and trips off the property. The whole family can enjoy potluck dinners by the pool, canoe trips, beach cookouts, ice cream socials, and so forth.

Baby-sitting is available for $3.75 per hour; just contact the Recreation Department to arrange it.

ACCOMMODATIONS: The resort refers to them as "full size vacation homes"—most have one or two bedrooms and are multi-level (the tallest are three floors). You can choose to be on the bay, at the Swim and Tennis Center, or at the golf course. Cribs are available at no charge; all accommodations have kitchen facilities.

RATES: A "Summer Family Vacation Package" that includes accommodations in a two-bedroom, two-bath townhouse or patio home, costs $599 for seven nights.

### Sundial Beach and Tennis Resort
1246 Middle Gulf Drive
Sanibel Island, Florida 33957
Telephone: 813-995-8014 or 800-237-4184
General Manager: Michael Peceri

IN THEIR OWN WORDS: "There's something mystical about this tiny paradise. When you cross over the three-mile bridge from mainland, Sanibel Island begins to cast its magical spell on you. It's a remote and relaxing place. Yet full of natural splendor and activity."

DESCRIPTION: There are 13 tennis courts in all, 7 Lay Kold, 6 Har-Tru. The pro shop will matchmake for you, give you private lessons or a clinic, and offer social tournaments. Golf is five minutes away at Dunes Country Club, or you can try sailing, biking, and swimming in five outdoor pools. Throughout the year there are a range of family-type activities scheduled by a full-time social director—face painting, tennis clinics, movies, bingo, mom and tot swims, scavenger hunts, and so on.

FOR KIDS: During the summer and from November to April, there's a camp for kids that runs every day of the week from 9:00 A.M. to 5:00 P.M. For Tiny Tots—kids who are potty-trained up to 5—there are arts and crafts, water play, creative dramatics, games, songs, riddles and stories, nature awareness, beach walks, and more. For kids 6 years and older there are water games, sports, crafts, cookouts, beach parties, water Olympics and shell crafts. The cost for the "camp" is $10 for a full day, $7 for half, and $45 for a full week.

Baby-sitting is available for the youngest, for $5 per hour.

ACCOMMODATIONS: Possibilities include 400 suites—effi-ciencies, one- and two-bedroom units with full kitchens. Most accommodations have private, screened balconies overlooking the gulf or courtyards. Cribs are available for $5 per night.

RATES: Kids under 14 stay free in the same room as their parents. A two-bedroom suite costs $125 to $205, depending on the season. An "Island Vacation Package" that includes unlimited tennis and the children's program costs $89 to $158 per person for a four-day, three-night stay for four in a two-bedroom suite (this package is not available at holiday time).

### Innisbrook Resort
P.O. Drawer 1088
Tarpon Springs, Florida 34286
Telephone: 813-937-3124 or 800-237-0157
General Manager: Cary Brent

IN THEIR OWN WORDS: "Innisbrook is wooded acres rich with gleaming lakes, rolling hills, emerald fairways. Innisbrook is hibiscus, azaleas, citrus groves, and Spanish moss on pine trees. Innisbrook is a natural habitat alive with peacocks, mallards, leaping trout and stately turtles. It even has a wildlife preserve."

DESCRIPTION: Besides the natural beauty of the spot, Innisbrook offers excellent golf and tennis, a Recreation Village, a basketball court, bike rentals, a game room, a playground and miniature golf course ($1 for unlimited play), a par course fitness trail, a Fitness Center with a full line of Universal and Future Exercise equipment, aerobics, fishing, and five heated swimming pools. There are three golf courses—the 27-hole Copperhead is ranked number one in the state of Florida, the Island course is the first constructed at Innisbrook, and the Sandpiper is the shortest of the three. The Innisbrook Golf Institute, directed by Jay Overton, is well known. The Institute offers a full three-night teaching package as well as daily clinics; private instruction is available, too, in what the staff calls "golf's most beautiful classroom."

The Tennis and Racquetball Center includes 18 courts (11 clay, 7 hard), 7 lighted for play at night; whirlpool baths; a complete fitness center and aerobics workout room; a video training room; a pro shop; and a cocktail lounge. There's a tennis clinic every morning at 10:30 covering a different stroke each day, and Innisbrook is home of the Australian Tennis Institute, founded and directed by former Australia Davis Cup player Terry Addison. The

Institute features stroke improvement, movement drills, strategy for singles and doubles play, slow motion video critique, and more. Students are grouped by playing level, never more than three or four students per instructor.

FOR KIDS: "Zoo Crew" is the name of the activities program Innisbrook operates for kids 4 to 11. Kids are divided into two groups—4- to 6-year-olds and 7- to 11-year-olds. Zoo Crew runs all summer long and during school vacations. Hours are 9:00 A.M. to 4:00 P.M. For 4- to 6-year-olds, a shorter 9:00 A.M. to noon stay is possible. Counselors are students of education who come from all over the United States to supervise the kids on excursions, at golf and tennis clinics, with arts and crafts, games, pool play, and a variety of theme days, such as "Kids Can Cook" or "Under the Big Top." Kids can be registered by the day or week. The cost is $12 per day, $9 per half-day, $3 extra for lunch, $60 for the week.

Lots of activities appropriate for teenagers are scheduled throughout the week at the resort, for instance, Junior Golf Clinics, bike tours, water games, basketball tourneys, and aerobics. Every Friday night there's a "Teen Happy Hour" followed by a "Teen Bash" for kids 12 to 17.

Baby-sitting is available for $3 per hour, day and evening.

And one more thing: Innisbrook offers a week-long Junior Golf Institute in July for kids 10 to 18 years of age. Kids staying with their parents can sign up and spend their days at the Institute.

ACCOMMODATIONS: Innisbrook's accommodations are all condos, which the resort prefers to call "lodges." They're two-story buildings with one to three bedrooms. Cribs are available at no extra charge.

RATES: For a sample, we asked for the rate for a golf package for a family of four, two golfing adults and two kids under 12 who don't play golf. At Christmastime (Innisbrook's shoulder season; peak is end of January to the end of April), the rate would be $262 per night for the two adults, no extra charge for the kids. (The price includes a two-bedroom, two-bath condo with a lounge, dining area, and fully equipped kitchen; unlimited golf; instructional clinic; reserved tee-times; and golf bag storage.) Remember that if your kids play golf, there'll be an additional charge.

**Sea Palms Golf and Tennis Resort**
5445 Frederica Road
St. Simons Island, Georgia 31522
Telephone: 912-638-3351 or 1-800-841-6268
General Manager: John Dow

IN THEIR OWN WORDS: "Since Sea Palms is both a country club and a resort, it caters to a variety of people and offers diverse activities. A beautiful resort, combined with the historical island itself, makes Sea Palms a perfect vacation choice. . . ."

DESCRIPTION: This is a resort/residential community set in the heart of St. Simon's Island, one of Georgia's 12 Golden Isles. Sea Palms has 27 holes of championship golf—courses that wind their way through old oaks and sparkling lagoons. The 18-hole Tall Pines course is the site of the annual Georgia PGA Challenge Matches. Mike Cook, the expert we quoted earlier, teaches golf at Sea Palms, and group and private lessons are available. For tennis enthusiasts, there's a three-year-old Health and Racquet Club with 12 composition courts, 3 of which are lighted for night play. Other possibilities for fun include swimming in a pool that's heated and covered in winter, an exercise room, saunas, a whirlpool, and a fitness course. Guests also like to take island tours, sail, horseback ride, and fish. During the summer there are weekly aerobic, weight, and exercise classes.

FOR KIDS: Keith Masengill is in charge of recreation services at Sea Palms, and he's organized an extensive program for kids. The "Children's Program" for kids 4 to 6 offers a choice of a morning or afternoon session. The hours are Monday through Saturday 9:00 A.M. to 12:30 P.M. or 1:00 to 4:30 P.M. from June 9 to August 23 and during holiday periods. Kids swim, make shell crafts, sing, hear stories, and make ice cream. The cost is $8 per kid. The "Youth Program" for kids 7 to 12 is a full-day program. Lunch is included, and kids play games, go on scavenger hunts, have their own Olympics, and so on. Day trips to Glynn County, Jacksonville, or Savannah are scheduled every Wednesday. The cost is $16 per kid. For teens (13 to 17) Sea Palms offers afternoon and evening activities—wind surfing, cable waterskiing, miniature golf, and so on. In the evening there are movies, tournaments, and teen dinners. Every Saturday a teen trip is scheduled.

Every day at 2:00 P.M. there's an all-family program activity—bingo or water basketball, and at 3:00 P.M. there's a pick-up game of volleyball. At night there are movies and other activities for the whole family to participate in together.

Baby-sitting can be arranged through the front office. All sitters are screened by the personnel department. During high season, give them a week's notice to find a baby-sitter and expect to pay $3 to $4 per hour.

ACCOMMODATIONS: The choices include hotel rooms and one-, two-, and three-bedroom villas and suites. Cribs are available for $5 per night.

RATES: A golf package, which includes accommodations, breakfast, and golf cart and fees, costs $112 to $114 per night for double occupancy with kids under 14, free.

### The Cloister
Sea Island, Georgia 31561
Telephone: 912-638-3611
General Manager: Ted Wright

IN THEIR OWN WORDS: "The Cloister is family-owned and family-oriented. Families visit every day of the year—there are always some children in the main dining rooms at night. . . . We don't even charge for children under 19—including their meals—at Christmas and New Year's and during the Summer Family Festival. . . . We get three and four generations of families these days, with parents who first came in 1928 or 29."

DESCRIPTION: Off the coast of Georgia, on sunny Sea Island, you can enjoy five miles of beach, championship golf and tennis, gardens, historic sites, and 10,000 acres of protected forests and serene marshes beside the sea. For golfers, there are 54 holes and complete teaching facilities; for tennis enthusiasts it offers 18 courts, all fast-dry clay composition; a staff of teaching pros; clinics; and guest round-robins. For nongolf/non-tennis hours skeet shooting, biking, fishing, swimming, jogging, and horseback riding on the beach or trails are available. At night there are torchlit plantation suppers, after-dinner entertainment, and dancing nightly to the Cloister's own orchestra.

FOR KIDS: From June to September and during school vacation periods, the Cloister offers a program for kids 4 to 8 from

9:00 A.M. to 3:00 P.M. every day except Sunday. Junior staffers take the kids for the day, playing with them and leading them in a variety of activities. Throughout the week there are also a number of special events for kids. We spotted a cooking class for kids 6 to 12 and a course in manners for kids 7 through the midteens. During the summer, there's no charge for tennis and golf for kids 19 and under, so there's plenty of chance for practice during the stay, and they may even get to be almost as good as you are. Kids 4 to 12 can spend 6:00 P.M. to 9:00 P.M. every evening with children's hostesses. Tennis lessons are available to kids as young as 5, and junior golf clinics are scheduled twice a week in summer.

Baby-sitters are available for small children, who may join play times and evening programs along with their sitters. The cost of baby-sitting is $3.50 per hour, day or evening.

ACCOMMODATIONS: There are several options: the main hotel, River House, guest or beach houses. Cribs are available at no extra charge.

RATES: All prices are full American plan—three meals per day—and include use of the Sea Island Beach Club, nightly dancing, and other of the resort's amenities. A sample rate is a tennis package that costs $121 to $173 per night per person from March to May. There's no room charge for kids sharing a room with parents; for meals it is $26 for kids 6 to 12, $18 for 3 to 5, and no charge at all for 2 years and under.

### Westin Mauna Kea
P.O. Box 218
Kohala Coast, Hawaii 96743
Telephone: 808-882-7222 or 800-228-3000
General Manager: Adi Kohler

IN THEIR OWN WORDS: "Mauna Kea was recently voted 'America's Number 1 Favorite Resort' in a national independent poll of over 15,000 CEOs and presidents of top U.S. corporations. This accolade is only the latest in a long lei of awards that stretches back to the opening by Laurence Rockefeller 22 years ago . . . you'll find a commitment to excellence in every detail. It begins with a spectacular location, a perfect climate, and Hawaii's finest white sand crescent beach."

DESCRIPTION: The hotel takes its name and inspiration

from the nearby snow-topped Mauna Kea, literally "White Mountain" in Hawaiian. The president of the United States and the emperor and empress of Japan have stayed there; art objects from all over the world adorn the grounds. Buildings are terraced to make the most of the panoramic views and, at the same time, to assure privacy for guests. Interior walkways and courtyards bloom with carefully landscaped gardens.

Mauna Kea may very well be golf heaven. Rated among "America's 100 greatest" and "Hawaii's finest" golf courses by *Golf Digest,* the course was designed by Robert Trent Jones, Sr., and built on a 5,000-year-old lava flow that spills into the Pacific. The course, the centerpiece of the resort, rolls over 230 acres of lava hills. The golf pro is John "JD" Elsberger. Jack Nicklaus, after competing in a tournament there, was quoted as saying, "It was more fun to play than any course I know." Not a bad review.

And for tennis lovers, too, Mauna Kea offers great possibilities. Rated one of the "50 great Tennis Resorts in America" by *Tennis* magazine and recipient of 5 star honors from *World Tennis* magazine, Mauna Kea's tennis park includes 13 plexiglass courts. As you'd expect, it has a pro shop, racquet rental, ball machines, and high-tech video-assisted private instruction. Tennis clinics and round-robin doubles tournaments are held every day. The director of tennis is Jay Paulson, who has served as practice partner for Bjorn Borg, Arthur Ashe, and Ken Rosewall.

Want more than tennis and golf? Mauna Kea offers a beach; a freshwater, palm-shaded pool; and snorkeling, surfing, sailing, wind surfing, scuba diving, horseback riding (kids must be at least 8 years to ride), deep-sea fishing, helicopter sightseeing (a bit pricy at $225 per person for an hour "volcanoes flight"). The resort offers three walking tours in the course of a week—a tour of the hotel and gardens, tours of the hotel's Pacific Rim collection given by a professor of art history, and a back-of-the-house tour. Interspersed throughout the week at the resort are Hawaiian crafts classes, movies (contemporary and vintage, complete with hot buttered popcorn), aquatics, volleyball, and dancercise. At night the resort has cocktail music on The Terrace or in the Batik Bar and dancing every night in the Batik Terrace and in the Pavilion. Once a week the resort hosts a luau, traditional food followed by a show of ancient chants and dances of the island of Hawaii.

FOR KIDS: Mid-June through Labor Day, again at Christmas

and Easter vacation time there's a supervised program for kids 5 to 12. Trained counselors are available 9:15 A.M. to 4:00 P.M. and again from 6:30 to 8:30 P.M. Some of the activities kids can expect are sand castle contests, Hawaiian crafts and games, nature walks, scavenger hunts, piñata parties, and hot dog roasts.

For kids too young for the organized program baby-sitters are available for $4 per hour day or night.

ACCOMMODATIONS: Families may choose guest rooms that feature spacious lanais (patios) facing the ocean, the beach, or the mountain. Beachfront accommodations feature bedroom/sitting rooms and give families direct access to the beach. The resort is proud of its interiors—rugs and cotton bedspreads loomed in India especially for the hotel and original art on the walls. Some families may prefer to rent one of the villas at Mauna Kea: full vacation homes with two bedrooms within walking distance of the hotel complete with individual pools, lanais, skylighted kitchens, and marble bathtubs overlooking private gardens. Another possibility are the Fairway Homes, three or four bedrooms completely furnished and including a private pool.

RATES: Modified American plan (MAP) rate, including breakfast and dinner, for a beachfront room is $368 for double occupancy; European plan (no meals) is $268 for the same room. A third person in the room, 7 or under, would cost $30 extra per night; 8 and over would be $50 per night. Infants under 3 cost $25, which includes the cost of a crib. Villas range in price from $600 to $700 per day, Fairway Homes from $400 to $800.

### Grand View Lodge and Tennis Club
Route 6, Box 22
Brainerd, Minnesota 56401
Telephone: 218-963-2234
General Manager: Fred Boos

IN THEIR OWN WORDS: "We are a National Historic Site located on Big Gull Lake and all of our business is families. . . . The phone starts ringing when the last snow melts. . . ."

DESCRIPTION: A long way from the Florida-style tennis and golf resort in miles and style as well, this one is open from early May to early October and is the quintessential northern lake spa, right down to the deer heads mounted on the wall of the pine-paneled lobby. The lodge is a cluster of 50 cabins with a cedar log lodge as a centerpiece, built along the north shore of Big Gull Lake. Golfers enjoy the nine-hole Grand View course carved through stands of white birch and pine trees, and tennis players can take advantage of seven courts. The tennis pro offers a range of tennis activities—instructional clinics, tournaments, and social mixer. Kids 8 to 18 get free group lessons. Use of the courts and golf course is free to guests of the lodge. Besides tennis and golf, a big attraction is the lake itself—motorboating, waterskiing, canoeing, swimming, and surf sailing are all possible, and the resort's marina can equip you for whatever water sport you choose. For those who prefer, there's a semienclosed, heated pool. Adult get-togethers include dances, bingo, backgammon lessons, bridge, and local sightseeing. The atmosphere is casual.

FOR KIDS: Four counselors supervise a children's program for kids 3 to 12. The kids are divided into two groups, 3- to 5-year-olds in one, 6- to 12-year-olds in the other. The day starts at 8:45 or 9:30—the choice is yours—and includes nature hikes, beach days, Olympics, arts and crafts, movies, gardening, and lots of other carefully planned activities. Excursions to places of interest nearby are scheduled, too, throughout the week. The hours of the program are until noon for the younger kids and then again 5:30 to 8:00 for dinner and more fun. The older kids meet until noon, then again from 1:30 P.M. to 3:30 P.M. and 5:30 P.M. to 8:00 P.M. (If you'd like, your kids can have lunch with the counselors; just be sure to arrange it by 9:30 in the morning.)

Baby-sitters are available for $1.75 per hour with three-hour advance notice.

ACCOMMODATIONS: Most guests stay in family cottages with one to six bedrooms. All have decks, views of the lake, fireplaces, and refrigerators, and some have kitchenettes.

RATES: The rates are structured according to the modified American plan (MAP), which includes accommodations; breakfast and dinner; golf; tennis; the children's program; use of fishing boats, canoes, and kayaks; maid service; and a variety of daily social activities. A stay in a family cottage that sleeps two to five would be $60 to $84 per adult per night with special rates for kids as follows: 6 to 12, two-thirds the adult rate; 3 to 5, one-half the rate; and under 3, $8 per night. Nonmeal plans are available early and late in the season. A few housekeeping cabins nearby are available for $450 to $850 per week.

### Kiawah Island Resort
P.O. Box 12910
Charleston, South Carolina 29412
Telephone: 803-768-2121 or 800-6-KIAWAH
General Manager: Ted Goodson

IN THEIR OWN WORDS: "The island's 10-mile stretch of wide, sandy beach along the Atlantic Ocean is one of the finest on the East Coast. Kiawah is a quiet place, designed with the family in mind. . . . Kiawah offers all the services and opportunities of most major resorts, but is part of a setting which is unlike any place else. The beach, the forests, the wildlife and the ambience of Kiawah are what people remember and tell their friends about."

DESCRIPTION: The island is divided into two sections, east and west, and each has its own golf course and tennis courts. The island has both residential and resort areas, and the two are kept quite separate. The West Beach Tennis Center features 12 composition and two lighted hard courts, ball machines, and a practice backboard. The staff there can pair you with a suitable partner and offers clinic and private lessons. The East Beach Center has nine clay courts, three hard courts, and audio-visual instruction facilities, a pro shop, and automated practice court. Two of the courts are designed for tournament play. (It was Kiawah's tennis pro, Roy Barth, whom we interviewed at the beginning of this chapter.)

The golf course on West Beach is the Marsh Point Golf Course, designed by Gary Player, with water on 13 holes, salt marsh on another 3. The Turtle Point Golf Course on the East Beach was designed by Jack Nicklaus and features three oceanside holes that offer golfers who can take their eyes off the ball a stunning view of the ocean.

Night Heron Park, a 21-acre park near the ocean, has playing fields, a bike rental shop with a video game room, a recreation building, and a 25-meter swimming pool. Guests at Kiawah also like to beachcomb, walk, and try out the 1.1-mile fitness course.

FOR KIDS: From June to August and during Christmas and Easter breaks, guests may take advantage of supervised activities for kids 4 to 12 such as face painting, ice cream making, treasure hunts, puppetry, and games. If you want a baby-sitter, the resort staff will supply you with a list of names. Tennis and golf lessons are available to youngsters.

ACCOMMODATIONS: You have a choice of rooms in an inn or a one-, two-, or three-bedroom villa all to yourself. The inn has 150 rooms, all with balconies. Villas may be beachside, parkside, or linkside; all have fully equipped kitchens, decks, and screened porches.

RATES: Double-bedded rooms in the inn are $125 per night; family packages of four days, three nights in a two-bedroom villa cost $495 for a family of four; eight days, seven nights $945. Cribs are available at no extra charge.

### Hyatt Regency Hilton Head
Oceanfront at Palmetto Dunes
P.O. Box 6167
Hilton Head Island, South Carolina 29938
Telephone: 803-785-1234 or 800-228-9000
General Manager: Ed Crovo

IN THEIR OWN WORDS: "This is a luxury oceanfront resort hotel that offers a relaxed, friendly atmosphere. Families are encouraged to visit. There's something about our wonderful ocean and outstanding recreational opportunities that make for a fun time for all."

DESCRIPTION: The hotel fronts on a three-mile stretch of private beach, and every conceivable kind of aquatic sport is possible—water skiing, wind surfing, sailing, shell collecting, and sunbathing. The resort features three 18-hole golf courses—the George Fazio Course and the Robert Trent Jones Course, over-looking the ocean, are among the nation's top-ranked courses. Tennis is what the public relations people call "only a serve away" at the Rod Laver Tennis Center with 25 courts, 6 lighted for night play.

FOR KIDS: "Pelican Kids" is a camp program for kids 6 to 12 that runs from Memorial Day to Labor Day, from 9:00 A.M. to 4:00 P.M. At other times of the year, there are scattered activities, too, for kids. Pelican Kids give prop plays, play "pillo polo," get swimming lessons, and do arts and crafts. The day, with lunch included, costs $20. The younger kids, 3 to 5, can go to "Possum

Tots" from 10:00 A.M. to 2:00 P.M. for $10. One-to-one baby-sitting is also available with 24-hour advance notice for $5 per hour. For teens, there are teen aerobics and every week, a Teen Night with fun, games, and music by the pool or on the beach.

ACCOMMODATIONS: There are 505 rooms altogether, all with two double beds or one king-size bed, a desk, sofa, television, and balcony. Cribs are available at no extra charge.

RATES: The "Family Vacation Package," which includes a gift for the kids, a coupon savings book, and a free breakfast buffet for kids under 12, costs $126 for two nights, $185 for three nights, and $372 for seven nights for a family of four in low season and $268 for two nights, $383 for three nights and $813 for seven nights in high season. This is for rooms with a sunset view; ocean view rooms cost more.

## Inter Continental Hilton Head
135 South Port Royal Drive
Hilton Head Island, South Carolina 29928
Telephone: 803-681-4000 or 800-327-0200
General Manager: Martin Seibold

IN THEIR OWN WORDS: "Golf, tennis, and croquet are immediately within reach, with some of the finest facilities in the world."

DESCRIPTION: The Guest Relations staff is available from 8:00 in the morning to 7:00 at night to help arrange for tennis at the Port Royal Racquet Club (16 courts, 8 clay, 6 Laykold, 2 grass, and 6 lighted for night games); golf at the Port Royal Golf Club, 36 holes of PGA-rated championship golf; horseback riding; massage; croquet; charter fishing cruises; or use of the health club with exercise equipment, saunas, steam room, and indoor pool.

FOR KIDS: From April to October, the Inter Continental offers "Kids' Corner"—a seven-day-a-week program for kids 5 to 12 from 10:00 A.M. to 4:00 P.M., Sunday–Wednesday; 10:00 A.M. to 10:00 P.M. Thursday–Saturday. Activities include pool games, beach games, scavenger hunts, arts and crafts, and, in the evening, a pizza party, movie, and quiet games. When it rains, there are indoor-type plans—charades, crafts, movies, and so forth. The program is free. Baby-sitting is available for $5 per hour with a $15 minimum.

ACCOMMODATIONS: Suites and connecting suites are available for families.

RATES: A Family Fun Package in high season (March to November) of three nights with connecting rooms—one for the parents, the other for up to three kids—costs $435 and $220, respectively. If your stay is in midweek, you can have a fourth night free.

### Marriott's Hilton Head Resort
130 Shipyard Drive
Hilton Head Island, South Carolina 29928
Telephone: 803-842-2400 or 800-334-1881
General Manager: Angus Cotton

IN THEIR OWN WORDS: "Here you can have a full vacation experience without ever leaving the hotel's 800 private acres."

DESCRIPTION: For your pleasure there are a health spa, indoor and outdoor pools, bikes to rent, 27 holes of golf, and 24 tennis courts, all within walking distance of your room.

FOR KIDS: "Kids World" is a structured program supervised by trained counselors that operates from 12:30 to 4:30 every day of the week. (There have to be at least six kids signed up to have the program.) It costs $8 per child, and lunch is available at an extra charge. Kids 6 to 11 play lawn games and pool games, go to the beach, have arts and crafts, and take bike hikes. Baby-sitting can be arranged for $4.50 per hour through the Hospitality Desk.

ACCOMMODATIONS: Rooms are in a multistoried complex; some suites are available. Cribs are available at no extra charge.

RATES: A family rate for up to four people in a room, use of two bicycles for three hours, and use of the Health Club, game room, and saunas, costs $179 for three days and two nights in high season, $499 for seven days and six nights.

### Palmetto Dunes Resort
P.O. Box 5606
Hilton Head Island, South Carolina 29938
Telephone: 803-785-1161 or 800-845-6130
General Manager: Wayne Whiteman

IN THEIR OWN WORDS: "At Palmetto Dunes you have as much activity (or peace and quiet) as you want—all in a lush setting enhanced by man's sensitive design . . . the beach at Palmetto Dunes is a vacation in itself."

DESCRIPTION: On the 2,000 acres that is the resort, there's a lot to do—three miles of beach, 24 swimming pools (plus kiddie pools), bicycle touring, boating (canoes are available to explore the resort's ten-mile system of inland lagoons). Hilton Head Island itself is a busy place with major golf and tennis tournaments, concerts, food festivals, theaters, shopping, and two movie theaters. For tennis buffs, the attraction is a 25-court Rod Laver Tennis Center with 23 clay and 2 hard courts, 6 lighted for night play. There's a full schedule of lessons, clinics, and demonstrations. Monday morning Wimbledon warm-ups give guests a chance to hit with the pros, on Monday evenings staff and guests watch professional exhibition matches. Golfers can choose from three courses designed by Robert Trent Jones, George Fazio, and Arthur Hills. PGA Class A professionals offer instruction, tournaments, and a variety of programs to keep things lively all year long.

FOR KIDS: During the summer, kids 5 to 10 are kept happy and busy as members of The Alligator Club. They play together, go crabbing and fishing, swim, and do arts and crafts. The cost of the program is $16 per day, and it operates Monday through Friday from 9:00 A.M. to 4:00 P.M. Lunch is included. The golf and tennis pros offer junior programs throughout the year, too.

Baby-sitting for $4 per hour is available day and evening; arrangements are made with the front desk.

ACCOMMODATIONS: All accommodations are privately owned, fully furnished one- to four-bedroom villas and homes. All have full kitchens, living and dining areas, washer/dryers, and either a balcony or a patio. Cribs are available for $3 per night or $15 for a full week.

RATES: The size and location of the accommodations you choose determine the rate. A Family Package offered by the resort—two nights and three days for a family of four, including four hours of bike rentals, free tennis (two hours per rental night per person), and a day's rental of an 18-foot motorboat—costs $310 to $360, depending on season. Tennis and golf packages are also available; check with the resort for details.

# 10

---

# SKIING

Skiing is another of our favorite topics. Skiing creates a wonderful family vacation just as long as you pick the right spot and make sure that there are facilities for every member of your family. Ski resorts have really been the leaders in providing family vacation facilities. In this chapter we first present some general information on planning a ski trip with some invaluable advice from experts—Billy Kidd, Christy Mueller Northrop, and Cal Coniff. Then we go on to list some mountains where we think you can have some fun. The information about each ski resort centers around their children's programs. We want you to take a look at what there is and then, when an area appeals to you, to contact the address listed for all the details. *Travel with Your Children* (TWYCH) publishes a guide called *Skiing with Children* every year. It's a compilation of almost 100 ski areas in the United States (we do a foreign version, too) with detailed information on each. The entire guide can be purchased for $29, or individual resort reports may be ordered for $1 each with a minimum order of five.

Another publication you should know about is put together by the people at Smuggler's Notch, one of the most family-oriented resorts around. It's called *The Book on Family Ski Vacations* and is free for the asking from The Village at Smuggler's Notch, Vermont 05464. The author, Kathleen O'Dell-Thompson, explains: "This book is for families—families who have tried skiing and are ready for more and families who have never skied together. It is for parents who may have skied years ago and for parents who have never tried this exciting sport. But, most of all, it is for families in search of a 'successful' vacation. By my definition that means one in which everyone has a wonderful time." We recommend this one highly.

## Choosing a Ski Destination

Start by evaluating the individual needs of your children, beginning with the youngest. Carefully determine whether each child will fit into the program geared to his or her age group. Then make certain that the ski terrain meets your own needs and that the resort has all the features beside skiing that you may want from a vacation: restaurants, interesting night life, swimming, tennis, and aerobics. Many ski resorts recognize how expensive it can be to get a family onto skis, so they've come up with special family packages. Shop around for savings, such as Steamboat's "kids ski free program" (free lodging, lifts, and rentals for kids), Okemo's free midweek nursery, and Smuggler's Notch's "Family Fest" weeks. Try to find a resort that has lifts and trails designed for all ages and levels. A variety of trails off one lift means a family can go up the mountain together and then ski down the trail that suits each one best. Remember that virtually all discounts are blacked out over the Christmas–New Year's period.

## Choosing Accommodations

Budget will have a lot to do with choice of accommodation. Remember what we've said before, though: a short, great vacation is better than a long unsuccessful one, so if you have to sacrifice time for comfort, do it. Stay as close to the lifts, child care, or ski school as you can afford. One quarter-mile may not seem like a long way, but at the end of the day when you're carrying ski equipment and an exhausted child, the distance will seem endless. Slopeside accommodations are particularly nice because not everyone has to come and go together. If a slopeside accommodation seems too expensive, compromise. Stay in a one-bedroom condo instead of a two-bedroom. Ask about daily maid service. Sometimes there's an extra charge for it, but we feel it's well worth it.

If you don't have your own transportation—and often it's not necessary that you do—check out the area's local transportation system and/or whether your accommodation facility has a courtesy van to and from the mountain.

### Evaluating Nursery Programs

Some of the questions you should ask about any nursery are the following:

- What age range do they accommodate?
- What are the daily activities?
- Do the kids go outside? Outdoor fun is one of the joys of a ski vacation even for the littler kids.
- What is the ratio of care givers to children? Children under 4 years need one adult to five children, infants need a higher ratio of adults.
- What do you have to provide? Always take a change of clothes and warm clothes. Label everything. Don't forget goggles and sun screen. (A good source of well-made, warm winter gear for kids is "Good Gear for Little People," a mail order company located in Washington, Maine 04574. One of their best items is their Bean Bag, a combination snowsuit/sleeping bag that zips on and off in seconds. It comes in two sizes, one for kids up to 15 pounds and one from 15 to 35 pounds.)
- Are hot lunches served? If your kid is a picky eater, can you pack a brown bag lunch?
- How important is "lunch included" to you? Think carefully about this one. Skiing down the mountain at noon may sound uncomplicated right now, but once you're on the slopes, it may not be.
- Are you allowed to visit and take your child out to play in the course of the day?
- Are reservations accepted? Are they necessary? When do you have to be there to ensure a place for your child? Can you think of anything worse than arriving at the mountain only to find your child locked out of nursery or ski school?
- How does the nursery program combine with the ski school?

## Evaluating Ski Schools

Ideally, your child should be in a group with others the same age. Because children get cold and tired, there should be a welcoming indoor space available. Although some kids do very well with formal structured ski instruction, most prefer an emphasis on fun and games. A combined nursery/ski school option is particularly nice for younger kids. Some questions to ask:

- How much time is spent out-of-doors?
- Is lunch served or supervised?
- Can kids ski with parents any time during the day without having to pay extra for a lift ticket?
- For the more experienced, is there a racing program? Or supervised skiing without structured instruction?
- Are the instructors experienced in teaching children?
- Are the areas for kids' instruction private enough so that kids won't feel inhibited by having people looking on?
- Are the facilities for kids—bathrooms and indoor play areas—close enough to the slopes for kids to get to them quickly?
- Are there any special programs? Teen programs for recreational skiers are a relatively new phenomenon, but they're happening at more and more resorts. Some of the spots that offer special teen programs are Snowmass, Vail and Beaver Creek, Copper Mountain, and Bolton Valley (more details in the listings later on). Many other places offer special après-ski programs or facilities for teenagers.

A WORD ABOUT SKIWEE: Although not the only game in town, SKIwee is a ski program we heartily endorse. Although there are lots of good schools that don't follow the SKIwee method, you should know something about it. The SKIwee program is sponsored by *SKI* magazine and several equipment suppliers. It's an all-day program that provides individual attention. Instructors are specially trained and must attend an annual clinic. SKIwee is game-oriented and based on the Montessori philosophy that play is learning. It begins with teaching kids how to put on their ski boots and continues on up to advanced levels of turns and freestyle techniques. The two basic keys to its success are the progress card and the use of a separate terrain garden. The progress card creates a universality of terms—a youngster going from one SKIwee area to another during the season simply picks up wherever he or she left off. Teaching is done through the use of familiar games, soccer, relay races, red rover, and so on. For instance, at SKIwee you don't hear *edging, wedges,* and *weighting.* Four-year-olds don't understand being told to push off and skate, but when trying to win a relay race, they find themselves skating automatically. A race through an obstacle course forces children to use their edges. And because kids seem to have such a hard time getting uphill on snow and cannot easily or happily herringbone or sidestep, many SKIwee areas use a carpet on the snow so that climbing becomes easy and fun. The SKIwee program is currently offered at approximately 50 ski areas in the United States. For a complete list, write to *SKI* magazine, 380 Madison Avenue, New York, New York 10017.

## What the Experts Say

We spoke to three well-known experts on the subject of skiing with kids. All are devoted skiers, and all have had personal experience getting their own kids on the slopes. Here's what they have to say:

*Billy Kidd, director of skiing, Steamboat Springs, Colorado, and former Olympic champion:*
For children under 5 there are three recommendations that I strongly feel will keep your kids on skis:

1. Have your child take a few professional lessons. Kids like to learn with older children and/or adults. And, most importantly, please find a ski resort which caters to children and their individual needs. . . .
2. Buy inexpensive equipment, i.e., plastic ski/snow shoes, often found in toy stores. Have your kids practice wearing these "short skis" on the living room floor to get a feel for balance and movement coordination.
3. Clothing—very important—make sure your children are properly dressed. Parents have a tendency to overdress their kids, who in turn become uncomfortably warm and can't move their arms and legs freely. This results in the child's disliking the sport from the start.

More importantly, kids want to have fun when they learn anything, especially skiing. If your children run into any snags or hang-ups during the first time out, they'll automatically be turned off. Make it as comfortable as possible in order to get them back on the slopes again. Otherwise, think about the beach for your next vacation.

Here are some tried and true hints: Don't modify old skis to fit your young children. Either rent ahead of time or buy—it is less money than you think. [Note from authors: Investigate buy-back programs where you can trade in one year's equipment for what will fit the next year. Many packages include equipment, so don't buy if this is true.] Choose warm sunny days to introduce your kids to skiing. Minimize your child's time to two to three hours a day on the slopes. Build confidence in your kids. Make sure they're comfortable with any new equipment before starting out on your trip. Get them in the right frame of mind for the ski trip. Familiarize them with the ski area with photos, maps, etc.

Kids naturally love to ski. They enjoy the freedom and independence it offers. Other sports are too team oriented. Skiing offers the first-timer an individual experience not matched by any organized sport. With just a few short lessons, your children will be able to ski down the easier slopes with the rest of the family, one of the key reasons you wanted to go on the ski trip in the first place. Spend time on the slopes with your children and don't try to teach them. Just go out and have fun.

*Christi Mueller Northrop, SKIwee national coordinator,* SKI *magazine:*

Since families that ski with their children, or are anxious to start skiing with their children, live in different geographical areas across the country, I have answered the question of when and how to start your children skiing according to their accessibility to snow and ski areas.

No matter where you live, it is best not to teach your children to ski yourself, but enroll them in a good children's ski school or special children's ski instruction program, such as SKIwee. Also, never push or force a young child to ski; it is a sport they must want to do and feel comfortable at.

If your family's availability and access to snow is

FREQUENT/EASY: If you live in the snow-belt with ample snow and easy, frequent access to skiing both at an area and in your backyard, children can start skiing as early as 30 months, depending upon the children's coordination.

The best way to start a child with good access to the slopes is to first let them play with their equipment indoors, then out in the backyard for short intervals. Once they are comfortable with the equipment, enroll them in a good children's ski program, since they will learn the most in a game-like atmosphere from their peers. Continue with the lessons, but let the child play on skis at home and at the ski area.

LIMITED/MODERATE: If you live an hour or two drive from the slopes and skiing, it is best starting children skiing at 4 years old at the earliest. If equipment is available, let the child play with it and try it out indoors. Enroll the child in a good program at an area, and try to have the child attend as frequently as possible. Again, the emphasis should be on fun, and the child should not be pressured to learn.

INFREQUENT/DIFFICULT: If you live several hours from skiing or a plane trip away, with the opportunity for only one or two trips a season, children with a very limited chance to ski each season are better waiting until they are five to start the sport.

When a long trip is involved to reach the area, there is a tendency to push the child to like skiing and learn fast. With children who see snow infrequently, it usually takes longer to adjust and learn to ski. If learning to ski is presented in a fun, relaxed way, the child will adapt more quickly. Since skiing is a relatively social sport, it is best that the child is enrolled in a fun program (such as SKIwee) to take advantage of the group, and the games. Also, with a group, a young child not used to snow is less apt to be scared.

No matter where you live remember, children will learn when they are having fun. Too much pressure, either from a ski school or the parents, takes the joy away.

### Cal Coniff, president, National Ski Areas Association:

Four or five years of age is a good time for children to take up skiing, and discover that winter is a great time for playing outdoors and having fun. Children take to skiing like ducks take to water, and learning to ski is a happy rewarding experience for children and parents alike.

Good inexpensive "starter sets" of equipment can be purchased at any ski shop. Most ski areas also rent children's equipment. Fancy ski clothes are not necessary but it is most important that children are dressed in outerwear that will keep them warm and dry. Good mittens and a warm hat are a must.

For the first few times on skis, just let your child walk around on a flat surface to get familiar with the strange "boards" attached to the feet. When you feel the child is at ease walking around, the next step is letting the child slide down the slightest incline that has a flat outrun free of obstacles. The parents should stay with the child at this stage to cheer the child on and, yes, help pick him up from the inevitable falls. This can be done on a little hill in your backyard or near your home. Remember, what may look like a molehill to the parent is Mt. Everest to the child.

For learning the technical maneuvers of skiing, such as turning and stopping, I strongly recommend that you enroll your child in ski school at a nearby ski area. Most have excellent learn-to-ski programs just for children, and many have full-day, learn-to-ski nursery programs where the children are well supervised and cared for. This will allow Mom and Dad a chance to go off and enjoy their day on the mountain.

At the end of the day when you head back to home, your child's pink rosy cheeks and big smile readily tell you it's been a great day full of new adventures and fun. And you won't have to worry about your child not going to bed early!

## CROSS-COUNTRY SKIING

Cross-country skiing is another great activity for families. It's nice and low-key and generally less expensive than downhill skiing. Experts recommend starting kids on cross-country skis at age 7 or 8—this kind of skiing requires strength, endurance, and balance that you can't expect from a younger child. The major consideration for families who want to cross-country ski with their kids is the kids' equipment. Gardner Lane, manager of the touring center at Bolton Valley, Vermont, says that "young children need well-fitting equipment. Families who cross-country ski know this and bring their own. The need for rental equipment has not been great enough to warrant a large supply of skis necessary to fit all sizes and abilities of children." It is unfortunate but true that many touring centers have a limited amount of equipment for young children. So you'll either have to take your own or check in advance as to the availability of your particular kid's size. Where should you go to cross-country ski? Practically all downhill ski areas have cross-country skiing nearby. The ones listed here do. But, all you really need is a place to stay where you're made to feel welcome, snow on the ground, proper equipment and clothing, and baby-sitting available for kids who don't want to go along or for cold, windy days. Many of the resorts listed in Chapter 8 offer cross-country skiing in season; check with some of the dude ranches, too, in Chapter 11. Some, like C Lazy U, have a full winter program that includes cross-country.

For specific information on 161 cross-country ski touring centers in the East, we suggest *Guide to Cross-Country Skiing in New England* by Lyn and Tory Chamberlain, published by Globe Pequot Press, Old Chester Road, Chester, Connecticut 06412 ($8.95).

## SKI RESORTS

We've listed the mountains that offer comprehensive services to families and covered the topics we think most important to you. These are not necessarily the best skiing spots from the point of view of a ski expert, but they're all great for families. Write to the ones that interest you for the reams of information most have on hand and compare.

Most of the resorts listed here offer summer programs, too. Some convert into tennis and golf spots, some continue to run the nurseries even when the snow goes, and most cost 20 to 50 percent less than in the winter. We spent a summer weekend at The Village at Smugglers' Notch and loved it. So when making your summer vacation plans, don't forget the mountains.

### Northstar-at-Tahoe
P.O. Box 129
Truckee, California 95734
Telephone: 916-562-1010 or 800-824-8516

DESCRIPTION: Skiers can get a view of the waters of Lake Tahoe from the top of Mt. Pluto. The sun shines 80 percent of the time in this corner of California, and the village at the base of the mountains includes on-the-slope lodging and a variety of restaurants, all with children's menus; a cross-country ski center; and a recreation center with saunas, outdoor spas, exercise room, and more.

FOR KIDS: All season long—end of November to end of April—kids 2 (as long as they're toilet-trained) to 6 are welcome at Minor's Camp Child Care for a full or a half day. Because the nursery is limited to 40 kids, reservations are recommended. Call 916-562-1010. The center is set up as a preschool with supervision in art, science, dramatic play books, blocks, cooking, music, and so on. All children play outside and in. The cost is $27 for kids who don't ski; $34 for kids who want to combine play school with 1½ hours skiing and are between the ages of 3 and 6.

Kids who attend Minor's Camp and have especially good motor skills can take a three-hour lesson at the Ski School, have lunch, and then spend the rest of the day at the Minor's Camp. The cost is $44. Special rates are available for the second child in the family.

Star Kids is an all-day (10:00 A.M. to 4:00 P.M.) lesson program for kids 5 to 12 that includes lessons, lifts, and lunch for $40. Sign-up must be by 9:30 A.M. The Minor's Camp has a list of sitters available for $2 per hour during the day, $3 at night. Check, too, at the Information Desk of the resort.

ACCOMMODATIONS: There are ten different lodging layouts ranging from hotel-type rooms to mountainside homes. All except Village Lodge Rooms have fully equipped kitchens and gas- or wood-burning fireplaces. Included in all lodging packages is use of the shuttle system and the Recreation Center with its saunas, outdoor spas, and exercise/game room. To give you an idea of cost, let's consider a three-night package for a group of three adults and two children (ages 5 to 12) in a two-bedroom condo with one child taking a three-day Learn-to-Ski program and one adult who is not a skier. The total, with tax included, would be just under $650. Cribs are available at $5 extra per night. For an additional charge you can get an interchangeable five- or six-day lift pass that's valid at Squaw Valley, Alpine Meadows, Heavenly Valley, and Kirkwood, too.

RATES: An all-day pass for an adult is $25; for kids 5 to 12 it's $13; and there is no charge for 5-year-olds and under skiing with an adult. Three-day passes cost $67 for adults, $35 for kids. Cross-country trail passes are $7 for adults, $4 for kids for a full day.

**Copper Mountain Resort**
P.O. Box 3001
Copper Mountain, Colorado 80443
Telephone: 303-968-2882 or 800-525-3878

DESCRIPTION: Copper Mountain is only 75 miles west of Denver, and the ski season is long—early November to late April. Of 75 trails, 25 percent are for beginners, 40 percent for intermediates, and 35 percent for advanced. When you're not skiing there's a Racquet and Athletic Club with indoor pool, tennis, racquetball, Nautilus, aerobics classes, and hot tubs. Guests of the Copper Mountain Lodging Services have free access to the club. Ice-skating, horse-drawn sleigh rides, dinner in the woods, and shopping in any of 35 shops in Copper Mountain Village are other possibilities. A good deal offered by the folks at Copper Mountain is the Copper Card; it costs $10 and entitles you to $5 off the adult lift ticket price (with the card lift tickets cost $22). It's good for a free day of skiing at the mountain in April and discounts on rentals, ski school classes, child care programs ($4 off), and specials at the Village's shops and restaurants.

FOR KIDS: Belly Button Babies welcomes kids 2 months to 2 years. The cost is $30 for a full day, 8:30 A.M. to 5:00 P.M., with lunch included or $20 for a half, 8:30 to12:30 or 12:30 to 5:00. A three-day rate is $80. Reservations are required; call 303-968-2882, extension 6344.

Combined with Belly Button Babies, the Belly Button Bakery facility is for kids 2 years and up. It got its name because the kids actually do bake there with help from the staff. Other indoor activities include blocks, music, water play, and dress-up. Kids 3 years and over can ski outdoors with instructors, while those under 3 play in the snow and go sledding. Kids who want to ski have to be registered by 9:30 A.M. for the morning lesson and 12:30 P.M. for the afternoon lesson. Reservations are necessary; call 303-968-2882, extension 6345.

In the Junior Ranch, beginners aged 4 to 6 get their own ski lift close to the indoor facilities. More experienced skiers have easy access to the entire mountain.

In the Senior Ranch, whether your 7- to 12-year-old is a beginner or a veteran skier, he or she can stay with the coaches all day, eat lunch with classmates, and ski as much as he or she wants. A full day, 10:00 to 3:30, costs $25; a half-day, 12:45 P.M. to 3:30 P.M., costs $19. Three consecutive days are $63. A lunch fee of $3.50 is charged. Special lift plus lessons plus rental packages are also available for kids. Reservations aren't required, but registration for the full day must be made by 10:00 A.M. of the day of the lesson. (Although lessons begin at 10:00, kids can be dropped off any time between 8:30 and 10:00.)

The Belly Button Bakery offers evening baby-sitting in guests' accommodations. Reservations must be made before noon of the day requested. Rates are $5 per hour, 50 cents more for each additional child. Call 303-968-2882, extension 6345, to make arrangements.

ACCOMMODATIONS: Your choice includes hotel rooms, and one-, two-, and three-bedroom condos and townhouses. Everything is within walking distance of the slopes; a free shuttle system is available when you'd rather not walk. There's a Club Med at Copper Mountain that includes a Mini Club open to kids 3 to 11 with four levels of ski instruction for kids age 6 and up. (No children under 3 are allowed.) It operates from 9:00 A.M. to 9:00 P.M. daily.

RATES: A week stay at the Club Med Copper Mountain ranges, depending on date, from $700 to $1,000 per adult and includes meals, accommodations, unlimited downhill skiing with lessons at all levels, unlimited cross-country skiing with lessons for beginners, aerobics, language lab, ice-skating, dancing at night, and evening entertainment. For kids, rates range from $250 to $460, 3 years; $350 to $600, 4 to 7; and $390 to $700, 8 to 11. For Club Med Copper Mountain information, call 800-CLUB-MED.

### Keystone Resort
Box 38
Keystone, Colorado 80435
Telephone: 303-468-2316 or 800-222-0188

DESCRIPTION: Skiing at Keystone (about 70 miles from Denver) can stretch from mid-October all the way into June. Night skiing at Keystone is big—it's the nation's largest night skiing operation with 13 beginner and intermediate runs lit up to 10:00 P.M. Adjacent to Keystone is North Peak, which is for advanced and strong intermediate skiers, and just 6 miles away, via a free shuttle bus, is Arapahoe Basin, the highest lift-served area on the continent. Lift tickets are interchangeable for all three mountains. Keystone Village has 11 swimming pools, a skating rink, a cross-country center, a teen center with video games, gift shops, a grocery, and indoor tennis with lessons and clinics available.

FOR KIDS: Keystone Children's Center operates year-round, unlike most ski-oriented resorts. The center is open from 8:00 A.M. to 5:00 P.M. When parents are night skiing, the kids can stay at the nursery, too. Applicable ages are 2 months and up; the nursery at Arapahoe takes kids from 18 months. Kids have free play, story hour, naptime, lunch, arts and crafts. For kids 3 and over, snow play is also offered. The cost is $25 for a half-day, $32 for full for infants 2 to 11 months, $20 and $28 for older kids. Lunch is included, and reservations are required. A special snow play program for kids 3 and over that includes sledding and building snowmen costs $32 per day, $25 half-day (8:00 A.M. to 1:00 P.M. or noon to 5:00 P.M.).

Mini-Minors Camp combines skiing and nursery with all-day supervision, indoors and out; lunch; and lift ticket, rental equipment, and sledding for kids 3 to 5. It costs $35 per day, $30 half-day. In Minor's Camp kids 5 to12 can combine lessons, lift, and lunch for $30 half-day, $40 full day with equipment, less without equipment, and for multiday packages. Night skiing lessons are available for $30, with equipment and lift tickets included. If you want to get serious about skiing with your kids, there's a Mahre Training Center at Keystone for four 5-day sessions each season. One of the Mahre twins will be at at least one of your sessions. Call 800-222-0188 for details.

Evening baby-sitting can be arranged in your accommodations. Call 303-468-4182. Cost is $4 per hour for the first child, 50 cents more per hour for each additional child. Requests for evening baby-sitting must be made by 1:00 P.M. that day.

ACCOMMODATIONS: One choice is Keystone Lodge, with a spectacular view of the Rocky Mountains from every window. Condos are available with studios to four-bedroom units possible, all with kitchenettes. Some private homes are also available for rent. Special packages that are available include free transfers to and from Denver, lift tickets, and no charge for children 12 and under. At the lodge, the per-person rate for a seven-night ski package is $494; in the condos, a "deluxe" two-bedroom unit is $289 per person in low season, $323 in regular season. For spring skiing, you can take advantage of two-day packages that represent a 22 percent discount over winter rates.

RATES: Lifts are $24 per day on multiple-day tickets for adults, $10 for juniors 12 years and under.

### Snowmass Resort
P.O. Box 5566
Snowmass Village, Colorado 81615
Telephone: 303-923-2000 or 800-332-3245

DESCRIPTION: Snowmass is 12 miles from Aspen and has lots to offer families. Besides skiing, 90 runs at all levels with a capacity of almost 19,000 skiers per hour, it has a great deal of other activities to lure you: sleigh rides in the moonlight, naturalist-guided snowshoe walks, cross-country skiing (25 miles of trails linking Snowmass and Aspen), swimming and hot tubbing, a genuine dog sled ride, a hot air balloon ride (kids have to be at least 9 years old), and at night, the Snowmass Repertory Theatre, and the Top o' the Rockies concert series. Another plus is the fact that 95 percent of the accommodations are slopeside. The resort is owned by Aspen Skiing Company, which also owns Aspen and Buttermilk Mountains, so lift tickets are usable at all three. A free shuttle bus connects all of them. Most of the restaurants in Snowmass Village have special children's menus, and another plus is the free Snowmass shuttle that runs all day from 7:15 A.M. to 11:25 P.M.

FOR KIDS: Kinderheim Ski School and Nursery, for kids 1 year to 6 years from the end of November to mid-April, offers indoor and outdoor play. Inside it offers arts and crafts, music, puppets, and stories, and outside there are skiing and sledding for kids 3 years and over. Hours are 8:30 A.M. to 4:00 P.M. In high season the cost is $245 per week with hot lunch and morning snack included. Call 800-525-9408 for reservations. For kids 3 to 10 there's evening care available from 5 to midnight with reservations.

Snowmass Snowbunnies is another toddler program for 1½- to 3-year-olds with a ski program for 3- to 6-year-olds. Games are played inside and out. Evening baby-sitting is available through Snowbunnies. Call 303-923-4620. The cost is $45 per day, less for stays of more than 4 days. At Happy Trails Day Care you'll find day and evening care for infants up to kids age 12. Meals, snacks, arts, crafts, music, and outdoor play are included. Call 303-923-5513. Little Red School House is for kids 2½ to 5 and is open from 8:45 to 5:30 P.M. Call 303-923-3756.

The Ski School at Snowmass gives classes for kids 5 to12. Kids meet at the Youth Center at 9:30 A.M. A noontime lunch break is supervised by instructors, and classes end at 3:00. Special events throughout the week include NASTAR, Ski School races, and a Children's Ski School Picnic. Classes are $22 for a half-day, $35 for a full day, with multiday packages available. The Ski School runs a program for 13- to 19-year-olds, who are grouped by age and ability. Instructors supervise a variety of activities, including ski racing, sled parties, picnics, and videotaping sessions. Instructors also plan after-ski activities such as movies, sleighride barbecues, and ice-skating parties. The program costs the same as the children's lessons. Snowmass Resort Association keeps a list of sitters at the Snowmass Information Booth on the Mall.

ACCOMMODATIONS: As we mentioned before, 95 percent of the accommodations at Snowmass are ski-in/ski-out, which is great for families. You have lodges and condominiums, studios to four-bedroom units. Most accommodations have kitchens, and many offer kids-free-in-parents' room deals. For information call 303-923-2010.

RATES: There are two distinct seasons at Snowmass: value season is November 27 to December 9, January 3 to January 30, April 4 to April 19; regular season is December 20 to January 2, and January 31 to April 3. In value season, 6-day adult lift tickets are $132, in regular season add $30. The kids' equivalent is $96 in either season. During value season you can save up to 50 percent on lodging.

### Steamboat
P.O. Box 774408
Steamboat Springs, Colorado 80477
Telephone: 303-879-0740 or 800-332-3204

DESCRIPTION: "Steamboat is so big; we have this corner of Colorado all to ourselves." A great advantage of skiing at Steamboat is that jets can land at the airport minutes away from the mountain. From Denver, Steamboat is about 40 minutes by air. The average snowfall at Steamboat is a total of 27 feet typically starting in November and lasting through April. Best of all, Steamboat has a "Kids Ski Free" plan: kids under 12 ski free when their parents buy a five-day or longer lift ticket and stay at a participating property. And if the parents rent equipment, the kids get theirs free (one child per parent, for the rental deal). Take proof of age for the older kids! The director of skiing at Steamboat is Billy Kidd, the expert we quoted at the beginning of this chapter.

FOR KIDS: From November 26 to April 19, the nursery operates from 8:00 A.M. to 5:00 P.M. It's open to kids 6 months to 6 years old. A full day for the first child is $25, for the second, $14; a half-day is $18 and the second, $12. Lunch is available for kids 2 and over for $4; you must provide food for the younger children. Kiddie Corral offers group lessons for kids 3 to 5. Half- and full-day lessons are offered. The full day includes lunch and a lift ticket. A half-day lesson costs $25 (including lift ticket), a full day $34. Three-day packages cost $90, 5 days, $125. Kids 6 to 15 may take group lessons at the Ski School. A two-hour lesson costs $16; a set of three is $40. Three all-day lessons, which include lunches, cost $90.

"Ski Week" is a package of five all-day lessons, five lunches, NASTAR racing, and a pin for $145. The ski school has specially trained staff for handicapped skiers, and there are Billy Kidd Racing Camps for three to six days at a time and daily NASTAR racing clinics.

Most lodges have access to baby-sitters. A list of baby-sitters is available from the Chamber of Commerce, 303-879-0740. Expect to pay $3 to 5 per hour and make arrangements in advance; early mornings are the most difficult time to get coverage.

ACCOMMODATIONS: There are hotels, motels, lodges, condominiums, houses, and guest ranches all within three miles of the mountain. There are lots of slopeside possibilities, too. Most have indoor pools, game rooms, hot tubs, and other amenities. All price ranges are covered, but for a sample let's consider a slopeside condo for a group of four, with a kitchen, maid service, laundry facilities, and a fireplace. The rate for seven nights would be $460 to $495 per person. For information on lodging, call 303-879-0740.

RATES: Remember that kids ski free as long as they're 12

years or under. The only time this deal is not in effect is during the Christmas–New Year's holiday. An adult daily lift ticket ranges from $25 to $27, depending on season. Multiday packages are a few dollars less. Seniors (65 and over) ski free, so invite the grandparents to come along.

### Vail Resort Association
241 East Meadow Drive
Vail, Colorado 81657
Telephone: 303-476-1000 or 800-525-3875

### Beaver Creek
P.O. Box 915
Avon, Colorado 81620
Telephone: 303-949-5750 or 800-525-2257

NOTE: We're listing Vail and Beaver Creek together because, although they're separate ski destinations ten miles from each other, they offer the same kind of facilities for kids because they are owned by one corporation, Vail Associates, Inc. Lift tickets are interchangeable between the two mountains.

DESCRIPTION: Vail Village nestles right at the foot of Vail Mountain and therefore offers all the extra attractions of a town. It has 92 named trails, and its longest run is the three-mile "Riva Ridge." It offers an outstanding variety of novice and intermediate trails and has lift capacity of almost 29,000 skiers per hour. It has three full-service restaurants, four cafeterias, and two lunch and snack spots.

Beaver Creek is a mountain 10 miles from Vail. There's shuttle service between Vail and Beaver Creek daily during the ski season. Beaver Creek is not so vast as Vail; it has 49 named trails. Its longest run is the Centennial, $2^{3}/_{4}$ miles, and its uphill capacity is 15,700 per hour. Cross-country skiing is also available on 12 miles of double-set track at the top of Beaver Creek Mountain. At Beaver Creek, as at Vail, the average annual snowfall is 300 to 350 inches, and there's sunshine for more than 70 percent of skiing days. There are three restaurants on the mountain and a fourth reserved for the exclusive use of property owners and members of the Beaver Creek Club. Lift lines are almost unknown at Beaver Creek.

FOR KIDS: Both mountains feature the Small World Play School, open from the end of November to mid-April from 8:00 A.M. to 4:30 P.M. Kids 2 months to 6 years are welcome and reservations are strongly recommended. Call 303-476-1088. Nursery ski lessons for $2\frac{1}{2}$- to $3\frac{1}{2}$-year-olds are available for $5 extra with equipment included. A day at the nursery costs approximately $30.

The Children's Skiing Center, operating from 8:00 A.M. to 4:30 P.M., is open to kids $3\frac{1}{2}$ to 12, who are divided into two groups: $3\frac{1}{2}$ to 6 and $6\frac{1}{2}$ to 12. The cost is $30 per day or $45 with a lesson and a lift ticket. (Lift tickets are interchangeable between Vail and Beaver Creek.) No half-days are available. There's inside staff available at all times to handle any problems.

Mogul Mice is for beginners $3\frac{1}{2}$ to 6. It's a package of $1\frac{1}{2}$-hour lessons, lunch, and equipment rental for $40 for a full day. Half-day is available as well. The SuperStar Program is for kids $3\frac{1}{2}$ to 6 who can stop on snow. All-day class lessons, lunch, and lift ticket cost $45 per day. Kids $3\frac{1}{2}$ to 6 may also take lessons without the rest of the program. The cost is $15 per lesson. Teenagers can take $5\frac{1}{4}$ hours of lessons for $32 per day. Lifts are extra, and this operates only during peak periods.

At Vail a privately operated facility called ABC Children's Acre provides day care to visitors and residents alike. The ages are 2 to 5, and the program includes art, music, stories, outdoor play, rest, and snack time. The cost is $30 per day. Call the director, Ann Hansborough, 303-476-1420 or 5684 for reservations at least one day in advance. In Vail and Beaver Creek, many lodges have baby-sitter lists, and in Vail the Youth Center, 303-475-7000, has a list of available sitters, who charge between $5 and $6 per hour.

ACCOMMODATIONS: In Vail, most hotels, lodges, and condos cater to families and may give children's discounts. Call 800-525-3875 outside Colorado, 303-476-5677 inside, for lodging information. In Beaver Creek, the number to call is 800-525-2257. A sample is the Charter at Beaver Creek, one-, two-, or three-bedroom condo facility at the base of the mountain that has ski season specials such as a two-bedroom suite for four nights at $920. Children under 12 are free, and cribs are available for no extra charge.

RATES: Through Beaver Creek's Central reservations number (given previously) you can arrange a Family Fun Package with savings on lodging, lifts, ski rentals, ski school, day care, and more. The Christmas–New Year's holiday period is not included. At both mountains, a regular adult lift ticket is $30 for a full day, with kids 12 and under $18. Multiday rates offer additional savings.

### Sun Valley Resort
Sun Valley, Idaho 83353
Telephone: 208-622-4111 or 800-635-8261

DESCRIPTION: Fifty-one years ago, a young railroad executive named Averell Harriman established the Sun Valley Lodge. Sun Valley's history is glamorous—Hemingway, Cooper, Crosby, Gable, Garland, Kennedy, Eastwood, and Ford all signed the register. One of the photos in the promotional brochure shows Louis Armstrong on the slopes with a group of ski instructors. No doubt, you and your family will be in good company at Sun Valley. Sun Valley has two mountains, Dollar for beginners, and Baldy for intermediate and advanced skiers. Free shuttle service takes you from the Lodge, the Inn, or the Village Condos to and from both. There are 66 runs on the two mountains. The first chairlift ever used in skiing was at Sun Valley; now there are 16 double and triple lifts.

FOR KIDS: At Sun Valley Playschool most kids are 2 to 6; younger and older ones are accepted, even infants. Children play indoors and out. A full day costs $30 per day for kids under 2, $27 for those over 2. Hourly rates are available, too. Lunch is included in the full-day price; it's $3.50 otherwise. The older kids can take two-hour skiing lessons at the ski school for $7.

There are 180 instructors under the direction of Rainer Kolb. Kids 5 to 12 can take beginner and intermediate lessons on Dollar Mountain. The cost is $37 for four hours of instruction, $95 for three days, $109 for five days. Reservations are recommended.

The Playschool can help you with nighttime baby-sitting with at least 8 hours advance notice; the cost is $4.50 per hour.

ACCOMMODATIONS: Sun Valley Village is within walking distance of the Lodge, the Inn, and Condominiums. Kids 11 and under stay free in the same room as their parents. Sample rates at the lodge for a family suite (two connecting rooms) are $190 per night; in the condos, a two-bedroom condo is $175 per night for up to four people. A seven-night package of lodging and lift tickets in the condo is $741 for each adult, and $73 for each child (for lift tickets only).

RATES: Lift tickets are $29 per day for adults, $19 for children; three days are $79 and $48; five days $128 and $73.

### Taos Ski Valley
Taos Ski Valley, New Mexico 87571
Telephone: 505-776-2291 or 800-992-SNOW

DESCRIPTION: Only 18 miles from the town of Taos, this resort offers an appealing combination of sun and snow. There are 71 slopes, and the easiest and steepest are accessible from the top of all lifts. Taos's Ski School's Learn-to-Ski-Better Week is popular with all levels of skiers. The Village includes shops, restaurants, and a pro shop and a shuttle bus to the town of Taos. Ski-related evening programs are offered throughout the valley; up-to-date schedules are available at the Ski School office; après-ski in the village includes dancing, movies, talent shows, and jazz festivals.

FOR KIDS: The Peek-a-Boo Child Care program for kids 6 weeks to 3 years operates in the "Hide 'n' Seek" building, about 100 yards from the center of the village year-round. It is open from 9:00 A.M. to 4:00 P.M., the same hours that the lifts operate. Kids 18 months and over play in the snow. Reservations are required; call 505-758-9076. The charge is $25 per day; you pack your own lunch for your child. In the town of Taos there's a day care center that will take drop-ins with advance registration. It's called Trudy's Discovery House, 505-758-1659, and is open from 7:45 A.M. to 5:45 P.M. during the week, 9:00 to 5:00 on Saturdays. Kids must be at least 6 months old, and prices range from $12 to $15 per day.

In the KinderKafig program kids 3 to 6 learn to ski all over the mountain. The 5- and 6-year-olds have two hours of lessons in the morning, lunch, and two hours of supervised skiing with an instructor. The 3- and 4-year-olds' program includes an hour of skiing in the morning and afternoon, play in the snow, and indoor activities such as crafts, games, puppets, and storytelling. The cost is $26 for a full day; $16 for a half. A lift ticket is included, and a six-day package is $150.

In the Junior Elite program kids 7 to 12 get morning and afternoon lessons and a lift ticket for $35 per day. Thursday at 2:00 is race time. The Elite program is for kids 13 to 18. Lessons are fast-paced and geared toward fun. Afternoons are free for skiing with new friends or for ski clinics on racing or other areas of special interest. Taos plans their ski programs to be as flexible as possible—groups can form their own race-oriented classes or challenge classes for kids who can ski and want thrills but aren't interested in racing. The lodges keep lists of baby-sitters who will sit either in their own home or at the resort.

ACCOMMODATIONS: On the slopes there are lodges, all with saunas, jacuzzis, or hot tubs and live entertainment and condos all with kitchens. (At this ski area, we recommend a lodge for a much more picturesque vacation.) If you plan to cook, you'll have to get groceries in town (no grocery store in the Ski Valley). Ski packages are also available at accommodations in the town of Taos.

RATES: If you stay on the slopes, the most popular package is the week-long Saturday to Saturday package. For lodges this includes the room, two or three meals per day, six days of lift tickets, and six mornings of ski school classes, and for the condos includes all of the above except the meals. A typical lodge is the St. Bernard, which charges $810 per adult for a ski week with $540 for kids 7 to 12 and $460 for ages 3 to 6 in the same room as the adults. For accommodations information call 800-992-SNOW. Lift tickets are $25 for an adult one-day ticket, $23 per day for a multiday ticket; a child (12 and younger) pays $15 per day, $13 for a multiday ticket. Equipment rental is $11 for the first day for adults, $9 every additional day; for kids it's $6 and $5.

### Ski Windham
Route 23W
Windham, New York 12496
Telephone: 518-734-4300 or 800-833-5056

DESCRIPTION: Ski Windham has 27 trails and a newly added third chairlift, raising skier capacity to 8,000 per hour. Snowmaking covers 97 percent of the mountain, and there are two lodges, The Wheelhouse and The Lodge at Ski Windham.

FOR KIDS: Kids from 6 months to 7 years may stay for a half- or full day of supervised activities at the nursery. Reservations and prepayment are required. The full-day session, from 8:30 A.M. to 4:00 P.M., is $25, a half-day from 8:30 A.M. to 12:00 noon or 1:00 P.M. to 4:00 P.M., is $15. Kids play inside and out. Smokey Bear Ski

School is a learn-to-ski program for kids 4 to 7. A single session is $15, $22 with equipment rentals; a full-day session, which includes two lessons, lunch, a lift ticket, and nursery supervision, is $40, or $48 with rentals. Beginner group lessons for first-time skiers 8 years old and up are given at 9:00 A.M. and 12:15 P.M. on weekends and holidays. Learn to Ski packages are available on weekdays for a rate of $82 for three days for adults and $75 for juniors 12 and under. The Lodging Bureau has a baby-sitter referral service. Expect to pay $5 to $6 per hour.

ACCOMMODATIONS: Ski Windham Lodging and Skier Information Service will help you find a place to stay. Call toll-free 800-833-5056.

RATES: Kids 5 and under ski free with a ticketed adult. Daily weekday rates are $18 for adults, $16 for juniors (6–12); five-day (nonholiday) rates are $82 for adults, $72 for juniors. Daily weekend and holiday rates are $27 for adults, $24 for juniors.

### Seven Springs Mountain Resort
R.D. 1
Champion, Pennsylvania 15622
Telephone: 814-352-7777
General Manager: James N. McClure

DESCRIPTION: Fifty plus years ago, Adolph and Helen Dupre bought 2½ acres of land, a natural snow bowl, that reminded them of their native Bavaria. They paid $13. Now the family has 12,000 acres, and the resort has room for 2,500 overnight guests, seven restaurants, shops, boutiques, lounges, a health spa, three swimming pools, an 18-hole golf course, a tennis center, and bowling lanes. It's Pennsylvania's largest ski area. Helen is quoted as saying, "Early on we realized we couldn't move all the snow we got, so we decided to take advantage of it." Now there are 11 lifts and three rope tows for 25 slopes and trails.

FOR KIDS: Kids 3 to 6 can spend 9:00 A.M. to 4:00 P.M. or 9:00 to 1:00, or noon to 4:00, at Tiny Tot Ski School. A full day costs $35, a half is $25, and lessons, snack, activities, lunch, and ski equipment are all included. The Junior Ski Program for the older kids, 7 to 12, offers four hours plus a lunch session every day from 10:00 to 2:00. The cost of the program is $35. It is meant for kids who can ride the chairlift by themselves. Equipment can be rented.

With 24 hours notice, the Customer Service Desk will arrange baby-sitting for you for $12 for the first one to four hours and $3 for each additional hour.

ACCOMMODATIONS: You have a choice of a room in the Main Lodge or its 10-story hotel wing, one of 5 cabins, 25 chalets, and 80 condos. Cribs are available at no extra charge.

RATES: A two-bedroom suite in the Main Lodge that is big enough for four people costs $265 (breakfast included). It has a sitting room, private bar, refrigerator, and private balcony or patio. Kids 16 and under stay free in the same room as parents in spring, summer, or fall. In winter, kids under 5 are free, with a $5 charge for kids 6 to 12. A two-bedroom apartment located three-quarters of a mile from the Main Lodge with two baths, a living room, balcony, complete kitchen, washer and dryer, and access to a private pool costs $575 for a week.

### Shawnee Mountain
Shawnee on Delaware, Pennsylvania 18356
Telephone: 717-421-7231

DESCRIPTION: A ski resort in the Poconos, this is a gentle hill compared to some of the other areas we've described here, but it is reputed to have one of the best SKIwee programs anywhere in the country. The mountain has 20 slopes and trails with snowmaking on all. Skiing doesn't stop when the sun goes down: night lights cover most slopes and trails with practically shadow-free illumination. Kids 7 and under ski free when accompanied by a ticketed adult. Shawnee Village and Shawnee Inn are 2½ miles from the mountain and have lots of family-oriented facilities.

FOR KIDS: Little Wigwam Babysitting, located at the base of the mountain, entertains kids 1 year and up from 9:00 A.M. to noon and 1:00 to 4:00 P.M. Rates are $2.50 per hour or $6.00 for a half-day. A lunch option is available, too. Children's Nest nursery is located at the Shawnee Village reception center, a few miles from the mountain, and one mile from the Inn and condos. Kids 1 to 8 are welcome from 8:30 to 5:00 on weekdays and 8:30 to 6:00 on weekends. Rates are the same as the Wigwam.

SKIwee offers kids 4 to 12 a full-day program or 1½-hour group lessons. The full-day program includes lunch and costs $35;

equipment rental is extra. All participants receive the individualized progress card and a SKIwee pin. Boys and girls aged 12 to 16 can join a holiday race camp during the Christmas holiday season. The package includes training on and off the snow, evening clinics, movies, and awards. Two nights' lodging, six meals, constant supervision, and swimming at Shawnee Inn are included for $150 with lift tickets, $110 without. A day camp option is available for $100 and $70 for teens staying with their parents. The Reception Center at the Village will help you find a baby-sitter.

ACCOMMODATIONS: The Shawnee Village/Shawnee Inn is located on the banks of the Delaware River about 2½ miles from the mountain. Free transportation from the Inn to the mountain is included with ski packages. If you stay in a condo, you'll need your own car. The activities staff provides a full schedule of daily activities, everything from crafts to aquacise classes in the pool to movies at night. Guests can use the facilities of the Shawnee Racquet Club, five miles away. You can choose from rooms at the Inn or two-bedroom villas. Sample rates, per night, are $52.50 per person double occupancy during midweek at the Inn and $375 to $750, depending on season, in the villas (which sleep up to six). Guests of the Inn and villas get two free lift tickets during the week and a one-third discount on weekends and holidays. Call 717-421-1500 for details.

RATES: Lift tickets are $27 for day and night (8:00 A.M. to 10:00 P.M.) during the week; $23 for 8:00 A.M. to 5:00 P.M. Children under 7 ski free when accompanied by a paying adult. Every Monday is bargain day: $18 for the day, $12 for the evening only.

### Bolton Valley Resort
Bolton, Vermont 05477
Telephone: 802-434-2131 or 800-451-3220

DESCRIPTION: "The Lodge at Bolton Valley and Trailside Condominiums are within steps of ski lifts, tennis courts, pools, and restaurants. Children can't get lost, cars are not needed, and programs provide a good mix of family time, children's time, and adult time together." Located in central Vermont, 19 miles east of Burlington, this destination resort is located on 6,000 wooded acres. There are 30 interconnected trails with summit views of

Lake Champlain and the Green Mountains. There's a cross-country touring center, too, with 100 kilometers of trails. The Sports Center includes two tennis courts, an exercise room, a whirlpool, a sauna, and an indoor pool. Night skiing is possible from 7:00 to 10:00, Monday through Saturday.

FOR KIDS: HoneyBear Nursery, open from 8:30 A.M. to 4:30 P.M., has a crafts area, a kitchen, a block area, and a separate room for infants and children. Infants through age 6 are welcome, with reservations necessary for children under 2. The cost for preschoolers is half-day with lunch $11, full day $20; 5 days for $80; infants half-day $16, full $25, and five days for $125. On Tuesday, Thursday, and Saturday nights the nursery is open from 6:30 P.M. to 9:00 P.M., and the fee is $10 for those hours.

The Ski School program for young children for 4- or 5-year-old kids enrolled in the nursery offers one or two SKIwee lessons. Instructors pick them up from the nursery and return them: half-day ($15) and full day ($28) sessions are available. Bolton Bears and Cubs SKIwee program is for kids 5 to 12. Operating 9:45 A.M. to 2:00 P.M. every day, it costs $34 with lunch and a lift ticket included; five days costs $125. The Teen Scene, available for school vacation times only, provides afternoon ski lessons exclusively for teenagers for $10 per day, five days for $40. The Pied Piper of Bolton is a dinner and evening activities program for kids 6 to 11 available three nights a week. It costs $14 with dinner; $9 without. Baby-sitting can be arranged with the front desk for $3 per hour, day or evening.

ACCOMMODATIONS: Right at the mountain there's the Lodge at Bolton Valley, a slopeside hotel (some rooms have kitchens), and Trailside Condos: one-, two-, three-, and four-bedroom units with kitchens and fireplaces and some separate chalets. A short drive from the slopes is Black Bear Lodge, a 20-room country inn. At the Bolton Valley Lodge and Trailside Condos, kids under 6 stay free in the same room as parents. Cribs are available at no extra charge.

RATES: Kids under 6 ski free. A variety of packages are available, for instance, an "All Frills Vacation," which includes lifts, slopeside lodging, breakfasts and dinners, daily ski lessons, use of the Sports Center, aerobic classes, night skiing, and cross-country skiing, for $249 per adult for five days; "Kidski All Frills Vacation" includes lodging in the same room as parents, enrollment in Bolton

Bears or Cubs full-day program, ski lifts, night skiing, sleigh-ride, breakfasts and dinners, and use of Sports Club, for $223 for five days.

### Mount Snow Resort Center
89 Mountain Road
Mount Snow, Vermont 05356
Telephone: 802-464-3333 or 800-451-4211

DESCRIPTION: Mount Snow has 75 trails and 16 lifts, and skiing is usually possible from early November through May. The facilities include three base lodges, all with cafeterias; a summit lodge; three rental shops; and a vacation center, which is the focus of the kids' activities.

FOR KIDS: The Pumkin Patch (that's how they spell it) is where kids 6 weeks to 12 years go for a variety of programs. The nursery is for infants up to age 8 and operates daily. Kids play indoors and out, and those under 2 have their own room where they can nap and play. Outdoor facilities include slides, monkey bars, rope ladders, and swings.

Ages 3 to 5 years participate in Peewee SKIwee, which includes two one-hour lessons a day. Kids 6 to 12 participate in the SKIwee program—five hours of supervised skiing and instruction each day with lunch included for all-day programs. All skiing lessons begin at the Children's Learning Center, a protected area with its own rope tow and terrain garden. Three weeks a year are designated "Teddy Bear Ski Weeks," which include free skiing for kids 12 and under, rides on a snow-grooming machine, a magic show, teddy bear parade, and more. Vacation Services at 802-464-8501 has details.

ACCOMMODATIONS: Mount Snow Vacation Services, 802-464-8501, represents 56 properties in the area. An example of a facility at the base of the mountain is Snow Lake Lodge, with two pools, a fitness center, and a lounge, which offers ski packages such as Fun Pack: three days of skiing and two nights lodging for $119 per adult, $30 for kids 3 to 12. Kids 4 to 12 ski free during the week.

RATES: Some sample package rates at the Mountain are $110 for adults, $60 for kids (at nonholiday time) for five days of skiing, $159 and $90 for skiing and lessons, and $142 for SKIwee.

**Okemo Mountain**
RFD 1B
Ludlow, Vermont 05149
Telephone: 802-228-4041 general information, 802-228-5222 for
  snow reports, 802-228-5571 for lodging service

DESCRIPTION: Located in central Vermont, Okemo has 60
trails, including a 4½-mile-long beginner trail from the summit.
The village of Ludlow has specialty shops, restaurants, antique
stores, and a variety of lodging possibilities.

FOR KIDS: Okemo Mountain lures families with

- free skiing for kids 6 and under
- free beginner lift regardless of age
- free lodging for kids 12 and under at Okemo Mountain
  Lodge, Kettle Brook, and Winterplace, all slopeside
  condos
- free day care with lunch included during the week at
  nonholiday times
- Saturday evening childcare from 6:00 to 10:00

From mid-November to late April, the nursery operates from
8:30 A.M. to 4:30 P.M. every day and on Saturday evenings from
6:00 P.M. to 10:00 P.M. as well. Kids 18 months to 6 years play
indoors and out, hear stories, play games, and do puzzles and arts
and crafts. The nursery is free midweek, otherwise $12 for a full
session, $8 for a half-session. Lunch is included. An Introduction to
Skiing option for kids 3 and 4 is available for $10 extra. The
SKIwee program, described in the introduction, offers half-day and
full-day sessions. Two-hour snow instruction is included morning
and afternoon for kids 4 to 8. At the Children's Ski School ages 6
and up may take lessons 9:45 A.M. to 11:45 A.M. and 1:45 P.M. to
3:45 P.M.

Young Mountain Explorers, for kids 8 to 12, is meant for kids
of average or better skiing ability and offers four hours of supervised skiing and instruction daily. Baby-sitting arrangements can
be made with Joyce Washburn in the main office of the resort; rates
are about $2 per hour. There's a Junior racing team program for
ages 8 to 18, divided into age groups. A NASTAR recreational

racing program for all ages and abilities is held every day except Monday.

ACCOMMODATIONS: Slopeside accommodations are available at Kettle Brook Condominiums—one- to three-bedroom units—and at Okemo Mountain Lodge with 72 one-bedroom units that can sleep four. Nearby are country inns and lodges, and motels as well. One of our favorites is the Combes Family Inn, a comfortable farm house filled with games and pets, a barn with goats, acres for cross-country skiing and sledding. Call 802-228-8799 or write to Box 275, RFD 1, Ludlow, Vermont 05149. For information about other accommodations, call 802-228-5571.

RATES: The cost of your vacation will depend on where you stay. The Okemo Mountain Lodge has five-day midweek packages of $520 for a family with two adults. Children under 12 are free. Full-day lift tickets at the mountain are $28 on weekends and holidays, $19.50 for 12 and under; half-day $21 and $15. A five-day package is $98 and $67.50, respectively. Ski school is $16 for a class lesson, $30 for a private lesson; the day care center is free midweek and $12 for a full day on weekends and holidays.

## The Village at Smuggler's Notch
Smuggler's Notch, Vermont 05464
Telephone: 802-644-8851
General Manager: Robert Mulcahy

DESCRIPTION: "We're a secluded self-contained village tucked away in the mountains. . . . Everything is within walking distance and there's a sense of freedom and casualness among guests. . . . Everything we do is with the family vacation experience in mind. . . . Our programs and activities are set up to give parents worry-free time to relax . . . while giving their children a chance to make new friends, be challenged and have a lot of fun." One of the nice things about Smuggler's philosophy about children's programming is that parents can always join in on an activity and kids can come and go whenever they'd like.

All amenities at Smuggler's are within a short walking distance of each other—the hot tub, the pool, the restaurants, a pub, all accommodations, and the lifts are all right there. There are three mountains to choose from: Madonna for the advanced expert skier; Sterling for the intermediate, and Morse for beginners.

Cross-country skiing is available through 23 miles of trails winding through wilderness with a Sugarhouse at the end of the trail.

FOR KIDS: Kids 6 months to 6 years may stay in the Slopeside Day Care Center from 8:30 to 4:00 daily with lunch available. The center is licensed by the state of Vermont, and advance reservations are necessary. The cost is included in ski packages; lunch is $4 extra. Kids 3 to 6 may spend the whole day at Discovery Ski Camp. The day includes 2¾ hours of ski lessons with breaks for snacks, lunch with friends, and games, ice-skating, sleigh rides, movies, arts and crafts, and Cookie Monster races. The full day costs $32 (without lunch, $28), and a special five-day rate of $85 is available. Little Smuggler's Ski School provides daily lessons for 3- to 6-year-olds; groups are small. Each lesson is 1¾ hours long with a hot chocolate break. Five lessons are $70; free with some packages.

Team Smuggler's Ski School is the same as Little Smugglers but for kids 7 to 12. Team Smuggler's Ski Camp gives 7- to 12-year-olds an all-day program that includes two 1¾-hour lessons at 9:30 A.M. and again at 1:00 P.M., lunch with friends, volleyball, soccer, ice-skating, challenge racing, and racing technique instruction. The full day costs $33 with lunch, $90 for five days with special packages.

Young Adults Ski School is the place for people 13 on into the early twenties who want to ski a lot, talk a little, and do some racing. A teen center, with a DJ and dancing, serves nonalcoholic beverages après ski. Baby-sitting is easy to arrange for $2 to $3 per hour. Parents' Night Out gives parents a chance to be together while the kids eat with staff and enjoy some after-dinner entertainment. The cost is $10 but is included in some packages.

ACCOMMODATIONS: These range from efficiency apartments to luxury homes. All are slopeside. A typical condo has a fireplace, fully equipped kitchen, queen-size bed, fold-out sofa in the living room, and patio or balcony. Cribs are available for $8 per stay.

RATES: Smuggler's offers many inviting packages. Our favorite is the Family Fest, which runs nine weeks of the season (including Christmas) and provides accommodations, a five-day ski pass, ski school classes, tennis club membership, use of the spa and hot tub, hosted parties and free rental equipment for kids 12 and under, free teens' racing clinic, free discovery and team ski camp, free Parents' Night Out, and half-price nursery rates. Prices start at $885 for a family of four in a studio, $1,025 for a one-bedroom suite.

### Jackson Hole Ski Resort
P.O. Box 290
Teton Village, Wyoming 83025
Telephone: 307-733-2292 or 800-443-6931

DESCRIPTION: When you're not skiing on the 3,000 acres of varying terrain, you can take a snow coach tour into Yellowstone National Park or a sleigh ride through the nearby Elk Refuge.

FOR KIDS: Kindershule operates for kids 24 months to 14 years. (There are a few spaces for younger kids.) Hours are 8:30 A.M. to 4:30 P.M. from early December to early April. Reservations are required. Write to Kindershule, P.O. Box 269, Teton Village, Wyoming 83025. Kids 3–5 may take two one-hour lessons each day at the ski school. Kids 6–14 are offered the SKIwee: a full day is $20; a half, $14. Lunch can be arranged for kids from noon to 2:00 P.M. for an additional $12, if parents want to stay on the slopes. Lodges and property management offices have lists of baby-sitters. Expect to pay $1.50 to $4 per hour.

ACCOMMODATIONS: For details, call 800-443-6931. At the ski area there are condos and lodges, and not far are two full resorts, Americana Snow King and Jackson Hole Racquet Club. One particularly nice-sounding lodge is the Alpenhof, a small (40-room) hotel that is the closest to the ski lifts. It has lots of Alpine atmosphere, a restaurant, jacuzzi, game room, and baby-sitting service. A seven-night package, which includes lodging, five days of lift tickets, and one half-day ski lesson on Sunday morning, costs $395 for two adjoining rooms in the low season, $493 in high season. The phone number of the Lodge is 307-733-3242.

RATES: A one-day adult ticket is $26, for kids 14 and under, $13.

# 11

---

# FARMS AND DUDE RANCHES

Dude ranches and farms are among our favorite categories. Whether you choose a working farm where your kids can help milk the cows and feed the chickens or an elaborate resort where dude ranching is the theme, this type of vacation can be lots of fun.

Here we list 3 farm-type vacation spots and 23 ranches. We've emphasized the facilities for kids, something no other book does. But for the most complete listing of farm and ranch possibilities in the United States, we recommend Pat Dickerman's book *Farm, Ranch and Country Vacations*. Pat's been updating the book for 30 years, and the latest edition includes 200 recommended places. It is available in some bookstores or by mail from Adventure Guides, 36 East 57th Street, New York, New York 10022 for $10.95 plus $2 for first-class mail. Call Pat at 212-355-6331 for advice.

The farms we list here all invite you and your kids to participate in the life of the farm. If possible, choose a farm where the kids of the family are close to the age of your own kids, in other words, instant friends.

The ranches we list fall into three basic types: working cattle ranches that have been established for a long while and now take a few guests, guest ranches where riding is the main activity, and resorts with a dude ranch theme that offer lots of other activities besides riding. All farms and ranches included here welcome children.

Most of the ranches we list are located out West, but there are a few on the East Coast as well—not quite as authentic, perhaps, but still fun.

## FARMS

**Glacier Bay Country Inn**
Box 5
Gustavus, Alaska 99826
Telephone: 907-697-2288
Owners: Al and Annie Unrein

IN THEIR OWN WORDS: "Deep in the woods, down a narrow, winding road, you'll find the inn. Its log beam ceilings, dormer windows, large porches, cozy wood stove and private baths provide a comfortable, relaxed atmosphere. . . . Al and I and our children, Havila, six, and Casey, three, treat you as a welcome friend who has come to share our home. Ask Havila for a guided tour to the 'bear tree'—she'll point out all the local flora and fauna along the way."

DESCRIPTION: Hiking and cross-country skiing are nearby, at Glacier Bay National Park. Just three miles away is a beach, and the fishing area is well known for king salmon in May; Coho salmon in mid-July, August, and September; and halibut all summer long. Guests at the inn are welcome to participate in farm activities, hike through the dense rain forest, listen for ravens, or watch for the Northern Lights.

ACCOMMODATIONS: All rooms at the inn have beamed ceilings, gorgeous views, and private baths. Each room has a theme; for instance, the Seaside room has brass porthole mirrors, a fisherman's net draped on the wall, and seagull wallpaper.

RATES: Rates are per person and include three meals and transportation to and from the airport in Gustavus: $76 per day for adults, $45 per day for kids 3 to 12, and no charge for under 3.

There are two cribs available at no extra charge. Baby-sitting can be arranged with a day or two notice for $3 per hour.

### Berkson Farms
Route 108
Enosburg Falls, Vermont 05450
Telephone: 802-933-2522
Owner: Sid Berkson

IN THEIR OWN WORDS: "Make your life simple. Come spend time with us and feel yourself in touch with the best things in life—fresh air, Vermont pasture and mountain greenery, farm animals and farm life, along with country home cooking."

DESCRIPTION: This is a dairy farm, and guests are welcome to help milk the 200 head of "county-honored" dairy cows, to collect eggs from the hen house, plant the garden, or help bring in the hay. During spring, maple sugar season, guests can even carry buckets of sap and help boil it down to maple syrup. The farm is located on 600 acres; the farmhouse is 100 years old, and guests are welcome all year round.

FOR KIDS: There are a children's pool, a playground area, and a room full of games for indoor play. There are bicycles, running trails, and swimming nearby.

ACCOMMODATIONS: The farmhouse has eight bedrooms, each with its own Vermont view. There's room for 12 to 14 guests altogether. Two cribs and two high chairs are available.

RATES: A six-night, seven-day stay at the Berksons' costs $275 for adults, $175 for kids under 12.

### Rodgers Dairy Farm Vacation
R.F.D. 3, Box 57
West Glover, Vermont 05875
Telephone: 802-525-6677
Owners: Nancy and James Rodgers

IN THEIR OWN WORDS: "We have a quiet, peaceful atmosphere for families to vacation with their children. We have five guest rooms in our home. Our guests live with us; we eat together as a family. . . ."

DESCRIPTION: The Rodgers' farm, operated since the early 1800s by Jim's family, is a working dairy farm with lots of open space. It has a swing set, sandbox, ponies to ride, and lots of cats, kittens, cows, and calves. Kids play in the hay barn, learn how to milk a cow, or go to the lake four miles away.

ACCOMMODATIONS: Five guest rooms have twin or double beds, and there's a crib available. The rooms are large, with homemade quilts on the bed. There's an enclosed porch for relaxing, and the large kitchen-dining area is where Nancy serves the meals.

RATES: Rates are per person so a family of four may take either two or three rooms; the choice is theirs. The rate per person is $175 per week, $100 for children under 12; daily it's $35 and $20. All rates include three meals.

## RANCHES

### Rancho de los Caballeros
P.O. Box 1148
Wickenburg, Arizona 85358
Telephone: 602-684-5484
Manager: Dallas C. Gant, Jr.

IN THEIR OWN WORDS: "Rancho de los Caballeros is an elegant, working ranch/guest resort set amid 20,000 acres of rolling hillsides and flowering Arizona desert."

DESCRIPTION: There are lots of things to do—swimming in an outdoor pool, tennis, trap and skeet shooting, golf, horseback riding, and at night square dances, movies, cards, and billiards.

FOR KIDS: From October to May, children 5 to 12 have an organized program run by counselors. The program begins at 8:00 A.M., when the counselor meets the kids for breakfast; the morning is spent riding and on nature walks. Afternoons are spent with parents until 6:00 P.M., when the counselor meets them again for dinner and after-dinner games until 9:00 P.M. Counselors are with the kids for all meals. The littlest kids can ring ride in the corral and play in the playground at any time during the day. Baby-sitting is available for $3 per hour. Instructions in horseback riding are available for $18 per ride, tennis and golf at $24 per hour.

ACCOMMODATIONS: Suites have one or two bedrooms, and some have kitchenettes. Cribs are available for $5 per night.

RATES: The basic per person adult rate in high season (February to May) is $87 to $103 per night for double occupancy. Connecting living rooms are extra. Ask for children's rates. Rates include meals, accommodations, and use of some, but not all, ranch facilities.

### Scott Valley Ranch
Route 2, Box 270
Mountain Home, Arkansas 72653
Telephone: 501-425-5136
Owners: Tom and Kathleen Cooper

IN THEIR OWN WORDS: "Here we really work at getting parent and child together. Games—either active or board games—are great. . . . We try to set up an atmosphere where parent and child can relate to each other. . . . Our guests become our friends and we place a high value on friendship. . . . Arkansas is one of the best kept secrets and hidden treasures in this country."

DESCRIPTION: In the midst of the Ozarks, the ranch is set among 214 acres of meadows, streams, and woodlands. There are six different trail rides offered each day (37 horses to choose from), a heated pool with a lifeguard on duty, tennis, volleyball, softball, baseball, badminton, and nature trails. At night expect cookouts and hayrides. There's world-class fishing on the White and Norfolk rivers (a box lunch and boat rental are available as an extra), and guided fishing trips and canoe adventures can also be arranged.

FOR KIDS: The Coopers are adamant—they don't believe in children's programs that separate kids and parents—"Granted our parents love the idea that the kids can and do go on supervised trail rides and they don't have to go every time, but that's not the intent and purpose of the vacation. Yes, they love to be able to have someone watch their toddler for a few hours while they canoe, go shopping or just lie in the sun, but that isn't the main point of the trip!" The Coopers go on: "Parents and children don't need more time apart; they need more time together learning how to interact. We do help with that." So the emphasis is clearly on togetherness, with lots of activities of interest to both parents and their kids. For the occasional adult trip, baby-sitters are available for $3.50 per hour with a five-hour minimum. All meals are family-style.

ACCOMMODATIONS: The facilities are motellike: 16 of the 28 units have two bedrooms and sleep up to six people. Each has a private bathroom and daily maid service, and all are on the ground floor.

RATES: Weekly rates are $300 for an adult, $228 for kids, 8 to 13; $147, 4 to 7; and free for kids under 4. Any family or group of four or more who come together are entitled to a 10 percent discount. Rates include all activities at the ranch, meals, and lodging. A one-day fishing trip with a guide on the Norfolk/White River is approximately $90.

### Coffee Creek Guest Ranch
Star Route 2, Box 4940
Trinity Center, California 96091
Telephone: 916-266-3343
Managers: Mark and Ruth Hartman

IN THEIR OWN WORDS: "The whole atmosphere is like a camp for families."

DESCRIPTION: Set in a canyon surrounded by wilderness, high peaks with lots of conifers, and Coffee Creek flowing right through it, the ranch hosts a maximum of 50 guests per week, keeping the staff to guest ratio at one to three. Horseback riding, swimming in the heated pool or a dip in Coffee Creek, gold panning, horseshoes, volleyball, hiking, and square dancing are all offered.

FOR KIDS: From Sunday through Thursday, from 8:00 A.M. to 5:00 P.M. there's a supervised program for kids 3 to 9 called Kiddie Korral. Mornings involve a nature hike and crafts, and the afternoon is passed in riding and swimming. Horseback riding lessons are available at $7.50 per lesson.

ACCOMMODATIONS: Cabins have one or two bedrooms. Some have fireplaces; all have full baths.

RATES: During the summer, the adult weekly rate for a two-bedroom cabin plus three meals and ranch activities is $335, for 13 to 17 it's $315, and for kids 2 to 12 it's $215; kids 2 and under stay free, but cribs must be rented for $10 per stay.

**Wilderness Trails Ranch**
23486 County Road 501
Bayfield, Colorado 81122
Telephone: 303-247-0722
Owners: Gene and Jan Roberts

IN THEIR OWN WORDS: "Parents rave about our wonderful children's and teen programs because the kids love it, and the parents don't have to worry about entertaining their children. The kids are never bored and are always ready for bed with no hassles! Many tears are shed at the end of a week's stay because they've had such a marvelous time."

DESCRIPTION: Located in the heart of the San Juan National Forest of southwestern Colorado, this is Colorado's last frontier. Riding, hiking, fishing at the ranch's private stocked pond or at Vallecito Lake (two miles from the ranch), waterskiing, wind surfing, relaxing in the spa, rafting down the Animas River, and playing volleyball are all favorites. Evenings may include a magic show, a square dance, or an old-fashioned hayride.

FOR KIDS: Children ages 6 to 12 participate in the riding program, with lessons all week long. They also have crafts, hikes, picnics, games, a hayride and a Frontier Day, which includes archery and Indian lore. The younger children ages 2 to 5 have pony rides each morning and afternoon and spend the rest of the time with their counselors in the tree house, on the swings, hiking, picnicking, or just playing outdoors. Although there's no specific programming for children under 2, staff members are usually available to baby-sit, during the afternoon or evening. Kids 6 to 12 usually eat lunch and dinner one hour before the teens and adults, but families may eat together if they prefer. Teenagers have their own counselors and go off on all-day rides and hikes with them. They picnic together, play volleyball, and have hot tub parties.

ACCOMMODATIONS: Families stay in log cabins with two, three, four, and five bedrooms, nestled among the pines, spruce, and aspens. Cribs are free.

RATES: The Sunday-to-Sunday package for adults is $545; for kids 12 to 17, $480; for kids 6 to 11, $450; for kids 4 to 5, $360; and 2 to 3, $310. Children under 2 are free. Rates include accommodations, all meals, daily maid service, children's program, horses, waterskiing, hayrides, and other ranch activities. The river raft trip is extra.

### Colorado Trails Ranch
P.O. Box 848
Durango, Colorado 81302
Telephone: 303-247-5055
Owner: Richard Elder

IN THEIR OWN WORDS: "A vacation at Colorado Trails Ranch is darn good therapy for anyone whether you are a family, a couple or traveling alone. . . . Remember, our job is seeing to it that you forget your job."

DESCRIPTION: Riding in groups of six, lessons for beginners and the more advanced, tennis on two courts (you can use their rackets), whirlpool spa, swimming in a heated pool, fishing on a lake 12 miles from the ranch, hiking, climbing, and photography are all possible during the day. River rafting on the Animas River can be arranged with a local outfitter, and an excursion to Mesa Verde National Park with a guide is easy to plan if you want to leave the ranch for a while.

FOR KIDS: The children are divided into three age groups—5 to 9, 9 to 13, and 13 to 18 years. The program runs from June 7 to August 30, and each age group has its own counselor. The kids do lots of riding; they swim and learn archery, riflery, and waterskiing. The program is flexible. The kids get a chance to schedule activities. Kids may eat with their parents or their new friends. Children under 5 are the responsibility of their parents, but arrangements can be made in advance for one-to-one baby-sitting.

ACCOMMODATIONS: There are two basic styles of cabins— Alpine cabins have full-size beds, and X-wing cabins have queen-size beds and full baths. Most have two separate sleeping rooms.

RATES: Rates vary according to the cabin chosen, but a sample would be two adults, two children in two rooms of the Alpine cabin for $2,275 per week. The rates include lodging, meals, horses, tennis, waterskiing, and all other ranch facilities. The only "extras" are the Mesa Verde trip ($20) and the overnight ($20 with their sleeping bag, $15 with your own).

## C Lazy U Ranch
P.O. Box 378
Granby, Colorado 80446
Telephone: 303-887-3344
Owners: George and Virginia Mullin

IN THEIR OWN WORDS: "We are the highest rated guest ranch in the country with the Mobil 5 Star and AAA 5 diamond ratings."

DESCRIPTION: This is ranching complete with wall-to-wall carpeting, high in the Colorado Rockies. Open all year, it's both a summer and a winter resort. In summer it offers fishing, skeet shooting, horseback riding, a sauna, whirlpool, racquetball, tennis, hiking, and hayrides; in winter, there are cross-country skiing, sleigh rides, ice-skating, snowshoeing, and holiday celebrations. Colorado River rafting trips, golf at a nearby course, boating, and wind surfing can also be arranged.

FOR KIDS: From mid-June to Labor Day and again during winter vacation time through New Year's, there's a full-day children's program for kids 3 to 17. Supervised by counselors, kids learn to ride and fish and appreciate western life. Teenagers 13 to 17 have their own program, which emphasizes riding (morning and afternoon rides), sports, hayrides, cookouts, and games. Everyone has breakfast together, and after breakfast counselors meet with the kids for a full day of activities. Lunches and dinners are eaten with the counselors; after dinner the kids join their parents for the evening entertainment—square dances, swing dances, or staff shows.

ACCOMMODATIONS: You have a choice of one- to three-room units, all with private bath, some with fireplaces. At the center of life at the ranch is the Main Lodge, which includes the dining room, bar, card room, and lounge.

RATES: In summer, weekly rates are $780 to $975 for two; children under 6 pay half-price but do not take trail rides. Winter rates range from $100 to $190 per day per person for two, kids 6 to 12 receive a 10 percent discount, and those 3 to 5 are half-price. From December 19 to January 14 there's a three-night minimum. There is a 10 percent discount all winter long for a stay of seven nights or more.

**Drowsy Water Guest Ranch**
P.O. Box 147
Granby, Colorado 80446
Telephone: 303-725-3456
Owners: Ken and Randy Sue Fosha

IN THEIR OWN WORDS: "A visit here in our secluded mountain home at Drowsy Water Ranch is a blend of our clean, rustic cabin and lodge accommodations, superb, homemade country-style food and our entertaining and friendly staff."

DESCRIPTION: The ranch borders thousands of acres of backcountry and the Arapahoe National Forest. Trail rides led by wranglers are available every weekday, and for nonriding times there are swimming, horseshoes, jeep trips, pack trips, and trout fishing. Nighttime activities are just what you'd expect at a ranch: square dancing, song fests, campfires, movies, and rodeos.

FOR KIDS: The littlest ones, under 5, spend time with counselors, riding horses, playing games, hiking, fishing, swimming, and doing crafts. Kids over 5 participate in the riding program: they get a horse of their own for the week, and after riding they swim, hike, learn to use a lasso, take archery lessons, and explore nature. Kids can be involved in supervised programming from 9:15 in the morning until 8:00 at night. The children's program runs from June 8 to September 14. Children may eat with or without their parents.

ACCOMMODATIONS: Cabins with one to five rooms are available to families. All are rustic but comfortable, sheltered by stands of aspen and pine and situated along the creek and ranch ponds.

RATES: For one week, a mother, father, or first two family members are $510 per person; all other family members are $460. Kids 5 or under are $290, and any nonriders among you can deduct $85. Rates include all meals, a horse for the week, the children's program, and all ranch activities except an overnight pack trip, a River Float trip, and golf.

**Lake Mancos Ranch**
42688 CR-N
Mancos, Colorado 81328
Telephone: 303-533-7900
Owners: Kathy and Lloyd Sehnert

IN THEIR OWN WORDS: "A guest ranch vacation is a unique family vacation. . . . Children have planned activities but still share experiences with parents. The atmosphere is casual and very friendly due to limited capacity. . . . Our ranch is really just an extension of our home. . . . We are right in the middle of cowboy country where cattle are worked with horses, the branding is still done out in the open and chaps and boots get plenty of hard use. . . ."

DESCRIPTION: Riding is available to everyone, as are swimming in an outdoor heated pool, a dip in the hot tub, jeeping into the high country with guides, and evening cookouts. Not far from the ranch are three golf courses, and fishing trips to nearby lakes and streams can be arranged easily. The ranch adjoins the San Juan National Forest. Easy side trips are to Mesa Verde National Park and its cliff dwellings or a ride on the Narrow Gauge Railroad from Durango to Silverton.

FOR KIDS: From June 7 to August 23 there's a program of activities for kids age 6 to 16 that includes lots of supervised horseback riding. The program is flexible, planned according to the participant's own interests. Kids can have dinner with their parents or with a counselor and the friends they've made at the ranch. It's possible to arrange to have a baby-sitter come in from town in order to entertain the little ones while you go out for a trail ride.

ACCOMMODATIONS: Family cabins have at least two bedrooms, two bathrooms, and a covered porch. For large families there are a few three-bedroom cabins. Cribs are available at no extra charge.

RATES: Rates include meals, accommodations, and all facilities. They are $550 per week for adults, $500 for 13 to 18, $457 for 9 to 12, and $410 for 8 and under.

**Bar Lazy J Guest Ranch**
477 County Road 3
Parshall, Colorado 80468
Telephone: 303-725-3437
Owners: Chuck and Phyl Brady

IN THEIR OWN WORDS: "Our ranch is relaxed and unstructured except for meal time and riding time. We want the entire family to have freedom and choice. This is every guest's vacation—from 2 to 80. Having reared three boys on the ranch we feel we have an outstanding children's program."

DESCRIPTION: Bar Lazy J is settled in a peaceful valley of the Colorado River. There's room for 38 guests at a time. Horse rides leave the ranch twice a day every day except Wednesdays. Instruction is available. The Colorado River flows through the ranch for "doorstep fishing," and right by the ranch is a 40-foot pool with a children's pool attached. Not too far away you can arrange a river rafting trip, or you can play tennis just five miles away at Hot Sulphur Springs. Every Saturday there's a rodeo, and for golfers there's an 18-hole course about one-half hour from the ranch.

FOR KIDS: The children's program here is for kids 2 and over and operates from mid-June to Labor Day. Local baby-sitters are available to take care of kids under 2. Just let the staff know you'd like one. The program is deliberately flexible and meant to suit the interests of each kid involved. After a family breakfast, a counselor checks with each child to see how much time he or she wants to spend with the counselor that day. The kids can have lunch and dinner in their own dining rooms if they'd like, and counselors are available from 8:30 A.M. to 7:30 P.M., for example, until after the nightly hayride. With their own counselors, kids ride, swim, fish, and hike, and if they're interested crafts and square dancing are scheduled. Each year there are some new lambs and calves that need to be fed. Usually the kids and their counselors are in charge.

ACCOMMODATIONS: Guest cottages accommodate from 2 to 8 people. They're situated along the Colorado River and all have a screened-in porch. Cribs are available at no extra charge.

RATES: Adults (that's anyone 9 or over) pay $495 for a week; children 5 to 8, $395; 2 to 4, $295; and under 2, $70. Rates include accommodations, meals, maid service, the counselor program, and all recreational facilities.

**Lost Valley Ranch**
Route 2
Sedalia, Colorado 80135
Telephone: 303-647-2311
Owner: Robert Foster

IN THEIR OWN WORDS: "Lost Valley is an authentic year-round working horse/cattle ranch situated in a beautiful valley on 40,000 acres of the Colorado Pike National Forest . . . our aim is to give the entire family a memorable vacation . . . 90 percent of our clientele are either returning guests or referred by a former guest. To understand you must come and experience the atmosphere that is created by the beauty of the mountains, the service attitude of our staff and the friendships formed with other families."

DESCRIPTION: Lost Valley is a working ranch, homesteaded in 1883. The owners, who say that most of today's young people have learned what they know about ranching from the TV show "Dallas," invite you to come and see the real thing in Louis L'Amour County. Riding is the main event with miles of scenic trails available; guests can help with the roundup or branding or plan an overnight pack trip into the hills. There are a heated pool, tennis courts and trap shooting, volleyball, and horseshoes. Trout fishing is great, and the chef will custom-cook a catch. Nighttime activities are typically ranchlike: barbecues, square dancing, and hootenannies.

FOR KIDS: From May 24 to September 1 and again from December 20 to January 4 Lost Valley offers a program for 6- to 12-year-olds and for teenagers. Three- to five-year-olds have a program available all year long; the littlest ones may have a baby-sitter for $2.50 per hour. Teenagers ride along with three college student staff members and are encouraged to do "their own thing" while the kids 6 to 12 have a more structured program, which includes riding, swimming, hikes, and picnics. Children may eat with or without their parents; some nights there are special meals just for kids. On Saturdays there are special family rides. Children 3 to 5 have group baby-sitting while adults are off on morning and afternoon rides. Parents can take their 3- to 5-year-olds on a horseback ride, but counselors won't.

ACCOMMODATIONS: Cabins have from one to three bedrooms. All have a living room, fireplace, and one or two baths. Cribs are available at no extra charge.

RATES: The basic adult rate is approximately $700; children 3 to 5, $400; 6 to 12, $579; and teens, $672; kids under 2 are free. Rates include meals, lodging, entertainment, all facilities, horseback riding, fishing, tennis, swimming, the children's program— everything except trap shooting and pack trips. Winter rates are lower.

### Flathead Lake Lodge
Box 248
Big Fork, Montana 59911
Telephone: 406-837-4391
Owner: Doug Averill

IN THEIR OWN WORDS: "Our clientele is entirely families— we have between 30 and 40 children each week."

DESCRIPTION: The Averills established the ranch in 1945 on the shores of the largest natural lake west of the Great Lakes, in the Rocky Mountains, just south of Glacier National Park. Horseback riding is the star attraction—trail rides along the mountain terrain, evening rodeos, breakfast rides, and cookouts over open fires. Guests can also sail, whitewater raft, fish, water ski, canoe, or swim in either the lake or a heated pool.

FOR KIDS: From mid-June to mid-September, the ranch has a children's program that operates from 7:00 A.M. all the way until 10:00 P.M. Kids 3 years and up can participate. The ranch offers horseback riding, of course, arts and crafts, swimming and boating, campfires at night, waterskiing for the older kids, tennis, inner tubing on the river. Lessons in sailing, waterskiing, horseback riding, tennis, and fishing are all available. Each week there's a guest rodeo and a special overnight campout in teepees. The kids' activities involve one wrangler (counselor) to every three children—good odds.

ACCOMMODATIONS: For families, there are rustic two- to three-bedroom cottages with room for four to seven people. There are "plenty" of cribs at no extra cost. Meals are eaten at the lodges, and outdoor barbecues of buffalo, roast pig, and fresh salmon are held on a patio overlooking the lake.

RATES: A seven-day package that runs from Sunday to Sunday costs $793 for an adult, $651 for teens, $539 for kids 4 to 12, and $96 for kids under 4. Included are meals, horseback riding, water sports, use of boats, waterskiing, tennis, volleyball, and lots of other ranch activities.

### Mountain Sky Guest Ranch
P.O. Box 1128
Bozeman, Montana 59715
Telephone: 406-587-1244 or 800-548-3392
Manager: Alan Brutger

IN THEIR OWN WORDS: "We're the perfect setting for a Western vacation—Swiss like peaks of the Absarokee-Beartooth Mountain Range, the Yellowstone River flowing through wide-open Paradise Valley, the Gallatin National Forest in our backyard and famous Yellowstone National Park only 30 minutes away."

DESCRIPTION: There are hundreds of miles of horseback riding trails surrounding the ranch. Everyone gets his own horse for the duration of his stay, and lessons for beginners are available. Big Creek, which flows through the ranch, is excellent for trout fishing, and there are also tennis, a heated swiming pool, hiking trails, a volleyball court, a hot tub, and a sauna. Kids have their own playground, game room, and private trout pond.

FOR KIDS: From June 1 to October 15, kids from 3 to 12 may participate in a full day of activities planned just for them. Breakfast and lunch are eaten with the family. Kids may eat in a supervised setting at dinnertime with other kids, allowing their parents to dine alone. The kids who are 3 to 5 years go on horseback rides with their counselor, do arts and crafts, and play in the playground. After lunch with their parents they go on another ride, swim, and fish. From 4:30 to 5:30 they get together with their parents, and from 5:30 to 8:00 they join their counselors for dinner and an after-dinner treat such as a cookout, a movie, or square dancing. Teens have a similar schedule but with kids their own age and at a different pace and level. The littlest ones, under 3, may have a baby-sitter; it's best to discuss individual needs for this age group with the staff.

ACCOMMODATIONS: A typical cabin at Mountain Sky has two rooms—a back bedroom and a front room with a hide-a-bed. Three- and four-bedroom cabins are also available.

RATES: The weekly package includes lodging, meals, a horse, and all ranch activities. In summers it's $825 per adult, double occupancy; $725 for kids 7 to 12; and $460 for those 6 and under.

### Shady Tree Ranch
Box 479
Livingston, Montana 59047
Telephone: 406-222-0570
Owner: Virginia Christensen

IN THEIR OWN WORDS: "We are in one of the world's most beautiful locations and we offer an ideal family vacation where families can spend a lot or very little time together. The parents don't have to worry about their children; the kids have a great time just experiencing regular ranch life. . . . Lasting friendships between families are formed here."

DESCRIPTION: This is a working ranch in Mission Creek Canyon, where guests join in on roundups and branding. Horseback riding lessons are available, and riding is the main event. Trout fishing in one of the nearby streams and excursions to nearby Yellowstone are popular with guests.

FOR KIDS: There's no formal kids' program, but baby-sitting can be arranged for $2 per hour.

ACCOMMODATIONS: There are two-, three-, and four-room cabins, some with two baths, tucked in among the aspen and pine.

RATES: A three-room cabin large enough for five costs $410 per person per week, including accommodations, meals, use of a saddle horse, riding instruction, and access to all ranch facilities. Pack trips are $45 per day extra.

### Rocking Horse Ranch
Highland, New York 12528
Telephone: 914-691-2927 or 800-437-2624
Owner: Billy Turk and his family

IN THEIR OWN WORDS: "Excellent for families . . . endless activity with supervision and instruction. Parents are pampered, too. . . . You arrive as a guest and become a friend."

DESCRIPTION: The long list includes horseback riding, waterskiing, fishing, swimming in an outdoor and an indoor pool, miniature golf, archery, tennis courts, saunas, ice-skating, sleigh rides, volleyball, a fitness gym, and on and on. Instructions in tennis, swimming, waterskiing, and horseback riding are all offered at no extra charge. At night, there's entertainment in the Round-Up Room Nightclub. Throughout the year there are special theme weekends—a "Who Dunnit" weekend, a "Festivale de Columbus," and so on.

FOR KIDS: A day camp for kids operates all summer and at holiday time. Kids from 6 to 14 are welcome to participate from 9:00 A.M. to 4:30 P.M., and in the course of the stay they can learn to ski, waterski, and horseback ride. Children can eat lunch and dinner with their parents or with their counselors. The choice is theirs.

ACCOMMODATIONS: Facilities are motellike, and many rooms are large enough for a family of six. Cribs are available at no extra charge.

RATES: Rates vary with season but as a sample: a weekend (three days, two nights) in the fall costs $155 to $210 for adults and $95 for kids under 16 staying in the same room. Included are all meals, riding, and all other ranch facilities.

**Pinegrove Resort Ranch**
Lower Cherrytown Road
Kerhonkson, New York 12446
Telephone: 914-626-7345
Owners: Dick and Deborah Tarantino

IN THEIR OWN WORDS: "Pinegrove is a small, family-owned resort specializing in warm hospitality and individual attention. People who came to Pinegrove as children with their families are now bringing their spouses and children to Pinegrove. We do a 90 percent repeat business and our guests return as friends. They have favorite horses, favorite waiters, meet and become friends with other guests and end up booking with them for next year. . . ."

DESCRIPTION: Pinegrove breeds its own purebred and half-bred registered Arabian saddle horses. Horses are trained in Western and English and carry guests over acres of picturesque mountain trails. Other activities include tennis, an indoor/outdoor pool, a rifle range, archery, minigolf, bocce, sauna, volleyball, a game room, a stocked lake for fishing, skiing in winter, boating, and hiking.

FOR KIDS: Pinegrove has a children's day camp, with a director and a staff of counselors, available to kids from 2 to 16. The littlest kids (2 to 3) spend time in the playground, at the animal petting farm, on hayrides, at storytime, and playing games. The 3- to 5-year-olds have a similar program, but they also have pony rides and an afternoon swim. For the 6- to 12-year-olds there are arts and crafts, minigolf, scavenger hunts, nature hikes, horseback riding, hayrides, swimming, and "Shirley Temple" parties. Teenagers play paddleball, volleyball, basketball, and softball; ride the trails; have disco and make-your-own-sundae parties; and so forth. Kids can eat with their family or their new friends. Baby-sitting for $3 per hour can be arranged for kids under 2 years old.

ACCOMMODATIONS: Some rooms are located in a two-level, motellike building. They have two double beds, private bath, and carpeting and are heated and air-conditioned. Others are in villas—with one, two, or three bedrooms; kitchen, and sitting rooms. Some have fireplaces. Cribs are free.

RATES: A week's stay for an adult ranges from $435 to $550 in the motel facilities; the villas range from $560 to $590. Kids 5 to 16 in a room with adults are $220, and kids under 5 stay free. Single parent's discounts are available as well. All facilities and meals at the ranch are included in the price.

### Rock Springs Ranch
64201 Tyler Road
Bend, Oregon 97701
Telephone: 503-382-1957
Owner: Donna Gill

IN THEIR OWN WORDS: "Special feelings at the ranch emanate from how easy it is to relax and have a good time. This is attributed to the setting, seclusion, quality of staff, and our extensive youth program in the summer."

DESCRIPTION: Rock Springs is about ten miles from Bend, adjoining the Deschutes National Forest. Days can be filled with horseback riding, swimming, tennis, or volleyball. If you're feeling lazy, just stroll through the woods, lie in the sun, or sit by the fire and read.

FOR KIDS: Rock Springs has a children's program that operates seven days a week from the end of June to after Labor Day. It operates from 9:00 A.M. to 1:00 P.M. and again from 5:00 P.M. to 9:00 p.m. and is available to kids 5 to 12. At the beginning of each day, the kids meet in the playroom to plan their day with their own counselors and wranglers. Horseback riding is most popular, but anyone who'd rather not ride can swim, try arts and crafts, or go on a nature hike. At night, there are hayrides, talent shows, dinner hikes, and lawn games. For teens, there are adventure trips and hayrides. Individual baby-sitting can be arranged for kids too young for the organized program, but to encourage parents to bring their own sitters, the ranch offers free accommodations and meals for the sitter in the family cabin (often on a roll-away bed).

ACCOMMODATIONS: Cabins are carpeted, sleep two to eight people, and generally include kitchens and fireplaces.

RATES: A week-long package including lodging, daily maid service, three meals, the horseback riding program (guided trail rides, luncheon rides, a weekly skills clinic, and corral rides), tennis and volleyball, outdoor spa, game room, and children's program costs $1,876 for a family of four during June and July and $2,046 from mid-July to September.

### Mayan Dude Ranch
P.O. Box 577
Bandera, Texas 78003
Telephone: 512-796-3312
Owners: Don and Judy Hicks

IN THEIR OWN WORDS: "My parents, Don and Judy, have owned the Mayan Ranch for 35 years and have been very successful running it with their 13 children. We are very family-oriented and feel we can nicely accommodate not only children's needs and wants but teenagers' and parents', too. Throughout the summer months, we have something planned every hour of the day for everyone."

DESCRIPTION: The ranch is situated in Texas hill country, and every day you can expect a morning and afternoon ride into the hills. There are a swimming pool and tennis courts, and golf is about two miles away at a neighboring guest ranch for nonriding hours. When there's been enough rain, you can float down the Medina River in an inner tube. When the sun goes down, there are barbecues, steak fries, mariachi bands, square dancing, and more.

FOR KIDS: All summer long, on Thanksgiving weekend and from December 21 to January 1, the staff at Mayan organize a children's program for kids 2 and over. The kids may eat with their families or, if they prefer, with their groups and supervising staff. Some of the activities planned for the kids are swimming parties, hayrides, horseback rides, coloring contests, and watermelon hunts.

ACCOMMODATIONS: There are two choices: "Western native rock cottages" with one, two, three, or four bedrooms or motel-type accommodations with two adjoining rooms, with a king-size bed in one and two double beds in the other.

RATES: The rate per day is $70 for adults, kids 13 to 17, $35; 2 to 12, $30; and, if you take your own crib, kids under 2 are free. (If you have to rent a crib, it's $30 per day!)

### Paradise Guest Ranch
P.O. Box 790
Buffalo, Wyoming 82834
Telephone: 307-684-7876 or 5252
Owners: Jim and Leah Anderson

IN THEIR OWN WORDS: "Our guests . . . say it is the best family vacation they have ever had. Many of our activities are geared so that the families can participate together—such as our talent night—or separately—such as our kids' overnight, when the kids go while the parents stay at the ranch for a gourmet dinner and an evening to themselves. . . . They feel like they are part of our family when they visit."

DESCRIPTION: The ranch is situated in a secluded valley in the Big Horn National Forest, along the edge of a forest of lodgepole pine and aspen and surrounded by over a million acres of national forest lands. Horses and horseback riding are the focus of a stay at Paradise. The staff matches horses and guests, and a horse becomes yours for the length of your stay. You can arrange anything from an hour-long ride to an all-day ride with a lunch packed on a mule and cooked along the trail. Lessons are available, and many guests like to take their horses to nearby mountain lakes to go fishing. A wrangler is always available to go with you. There's fishing galore (they even supply you with bait), as well as a whirlpool spa, volleyball, badminton, and, of course, horseshoes; and for rainy days, there's an indoor game room. The people at Paradise will also arrange a four-day guided trip into a base camp at Frying Pan Lake. Some guests like to combine the pack trip with a stay at the ranch. Ask for details.

FOR KIDS: The children's activities are unstructured and cater to individual needs. For the youngest, baby-sitting can be arranged, or they may want to play in the Kiddies' Corral, which includes swings, a sandbox, playhouse, and crafts. For the 3- to 5-year-olds there are crafts and games and rides on kids' ponies. They're supervised in the pool and spend time in the Kiddies' Corral. As soon as the kids are old enough—usually 6 years and up (but they are flexible)—their time is centered around horses and trail rides. One night a week is "Kid's Night Out," a camping overnight much enjoyed by all. Teens do lots of riding and fishing and socializing with the crew, some of whom are teenagers themselves. A special counselor with a degree in early childhood education coordinates activities for kids under 6, and several weeks are set aside each year to cater to families with young children. At night families get together for a variety of activities: a sing-along around a bonfire, a slide show about the area and the ranch, a barbecue on a hill overlooking the ranch; talent night featuring guests and the crew, too; a chuck wagon dinner in Bald Eagle Park; and a steak fry and a square dance. Every Saturday there's a rodeo for kids and adults, and that same night awards are given to all children who participate.

ACCOMMODATIONS: Guests stay in deluxe log cabins, all recently renovated, built into the hillside overlooking the valley. All cabins have full baths, a separate living room, a fireplace (all ready for lighting), and spacious porches. Three cribs are available, and all cabins have kitchens. Cabins range in size from one to three bedrooms. Housekeeping services are provided.

RATES: Rates include lodging, three meals, and all regular

weekly activities. They're based on a Sunday-to-Sunday stay and cost from $575 to $675 for adults, $475 to $525 for children 6 to 12. Because most children under 6 don't participate in the regular riding program, a $190 rate is charged, and baby-sitting and activities for this age group are provided while the older kids and adults are riding. The four-day pack trip costs $100 per person for four or more people and includes tack, horse, sleeping bags, cots, food, and the services of a cook.

### Castle Rock Centre for Family Adventures
412 Country Road 6N5
Cody, Wyoming 82414
Telephone: 307-587-2076
Owner: Nelson Wieters

IN THEIR OWN WORDS: "Castle Rock is an unusual 'guest-ranch' in that it provides a wide range of adventure activities for families, all with the theme of environmental awareness and challenge-achievement. The program is especially designed so that all family members are on common ground—they all approach a variety of new experiences on an equal basis."

DESCRIPTION: Activities include llama treks, horseback trips, whitewater rafting, backpacking, fishing, rodeos, ranch chores, arts and crafts with artists-in-residence, photography safaris, exploration of Yellowstone National Park, square dancing, and mule-team trips. Families, assisted by staff, choose and plan their own program.

FOR KIDS: Kids 8 years and over participate fully in the activities planned; staff encourage parents to take an "attendant" for younger kids, and a counselor will be available to help the attendant plan activities.

ACCOMMODATIONS: Families stay in housekeeping cabins with two bedrooms, kitchen, and private bath. Cribs are available at no extra charge.

RATES: Sessions, scheduled to coincide with the time just before or just after the kids go to summer camps, are $600 to $750 per person per week.

### Rimrock Dude Ranch
2728 North Fork Route
Cody, Wyoming 82414
Telephone: 307-587-3970
Owners: Glenn and Alice Fales

IN THEIR OWN WORDS: "There are no 'musts!' Rimrock is a place where everyone does what he pleases. . . . We offer a wonderful family vacation."

DESCRIPTION: Horses are assigned to suit the guests' experience. Anyone who has never ridden before is taught Western-style riding. Offered are fishing in the north fork of the Shoshone River, swimming in the river or at De Maris Hot Springs, and hiking, at night there are square dancing, games, parties, and rodeos. Rimrock also offers wilderness pack trips of varying lengths during the summer.

ACCOMMODATIONS: Guests stay in cabins with private baths. Some have stone fireplaces, and all are heated. Cribs are available at no extra cost.

RATES: Rates per person for a one-week stay are $64 per day per person for four people, including meals and all ranch activities. Pack trips are $95 per person per day for a group of four or more.

### Bitterroot Ranch
Dubois, Wyoming 82513
Telephone: 307-455-2778 or 800-545-0019
Owners: Bayard and Mel Fox

IN THEIR OWN WORDS: "We have a 7-year-old boy ourselves and there are two girls aged 7 and 10 who live here. Visiting children are drawn into the life at the ranch. . . ."

DESCRIPTION: This is a working ranch where riding is the main focus.

FOR KIDS: There's no organized children's program, but there are ponies for the children to ride, and the older ones go off on supervised rides. There are a number of other resident animals—lambs, angora rabbits, ducks, and geese, and a stocked trout pond where kids can learn to fish. A baby-sitter is available every afternoon, so that parents can go off on a ride by themselves.

ACCOMMODATIONS: Log cabins have one, two, or three bedrooms and are heated.

RATES: Adults pay $100 per day, which includes accommodations, riding, and all meals; kids 4 to 16 pay 25 percent less; and those 3 years and under pay $20.

### Crossed Sabres Dude Ranch
Wapiti, Wyoming 82450
Telephone: 307-587-3750
Owners: Fred and Alvie Norris

IN THEIR OWN WORDS: "The mountains here and the tall, tall pines combine to make up what is considered to be some of the most beautiful country in all of the world. . . ."

DESCRIPTION: The ranch is located just nine miles east of Yellowstone in the Shoshone National Forest. A week at Crossed Sabres includes lots of riding: scenic rides, picnic rides, short rides, long rides, and even an overnight pack trip. In between the riding, the ranch offers fishing, usually a day trip to Yellowstone, a day in historic Cody with a visit to a rodeo, a raft trip on the Shoshone River, cookouts, square dancing, and more.

FOR KIDS: There's no special kids' program; they go along with the grown-ups.

ACCOMMODATIONS: The two-room cabins are rustic but modern, and all are heated.

RATES: Weekly rates for adults are $495; kids 8 to 17, $445, 4 to 7, $395; and 3 and under free. Rates include accommodations, meals, your own horse and tack, cowboy guides, an overnight pack trip, a rodeo trip and visit to Cody and Yellowstone, and transfer to and from the Cody Airport.

# 12

---

# CAMPING AND CABINS

Camping can range from rustic—sleeping bags under lean-tos along the Appalachian Trail—to luxury—queen-size beds in a sleek recreational vehicle (RV) parked at a spot complete with electricity and hot and cold running water. The kind of camping you choose will depend on you and your family, but whatever style you choose, don't embark on a two-week-long camping vacation until you've tried it for a weekend and are sure that you like it. Your first trip should be close to home and civilization.

In this chapter we include information on tent camping, RV camping, as well as a listing of rustic-type "resorts" where families stay in cabins and spend their days enjoying the outdoors. In the West, many of these types of places are called ranches, so check Chapter 11.

Other possibilities for camping families are the outfitters described in Chapter 6.

Our own families have had wonderful camping vacations, usually tenting and often in state or national parks. Naturalist-led walks into the woods or along the coast at low tide have taught our kids a lot about nature; storytelling around the campfire at night is something they talk about all the time. There's nothing quite as nice as life without telephones, televisions, and clocks. Camping gets its rhythm from nature: the beauty of the surroundings takes over, and the stress of everyday life loses its hold on everyone in the family.

Camping is also one of the most economical vacations you can take. Campsites cost only a few dollars per night, and food costs can be kept to a minimum.

## FINDING A CAMPGROUND

The United States has over 13,000 campgrounds, 5,000 publicly owned and over 8,000 privately owned. Some national parks are so popular that they need to be booked months ahead and can be reserved through Ticketron outlets. For a list of the 104 areas maintained by the National Park Service and information on their facilities, send $1.50 to the Superintendent of Documents, U.S. Government Printing Office, Washington, D.C. 20402, and ask for *Camping in the National Park System*. For $1.50 more you can also order *Lesser Known Areas of the National Park System*. If the idea of camping on Indian lands interests you, write to the U.S. Department of the Interior, Bureau of Indian Affairs (BIA), Washington, D.C. 20242, and ask for its map of Indian areas. On the back of the map are listed the addresses of areas and agency offices of BIA where you can write for specific information on existing sites.

Probably the best guide to campgrounds is the one revised yearly by Rand McNally. Published in East and West editions, the *Campground and Trailer Park Guides* are particularly useful because they include maps of each state with every campground marked. We've been able to plan lots of our trips using the guide to locate overnight camping stops. Both editions cost $7.95. Free campground information is usually available from local and state government tourist offices; see the appendix in the back of the book for addresses. Many of the state and national parks have cabins where families can enjoy a bit more comfort than in a tent. Two books that list these cabins are *The Complete Guide to Cabins and Lodges in America's State and National Parks* by George Zimmerman, published by Little, Brown and Company ($12.95), and *State and National Parks; Lodges and Cabins* by John Thaxton, published by Burt Franklin and Company as part of the Compleat Traveler series ($8.95).

## RV CAMPING

The RV industry's public relations voice, the Recreation Vehicle Industry Association, will be more than happy to send you a bulging packet of information on the benefits of RV travel. You'll get information on rentals, purchase, campgrounds, state and regional RV associations, and more. Their address is P.O. Box 2999, 1896 Preston White Drive, Reston, Virginia 22090. Two specific sources of information on renting RVs are Cruise America, American Land Cruisers, 7740 N.W. 34th Street, Miami, Florida 33122, 800-327-7778, and U-Haul International, Inc., 2727 North Central Avenue, Phoenix, Arizona 85004, 800-528-0463.

## PREPARING A CAMPSITE

Once you have chosen a campsite, the first thing to do is to set specific boundaries for your kids. We like the idea of taking balls of yarn, a different color for each kid, and using it to mark off the "safe" area for each child. Arrange a play area for your youngest while you set up camp and have everyone participate in the setting-up process. There's plenty for even the youngest to do: spreading the ground cloth, hammering in the tent posts, or filling a pot with water. Older children may enjoy having their own tent. Parents: think of how nice a little privacy will be.

A camping trip gives you the perfect opportunity to work as a team and to teach your kids real respect and love for nature. Two excellent books to help you do the latter are *Starting Small in the Wilderness* by Marilyn Doan and *The Nature Observer's Handbook* by John W. Brainerd. *Starting Small* is a how-to book for parents who are introducing kids to wilderness adventure and a source book for safe, responsible, and enjoyable activities for the youngest campers; the age range is infancy to 12. Information on the right gear for adults as well as kids is also included. It costs $6.95 and is published by Sierra Club Books. *The Nature Observer's Handbook* presents ways to observe, experience, and record the "intricate beauty of nature." Brainerd includes excellent advice on "nature touring" with children; he suggests starting with a tour of your backyard on your hands and knees. The book, published by Globe Pequot Press, Old Chester Road, Chester, Connecticut 06412, costs $9.95.

## CABIN VACATIONS

The following places offer cabins and a range of outdoor possibilities, a bit more luxurious than tent camping, perhaps, but still very much in the camping mood.

### Sandy Bay Camps
Box 1173
Greenville, Maine 04441
Telephone: 207-695-2512
Owner: John Connelly
Operating Season: Summer

DESCRIPTION: Sandy Bay Camps is located on 40-mile-long Moosehead Lake. It offers both housekeeping cabins and a campground with primitive tent sites. Guides are available to help you locate the best fishing spots, and families can hire guides for a day or more of canoeing or hiking in the backcountry.

ACCOMMODATIONS: The cabins can accommodate up to 11 people, and they're located only steps away from lakeside. They have kitchens, hot showers, screened porches, and easy access to lakeside picnicking. "Unlike in modern motels, guests should not be surprised to find mice in the porch woodpiles, bare floors and just enough of the necessities to get by." The owner provides bed linens; guests take their own towels.

RATES: Cabins cost $32 per night for two people, $8 for each additional person. Kids under 2 stay free. If you stay a week or more, there's a 10 percent discount.

### Kawanhee Inn Lakeside Resort
Webb Lake
Route 142
Weld, Maine 04285
Telephone: 207-585-2243 in summer; 207-778-4306 in winter
Manager: Sturges Butler
Operating Season: Summer

IN THEIR OWN WORDS: "We have a lodge-type atmosphere here. Our huge living room—the Moose Room, with its fieldstone fireplace, puzzles and a library—is perfect for rainy days. There are no required activities—just an outdoor environment that families love. Our white sandy beach with water that drops off slowly is safe even for toddlers. We have the best family hiking trails in the state. . . ."

ACTIVITIES: There's a main lodge situated on a high knoll overlooking the lake and mountains. The lodge has 14 rooms, but for families the housekeeping cabins are best. Guests like to swim, play tennis, sail on the lake, bicycle, and hike. From time to time, watercolor workshops are offered. All-day climbing trips to Mt. Blue, Tumbledown, and Bald Mountains are popular with hikers of all skill levels. The dining room features half-price meals for kids.

ACCOMMODATIONS: The cabins face the lake and mountains, and none is far from the shore. They vary in size and can accommodate from two to seven people. Each has a living room with a large stone fireplace, a complete bath, and a screened porch. Extra cots and cribs are available.

RATES: Cabins are rented by the week. Rates are $300 for a family of four.

### Appalachian Mountain Club
5 Joy Street
Boston, Massachusetts 02108
Telephone: 617-523-0636
Owner: Private, nonprofit organization
Operating season: Summer

ACTIVITIES: The Appalachian Mountain Club (AMC) operates a number of camping areas that are available to members and nonmembers alike. The four camps that are recommended for families with young children are the Cardigan Lodge, Echo Lake, and Cold River camps in New Hampshire and the Echo Lake Camp in Maine. Accommodations range from lodges to platform tents to cabins. Family-style meals are served in main dining rooms. Let's take Cold River Camp as an example. It is located on a 90-acre site in a secluded valley on the Maine/New Hampshire border. From the site, the hiking possibilities are unlimited— woodland walks, easy climbs, or more challenging full-day hikes are possible. The camp rents canoes, and the area is great for biking. For kids, there are a sandbox, slide, and swings and play equipment in the recreation hall.

ACCOMMODATIONS: Family cabins are located in the pine grove, surrounding the meadow and overlooking the ravine. The main lodge has a massive stone fireplace and a central dining room.

RATES: At Cold River, adults pay $165 per week (with an additional $20 for nonmembers); children 8 to 15 pay $145 and under 7, $98.

### Ludlow's Island Lodge
Box 1146
Cook, Minnesota 55723
Telephone: 218-666-5407
Managers: Mark and Sally Ludlow
Operating Season: Summer

IN THEIR OWN WORDS: "We think our resort is extremely family-oriented. (We have four children ourselves—11, 9, 6, and 4.) Everything here is set up for parents and children to use as they need or want to. . . . Most of our guests take several vacations—Ludlow's is their choice for their family vacation."

ACTIVITIES: There's no lack of things to do at Ludlow's. Much of the activities center on Lake Vermilion and its 1,200 miles of shoreline. There are swimming, boating, tennis, racquetball, golf a ten-minute ride away, waterskiing, sauna, and hiking trails. During the summer, Ludlow's has activities scheduled for kids 2½ years and older, three to five days a week. There's no extra charge for the program. Some of the activities you can expect are pontoon rides in search of beaver dams or bald eagles, nature hikes, breakfast cookouts, and treasure hunts. Kids can sign up for lessons in tennis, waterskiing, and racquetball. Baby-sitting is available for $3 per hour with four hours notice.

ACCOMMODATIONS: All cottages have fireplaces and decks, are fully carpeted, and have kitchens. There are dishwashers, microwaves, blenders, and automatic coffee pots. All are situated in birches and pines and within 50 feet of the water's edge. Cribs are available at no extra charge. There's no main dining hall; everyone does his own cooking. There's a small grocery store that's open 24 hours.

RATES: Weekly rates based on two people in a cabin ($40 for each additional person) range from $500 to $885. Maid service is $50 per week for two, $15 for each additional person. Children under 12 stay free before June 15 and after Labor Day.

## Gunflint Lodge
Box 100 GT
Grand Marais, Minnesota
Telephone: 218-388-2294 or 800-328-3325
Owners: Bruce and Susan Kerfoot
Operating Season: Summer

IN THEIR OWN WORDS: "The single thing that makes families enjoy a vacation at Gunflint is that children are truly welcome here. We avoid having a lot of rules. We cater to kids at meals—if a child wants a cheese sandwich for dinner, we make it for him or her even though it's not strictly 'on the menu.' Games and puzzles can be left unfinished overnight in the Lodge. . . ."

ACTIVITIES: During the summer, staff naturalists lead a variety of activities based on the forest, lakes, plant life, animals, and wilderness that surround the lodge. Twenty or more activities are offered each week, from nature hikes to berry picking (early August is raspberry and blueberry season), from an evening moose search to a breakfast cookout and paddle. Gunflint has a resident fishing pro, and for kids 6 to 15 staying one week or more, there's a free half-day guided fishing trip led by the pro or one of the guides. Baby-sitting, at a cost of $1.50 per hour, can be arranged with two hours advance notice.

ACCOMMODATIONS: Lakeside cottages have from one to four bedrooms, a living room with a fireplace, a full bathroom, carpeting, and electric heat; some have kitchens. Cribs are available at no extra cost.

RATES: A seven-night package that includes room, all meals, a motorboat, two canoes, gas, unlimited waterskiing, and the family naturalist activity program costs approximately $600 for the first two adults and $250 for each child 4 to 15. Children under 5 are $5 per night. Other packages are available for two to six nights.

**Brookside Resorts**
HC 05, Box 240
Park Rapids, Minnesota 56470
Telephone: 218-732-4093
Manager: Dave Keller
Operating Season: Summer

IN THEIR OWN WORDS: "We are a very family-oriented summer resort. We concentrate on activities and care for children 2 to 18. . . . We offer families a chance to enjoy each other and give each family member the opportunity to pursue their personal recreational interest. . . ."

ACTIVITIES: Brookside, located in the north woods of Minnesota, boasts lots and lots of recreational facilities—a golf course, tennis courts, and indoor-outdoor swimming pool (one end in the lodge, the other outside, surrounded by a deck), fishing, boating, and waterskiing on Two Inlets Lake. On rainy days it offers Ping-Pong, movies, a pool table, and a sauna in the lodge. From Memorial Day to Labor Day, there's a seven-day-a-week Kids' Program that begins at 9:00 A.M. and ends at 9:00 P.M. and is available to anyone 2 or over. For kids 2 to 7, there's a Kindernook program that runs from 9:30 A.M. to 11:30 A.M. Monday to Friday. The program combines free play, storytelling, nature walks, and crafts. The Kindernook area is a large, fenced-in playground with a log cabin, swings, toys, and a walk-in bunny cage. For kids under 2, baby-sitting is available for $2 per hour with advance notice.

ACCOMMODATIONS: All of the 28 cabins have kitchens and a knotty pine interior. There are two- and four-bedroom cabins, and a boat is supplied with each cabin. Some are carpeted; others have room-size braided rugs. Appliances are modern, and all the basics for cooking and eating are supplied. Guests take their own sheets and towels or rent them from Brookside.

RATES: Rates vary with the season and the size of cabin. A sample: a two-bedroom cottage for four people costs $530 for the week of August 9 to 16. Before June 13 and after August 16, kids under 17 stay free; children under 3 are always free.

### Holland Lake Lodge
Box 2083
Condon, Montana 59826
Telephone: 406-754-2282
Owners: The Schaeffers
Operating Season: Year-round

IN THEIR OWN WORDS: "Holland Lake Lodge is that special place for your family if the outdoors appeals to you. We feel our atmosphere offers the family a relaxed place to come without costing a year's salary. Our lounge has a toy box and children's books. . . . Many families book one to twenty years in advance."

ACTIVITIES: The Lodge is located in the heart of Montana's scenic Rocky Mountains at the gateway to the Bob Marshall Wilderness. In summer, guests horseback ride, canoe, fish, swim, and hike; in winter, they cross-country ski, ice fish, skate, and snowmobile. All meals are served in the Lake Room of the Lodge, and there are special meals for children. Baby-sitting is available at $2 per hour.

ACCOMMODATIONS: There are rooms in the lodge, but for families the cabins are best. The cabins are rustic but comfortable; all but one has a kitchen, and they can accommodate from four to eight people. Cribs cost $5 per night to rent.

RATES: The cabins rent for $42 to $68.50 per night. Meals are extra and moderately priced. Canoes and rowboats are available for rent for $3.50 per hour, and a guided four-hour horseback ride costs $30.

### Loch Lyme Lodge
Route 10, RFD 278
Lyme, New Hampshire 03768
Telephone: 603-795-2141
Owners: Judith and Paul Barber
Operating Season: Year round; cabins in summer only

IN THEIR OWN WORDS: "My husband and I have a son, age 5, who has certainly taught us a lot about vacationing with children during the past years. We have found this very helpful in working with our own summer guests. We do not offer, and do not intend to offer, the following: televisions, telephones in cabins, video game room, soda machines, or organized social programs. . . . What we *do* have is 125 acres of New Hampshire fields and woodlands bordering Post Pond, a spring-fed lake."

ACTIVITIES: During the summer Loch Lyme operates as a summer resort, with housekeeping cabins; in the fall and winter it becomes a small bed and breakfast operation using just the main lodge. Located near Dartmouth College, the lodge features a waterfront with a safe, sandy beach for toddlers. Boats and canoes are available, and fishing on the lake is reported to be good. There are two clay tennis courts and hiking trails. Baby-sitting can be arranged with six hours notice for $2 per hour during the day and $2.50 at night. Usually the baby-sitters are the teenage girls who work and live at the lodge during the summer. Children's portions are available in the dining room, and most of the vegetables are grown in the garden by Mrs. Barber's father.

ACCOMMODATIONS: Cabins are spread out through the woods and along the lakeshore so that there's a feeling of privacy. A typical cabin has a living room with a fireplace, a bath, a kitchen or kitchenette, one to four bedrooms, and a porch. Most cabins have daybeds in the living rooms for additional lodging. Cribs are available for $5 per stay.

RATES: The weekly rental for cabins ranges from $205 to $350. Daily rates on a European Plan (no meals) or Modified American Plan (MAP) (breakfast and dinner) are also available. The MAP is $40 per day for cabins for adults, $20 for kids 5 to 12. Children under 4 are free. "Children visiting Loch Lyme on their birthdays will be our guest."

# 13

# CRUISES

Before we set out on our first cruise with the kids we were less than enthusiastic about the idea. We were afraid we'd be bored, that all we'd do was eat ourselves into oblivion, that we'd go stir crazy sharing a tiny cabin with our kids, and that the kids would be restless. None of these came to pass. We had a great time, and we've become real fans of cruising with kids. Our cruise was on Sitmar's *Fairwind*, which has a Youth Center open from 9:00 A.M. to midnight, a pool just for kids, a kids' program that operates even when the ship is in port, and other services just right for families.

Our route took us to some scuba diving meccas, and my husband and I wanted to dive at as many ports as possible. We were able to arrange several dives; we spent the morning together and had lunch with the kids, and then dropped them back at the ship. On many ships we couldn't have done that because sometimes the children's program doesn't operate when the ship's in port.

More and more cruise ships are tuning in to the needs of families. Fortunately, single parents traveling with their kids are getting attention, too. Combination sea/land packages, free airfare, and other enticements are making cruising with your family more and more affordable. The typical cruise price includes accommodations, meals, snacks, and entertainment, so even if the price quoted seems high at first, consider what's included. More and more ships are offering kids' and teens' programs. Not only does that mean that you'll have a chance for free time yourself but also that other kids are more likely to be along on the ride. New friends are a very,

278

very important part of a successful vacation for your kids. Not every cruise ship is right for families. Here are some guidelines to help you decide which ones are.

- Accommodations: Look for a cabin to accommodate all of you in a category you can afford. Family cabins can accommodate three to four people or have room for a crib. Adjoining rooms are nice but, of course, more costly. Your youngest may not take kindly to a shower, so ask whether you can have a cabin with a tub. And if you need a crib, be sure to ask for it at booking time; this also applies to booster seats, special menus, early seating, or any other requests you have. Even when the cruise line indicates that these options are always available, be sure to reserve what you need.
- Shore excursions: Wherever you dock there will be planned excursions. We think it's better to explore on your own. It's less expensive, and you can control the pace. Consider joining up with another family for a shore adventure. Some ships have shore excursions just for kids. Ask about them.
- Baby-sitting: Most, but not all, ships have some kind of arrangement for baby-sitting. Even if there's no formal baby-sitting arrangement, you can usually make a private agreement with a crew member or find a willing teenager on board.
- Refrigerators: These are always a plus with kids. If there aren't any, take along an insulated bag and ask the steward for ice. If the ship has 24-hour room service, this won't be necessary.
- Pricing: A child with 2 adults usually pays third or fourth person rates, less than the rate of the first two people in the cabin. Although more cruise lines are taking single parents' needs into consideration, the second person in the cabin, even when a child, will be charged an adult rate. Also, look for special "kids cruise free" deals.
- Early dining: When there are two seatings, sometimes kids can eat at the early one and parents can eat at the second. Ask at booking time. Full meals may not be available from room service, but substantial snacks are often available.

Every year, TWYCH (Travel with Your Children) publishes a special guide called *Cruising with Children*,™ which lists almost 100 ships and all their child-related services. Copies are $20, and single ship profiles are $3.50 each. Write to 80 Eighth Avenue, New York, New York 10011, or call 212-206-0688 to order.

An organization you may want to know about is South Florida Cruises, which offers savings up to 45 percent in various accommodation categories on ships worldwide. They know a lot about facilities for kids. You can contact them at 2005 Cypress Creek Road, Fort Lauderdale, Florida 33309, 800-327-SHIP.

And now for some specific cruise possibilities for you and your family, listed alphabetically, by cruise line.

## Admiral Cruises, Inc.
1220 Biscayne Boulevard
Miami, Florida 33132
Telephone: 305-373-7501 or 800-327-2693

THE SHIPS: SS *Emerald Seas,* Miami to Bahamas; MV *Stardancer,* Vancouver to Alaska and Los Angeles to Mexico; SS *Azure Seas,* Los Angeles to Ensanada, Mexico, and San Diego, California.

IN THEIR OWN WORDS: "With its three- and four-night short cruises, the *Emerald Seas* offers families a great opportunity to spend some quality time together without taking up all their vacation time or their money. . . . The *Stardancer* is a newer, sleeker ship with all the activities and amenities of a resort hotel. Families can even bring their cars or RVs for land touring in Alaska or Mexico."

DESCRIPTION: *Emerald Seas* has room for 980 passengers with 450 crew members to serve them. It has the largest cabins of any ship afloat and full bathtubs and showers in most cabins. *Azure Seas* has room for 740, nine decks, and a crew of 370. It has an exercise room and gymnasium and a video game room. And, finally, *Stardancer* can accommodate 980, with ten passenger decks, room for 350 cars, and a crew of 380. It features an outdoor track with par course stations, an outside sliding glass domed swimming pool, and a children's playroom and Teen Club.

FOR KIDS: Probably the best bet of this line for a cruise with kids is *Stardancer.* From October to May it sails from Los Angeles to Puerto Vallarta, Mazatlán, and Cabo San Lucas; from May through September from Vancouver to Juneau, Skagway, Haines, and Ketchikan. It has an organized children's center and a full-time director for kids on every sail. The Teen Center has video games, Ping-Pong, and other games; activities are not supervised. There are no children's programs while the ship is in port.

ACCOMMODATIONS: *Stardancer* has 132 three-bed cabins and 244 that have four beds. There are 50 interconnecting cabins on the two upper decks with two people per cabin.

RATES: Kids are charged the regular third and fourth person rates (for the *Stardancer* it's $55 per night). For kids under 16 traveling with one parent on the *Emerald Seas,* the pricing is half the regular room rate as long as the cabin has an upper and lower berth, an interesting possibility for single parents.

### American Hawaii Cruises
550 Kearny Street
San Francisco, California 94108
Telephone: 415-392-9400 or 800-227-3666

THE SHIPS: SS *Independence,* Honolulu to Hawaiian Islands; and SS *Constitution,* Honolulu to Hawaiian Islands.

IN THEIR OWN WORDS: "The emphasis on the *Independence* and the *Constitution* is on bringing the destination on board with Hawaiian food, island shows, and a relaxed 'aloha' feeling in everything—from the guests' attire to the warmth of the all-American crew."

DESCRIPTION: The ships have two outdoor pools; the *Constitution* has a children's pool. Both have a children's playroom, a library with children's books, and a movie theater. A full-time recreational/social director is always on board.

FOR KIDS: Both ships have children's programs, but they only operate when there's a sufficient number of kids, usually ten or more, on board. You can be fairly sure that there will be activities during vacation periods and the summer. The programs are for kids 2 to 6, 7 to 12, and 13 to 18 years. There's no nursery for kids 2 years or under, and baby-sitting services are not generally provided. The kids' recreational center has a jukebox, dance floor, and soda fountain.

ACCOMMODATIONS: On the *Constitution* the average cabin

size is 162 square feet. There are 397 cabins in all, 41 with three beds and 81 with four beds. The "A" suites have two adjoining rooms; two bathrooms, one with a tub; refrigerator; and two sofa beds and can accommodate six people in all. On the *Independence* cabins are a bit smaller, an average of 143 square feet. There are 77 with three beds and 78 with four beds. Two adjoining suites, with a bathroom in each room, are available to families.

RATES: On the *Independence* and the *Constitution* there's a special 18 and under rate of $99 for kids sharing a cabin with two full-fare adults.

### Holland America Lines
300 Elliot Avenue West
Seattle, Washington 98119
Telephone: 206-281-3535 or 800-426-0327

THE SHIPS: SS *Rotterdam*, Fort Lauderdale; Norfolk, Virginia; and New York to the Caribbean; and San Diego and Vancouver to Alaska; MS *Noordam*, Fort Lauderdale to Mexico, Vancouver to Alaska; MS *Nieuw Amsterdam*, Tampa to Caribbean and through the Panama Canal and on to Vancouver and Alaska.

IN THEIR OWN WORDS: "Kids will like our attentive crew, our movie theater and our arts and crafts program."

DESCRIPTION: The SS *Rotterdam* can accommodate 1,114 guests. It has two swimming pools—one inside, one out—full orchestras with vocalists, golf lessons, tennis practice courts, blackjack and slot machines, a gymnasium, and a masseuse. The *Noordam* and the *Nieuw Amsterdam* are even larger: they can hold 1,214 people each. They've got all the features listed for the *Rotterdam* plus roulette, a whirlpool, and dual saunas.

FOR KIDS: On cruises that are likely to have quite a few kids, for instance, at Easter or Christmas vacation time, there are organized kids' programs. You can expect games and sports contests, pizza parties, "coketail" parties. Check to see what will be available when you plan to go. Babysitting can be arranged for $5 per hour through the ship's front office.

ACCOMMODATIONS: On the *Nieuw Amsterdam* and the *Noordam* there are 20 deluxe staterooms with king-size beds and sofa beds; 72 cabins with two uppers and two lowers; 24 adjoining cabins, and bathtubs in 142 of the top three category cabins. The

*Rotterdam* has 180 three-bed cabins, 73 four-bed cabins, including four three-bed and 18 four-bed suites with separate sitting areas and a couch. There are 42 adjoining rooms and 70 rooms with a common hallway. Cribs are available and can be accommodated in any category.

RATES: For Caribbean cruises, kids are charged third and fourth person fares; those under 3 years are free when accompanied by two full-fare-paying people. For the Alaska cruise, kids up to age 12 pay one-half the regular fare if they're sharing with one adult.

### Premier Cruise Lines
101 George King Boulevard
Cape Canaveral, Florida 32920
Telephone: 305-783-5061

THE SHIPS: SS *Oceanic* and SS *Royale,* Port Canaveral to Nassau, Bahamas.

IN THEIR OWN WORDS: "Both ships are festive and family-oriented. The mood on board is casual . . . great fun and excitement."

DESCRIPTION: The *Royale* has room for 1,100. The *Oceanic* can accommodate 1,500. Both have outdoor pools. The *Oceanic* has a separate children's pool and a Teen Center. Premier is the official cruise line of Walt Disney World, which means that for the price of a four-night cruise you have a pre- or postcruise stay at a Disney World hotel for three days and get a rental car, a free tour of Spaceport USA, and a three-day passport to Walt Disney World at no extra charge.

FOR KIDS: There are activities for kids 2 years and over from 9:00 to noon, 2:00 to 5:00, and 7:00 to 10:00. The center of the program is the Children's Room. Activities include arts and crafts, storytelling, disco classes, pool games, and movies. For older kids, there's a teen center. If kids don't want to go on shore excursions, there's programming on board for them. Baby-sitting can be arranged through the youth director for $3 per hour.

ACCOMMODATIONS: The *Royale* has 110 three-bed cabins and 84 four-bed cabins. There are two sets of connecting suites, and one with a queen-size bed connecting to a cabin with three berths. Twenty-six five-berth cabins are available. The *Oceanic* has 196 three-bed cabins, 149 with four beds, 75 with five beds, and eight Nevada Suites that have their own balcony.

RATES: Kids under 2 are free; otherwise they pay the third, fourth, and fifth person rates.

## Royal Caribbean Cruise Lines
903 South America Way
Miami, Florida 33132
Telephone: 305-379-2601

THE SHIPS: *Song of Norway,* Miami to Cozumel, Grand Cayman, Ocho Rios, and La Badse, Haiti; *Song of America,* Miami to Labadee, San Juan, and St. Thomas; *Nordic Prince,* Miami to Labadee, San Juan, St. Thomas; St. Thomas, Antigua, Martinique, St. Maarten, and New York to Bermuda; *Sun Viking,* Miami to Labadee, San Juan, St. Thomas; Antigua, Barbados, Martinique, St. Maarten; St. Thomas, St. Kitts, Martinique, Barbados, Dominica, Guadeloupe, St. Maarten, St. Thomas.

IN THEIR OWN WORDS: "Passenger pampering is what sets us apart—our ship's staffs really like passengers and work sincerely to serve them, adults and youngsters."

DESCRIPTION: The *Sun Viking* is the smallest, with a capacity of 882, the *Song of America* is the largest, with room for 1,551. All ships have two outdoor pools, and a full-time recreational/social director.

FOR KIDS: All Royal Caribbean ships have organized programs for kids during the summer and vacation times. There are two programs, one for ages 5 to 12 and one for 13- to 17-year-olds. The program is supervised by counselors, who are usually teachers. Activities are scheduled from 9:00 A.M. to noon, 2:00 P.M. to 6:00 P.M., and 9:00 P.M. to 10:00 P.M. and include tours of the ship, ice cream and pizza parties, video games, movies, swimming, games, and tournaments. Although there are no public rooms exclusively for kids on the ships, special children's hours are scheduled for the pool and other facilities. Programs are available while the ship is in port for kids too young to go on shore excursions. Baby-sitting usually is available in the evening, but the price is steep, $8 per hour. Shore excursions are free for kids, and some special kids' tours, for instance, to the Coral World in St.

Thomas, are available. Each evening a newsletter with the next day's activities for kids is distributed so your kids can choose what they want to do.

ACCOMMODATIONS: Cabins are 130 to 160 square feet, and each of the four ships has over 14 cabins with four beds. All but the *Song of America* have adjoining cabins. Cribs can be arranged through the courtesy department.

RATES: Kids pay the standard third and fourth person rates when traveling with two full-fare adults.

### Sitmar Cruises
10100 Santa Monica Boulevard
Los Angeles, California 90067
Telephone: 213-553-1666 or 800-421-0880

THE SHIPS: *Fairsea,* Mexican Riviera, trans-Panama, Canada, Alaska; *Fairsky,* Caribbean, Mexican Riviera, trans–Canal, Canada/Alaska; *Fairwind,* Caribbean, trans–Panama Canal.

IN THEIR OWN WORDS: "We feel that the service, warmth and friendliness of our Italian crew members make the difference. They make you feel at home and do their utmost to make your vacation a special experience."

DESCRIPTION: *Fairsky* is the largest ship, with room for 1,200 on board; the other two can accommodate 925. There are two outdoor pools, one for adults, one for kids; a library with children's books; video games; and Ping-Pong.

FOR KIDS: Sitmar is one of the leaders in providing amenities and services for kids. Each ship has a youth coordinator and at least four counselors. From June through August, the staff includes a teen coordinator, a performing arts director, and at least eight counselors. Youth Center counselors are on duty from 8:00 A.M. to midnight, every day of the week. Hours of the center are flexible: they open early or stay open later when the ship is in port. For nursery-age kids, the Youth Center has cribs and cots. Formula should be requested two weeks in advance of sailing. Parents are asked to feed and diaper their little ones, but the staff will pinch hit in an emergency.

The Youth Center is open to kids through age 12 and is stocked with games, books, art supplies, and plenty of prizes for various games played throughout the day. Activities include magic shows, ice cream and pizza parties, cartoons, talent shows, board games, bingo, disco dancing, and a ship's tour. Planned activities are available during lunch and dinner hours. Parents are asked to check in with their kids frequently throughout the day.

The Teen Center is meant for kids 13 to 17 and has a dance floor, jukebox, and video games. The teen coordinator schedules sports, aerobics, drama classes, Italian lessons, midnight films, swimming competitions. High chairs and booster seats are available. Request them two weeks before sailing. Although there's no special children's menu, kids can order just about anything they'd like. Kids can eat at the early or the late seating, and room service is available 24 hours.

Baby-sitting is not available because the Youth Center is open for so many hours. At night there's a supervised "quiet environment" area in the center with cribs and cots where kids can go off to sleep until closing time.

ACCOMMODATIONS: The average size of a family cabin is 110 to 130 square feet. Most cabins except suites and minisuites have two lower beds and two upper pullman beds. The *Fairsky* has no adjoining rooms, but the other two ships have sets of rooms that share a small common hallway.

RATES: Kids to 17 years pay approximately one-half the third or fourth person rate when they're with two adults. A child with one adult pays double occupancy rate.

### World Explorer Cruises
550 Kearny Street
San Francisco, California 94108
Telephone: 415-391-9262 or 800-854-3835

THE SHIP: SS *Universe,* Vancouver to Alaska.

IN THEIR OWN WORDS: "Our cruises are friendly, relaxed, casual, informative, fun, and adventurous. . . . We feature classical music, string quartets. . . . Leave your tuxedo at home—the atmosphere here is comfortable and casual and the accent is on fun, not formality."

DESCRIPTION: There is room for 550 guests on board. The library of the *Universe* is supposed to be the finest on any cruise ship, and in the course of the cruise (14 days) there are many opportunities to learn about the art, culture, ecology, and history of each port. (It's even possible to earn college extension credits on board.) The ship has seven decks, five lounges, a nightclub and bar, a 200-seat theater, and a glass-covered promenade deck, for protected views of Alaska's landscape.

FOR KIDS: Practically all scheduled cruises have programs for kids 7 to 16 years. Activities include board games, exercise classes, sports tournaments, and movies. Evening fun is also scheduled. If five or six kids under 7 years of age are on board, the youth director will arrange suitable activities: games, arts and crafts, ice cream parties, and dramatic play, for example. Baby-sitting is available through the cruise office. There are no booster chairs or high chairs in the dining rooms; this seems a little strange because children do seem to be welcome otherwise. If children don't want to go on shore excursions with their parents, activities can be arranged for them instead. Older kids will probably want to attend some of the lectures on board.

ACCOMMODATIONS: There are 110 four-bed cabins, four adjoining cabins, and although there are no cribs, there are guard rails that attach to the bed. Request them at booking time.

RATES: Kids under 2 years travel free; over 3 years old they pay the third and fourth person rate of $595 plus port charges.

## ABOUT OUR LISTINGS:

The properties we list in this book all welcome kids and all willingly responded to our many, many questions. We're relying on you, our readers, to let us know about your own experiences with our choices—good and bad—and to tell us about any new places we can list in the next edition.

## ONE MORE REMINDER:

If you're looking for a place to play tennis, check the tennis and golf chapter but don't overlook Chapter 8 on resorts, Chapter 10 on skiing (many ski resorts turn into tennis and golf spots once the snow melts), and Chapter 11 on farms and dude ranches.

And don't forget the None of the Above listings beginning on page 289.

NOTE: Rates quoted here were accurate at press time but are subject to change.

NOTE: Be sure to check pages 297–99 for a list of publishers' addresses. Some books published by smaller publishers may not be readily available in bookstores but can be ordered directly from the publisher.

Send us your cards and letters. We want to hear from you about your great vacation choices so that we can include them in the next edition.

# None of the Above

In the course of writing this book, we discovered many hotels/resorts that welcome families but don't fit neatly under any of our chapters. Even so, we want you to know about them so that if you're traveling in their direction you can consider them. We've listed them here by state:

## California

### Dana Inn and Marina
1710 West Mission Bay Drive
San Diego, California 92109
Telephone: 619-222-6440
General Manager: Thomas Cartwright

Right next door to Mission Bay Aquatic Park, this inn has an outdoor heated pool. They're happy to have kids stay: those under 18 stay free, and most rooms have two double beds. Cribs are available, and one room has a kitchenette. Baby-sitting can be arranged for $5 per hour through the front desk with six hours advance notice.

### Hotel Inter-Contintental San Diego
333 West Harbor Drive
San Diego, California 92101
Telephone: 619-234-1500 or 800-327-0200
General Manager: Sandor Stangl

You'll find rooms with a view: San Diego Bay and the downtown skyline. A free-form heated pool and four all-weather tennis courts are available to guests, and there's an outdoor children's pool as well. All rooms have a king-size or two double beds and a pullout sofa. Cribs are free, and all rooms have minibars. The children's menu is also available from room service, and baby-sitting costs $25 for the first three hours and $6 per hour after that.

### Humphrey's Half Moon Inn
2303 Shelter Island Drive
San Diego, California 92106
Telephone: 619-224-3411 or 800-542-7401
General Manager: Lance Clements

Humphrey's is located on Shelter Island, 10 minutes from the airport, and 15 minutes from downtown San Diego. The atmosphere is tropical, surrounded by San Diego Bay and the Yacht Harbor Marina. The property has been recently landscaped and the sleeping rooms refurbished; the rooms are built in a two-story bungalow style with lots of open space around them.

Kids under 18 stay free with their parents; cribs are free, and 30 of the rooms have kitchenettes. The special children's menu is offered at Humphrey's Restaurant and through room service. Baby-sitting can be arranged for $5 per hour with the front desk. A double room with a bay view or at poolside is $125; luxury suites are $175 to $250.

### Monterey Bay Inn
242 Cannery Row
Monterey, California 93940
Telephone: 408-373-6242 or 800-424-6242
General Manager: David Jones

Here's a new hotel on the beach, on the bay, and on the park. It has 47 rooms, all with a private balcony, dry bar, refrigerator, king-size bed, and double sofa sleeper. Guests can use the two jacuzzis, a sauna, and an exercise room. Cribs are available for $5 per night, and baby-sitting is offered for $5 per hour with a day's advance notice. Rooms range from $95 to $165, depending on the view. A Continental breakfast is included.

### The Ritz Carlton
33533 Shoreline Drive
Laguna Niguel, California 92677
Telephone: 714-240-2000 or 800-241-3333
General Manager: Henry Schielein

Located on a 150-foot bluff above the Pacific Ocean, this Mediterranean-style hotel has the feel of a fine home, albeit a rather large one, with 393 rooms. Midway between Los Angeles and San Diego, it has four tennis courts, a nearby 18-hole golf course, and two miles of unspoiled beach at its doorstep. All rooms have refrigerators, and cribs are available. There's a children's menu, which is also offered through room service. Baby-sitting can be arranged for $6 per hour through the concierge with a minimum of one day notice. A junior suite—a bedroom plus living room with a sleep couch—costs $155 per night on weekends, $275 during the week.

### Yosemite Lodge
Yosemite National Park
Yosemite, California 95389
Telephone: 209-252-4848
General Manager: Bill Johnston

The atmosphere is relaxing, and the views are spectacular in the midst of this most beautiful national park. Rooms in the lodge have two double beds, and cribs are available at $5.35 per night. A pool, tennis, golf, hiking, skiing, and horseback riding and rafting are offered nearby. Cabins with and without baths are also available. Doubles, at ski season, are $72.75 per room for two, with $8 for additional people in the room.

## Colorado

### Beaver Village Condominiums
50 Village Drive
P.O. Box 3154
Winter Park, Colorado 80482

Telephone: 303-726-8813 or 800-525-3304
General Manager: Christine Harris

These one-, two-, and three-bedroom condos are adjacent to Arapahoe National Forest and 1½ miles from the Winter Park/ Mary Jane Ski Areas. Guests can shuttle free to downhill skiing or go cross-country skiing right outside their condo door. To warm up there are jacuzzis, an indoor pool, and a steam room. Tennis, sailing, golf, hiking, and horseback riding are all possible when the snow melts. Cribs are available for $5 per stay, and baby-sitting can be arranged for $1.50 per hour. A two-bedroom condo large enough for six costs $90 to $210, depending on the season; a one-bedroom for four costs $160.

## Florida

### Cheeca Lodge
P.O. Box 527
U.S. Highway 1
Islamorada, Florida 33036
Telephone: 305-664-4651
General Manager: H. P. Galloway

This lodge offers an outdoor pool, and one for kids, too, as well as tennis, sailing, golf, and biking. There's no charge for kids in rooms with their parent. Rooms have two double beds, and cribs or roll-away beds are available. Ten of the rooms have kitchenettes. Per-night rates are $170 to $205 (December 20 to April 21) and $110 to $125 (at other times).

### Fontainebleau Hilton
4441 Collins Avenue
Miami Beach, Florida 33140
Telephone: 305-538-2000 or 800-HILTONS
General Manager: Andre Schaefer

This elaborate hotel has recently had $30 million worth of "refinements" as the management calls them. You'll find seven tennis courts, a swimming pool as big as an island lagoon, and a 1,200-foot beach. For kids 5 to 13 there are activities originating at the Kids' Korner—arts and crafts, sand castle building, T-shirt painting, and exercises. A double room costs $145 to $215 per night; a parlor plus one bedroom is $325 to $450. Packages such as a seven-day, six-night version cost $40 per person double occupancy and include a breakfast in bed, a chaise longue poolside, and a day at the spa.

### Fortune Place
1426 Astro Lake Drive
North Kissimmee, Florida 32743
Telephone: 305-847-9661 or 800-624-7496
General Manager: Jim Schroeder

These are condos with two, three, or four bedrooms; full kitchens; an outdoor pool; a children's game room; and a children's playground. It's near Walt Disney World, Sea World, and so on. Cribs are available. Rates range from $79 to $99 per night for a two-bedroom condo, depending on season.

### Hilton at Walt Disney World Village
1751 Hotel Plaza Boulevard
Lake Buena Vista, Florida 32830
Telephone: 305-827-4000 or 800-HILTONS
General Manager: James L. Claus

One of the six official hotels of Walt Disney World, this features a Youth Hotel complete with activities for kids 3 to 12, a big-screen video room, lots of toys, and plenty of Mickey Mouse lookalikes. The hotel provides complimentary transportation to Epcot and the Magic Kingdom and character breakfasts in season. Baby-sitting can be arranged through the Youth Hotel for $3 per hour.

Kids stay free in their parents' room; a sample package is called "The Donald Duck Package"—it costs $54 per person per day and includes breakfast.

### Southern Sun Inn
3300 South 441 and 14
Orlando, Florida 32805

Telephone: 305-422-4521 or 800-352-4667
General Manager: Mike Harding

There are two outdoor pools at this motel and cribs to rent for $12 per day. A two-night, three-day package costs $64 double occupancy. Baby-sitting is available for $5 per hour with four hours advance notice.

### Sun Viking Lodge
2411 South Atlantic Avenue
Daytona, Florida 32018
Telephone: 904-252-6252
General Managers: Frank and Mindy Forehand

The lodge caters primarily to families. During vacation season, they feature game days for all ages complete with prizes. The 60-foot-long waterslide is a hit with everyone, and for cooler weather, there's an indoor pool. The kiddie pool is best for little ones, and for everyone there are two game rooms and a sauna, hot tub, shuffleboard, and basketball. Family packages for two-room suites with room for up to six people and kitchens are $70 to $120 per night, depending on season. Cribs are available at no extra charge. Baby-sitting for $3 per hour can be arranged at the front desk.

## Michigan

### Grand Traverse Resort Village
Grand Traverse Village, Michigan 49610-0404
Telephone: 616-938-2100
General Manager: Jim Gernhofer

Set along the sandy shores of East Grand Traverse Bay, this 850-acre property offers tennis, an indoor pool, an exercise room, saunas, a beach club with boat rentals, skiing in winter, and 36 holes of golf, including "The Bear" designed by Jack Nicklaus. For kids 5 to 8 there's a supper club three nights a week from 6:00 P.M. to 9:00 P.M., and older kids 9 to 12 have evening activities on the same nights. The tennis pro gives group lessons for 5- to 8-year-olds every Saturday from 9:00 A.M. to 10:00 P.M. Baby-sitting is available at $3.50 per hour for one child, 50 cents more for every child after that. Guests choose from hotel or condo accommodations. A hotel room costs $64 to $80; kids are free when they're with two adults; condos are $75 to $195, depending on the number of bedrooms.

## New Hampshire

### Snowvillage Inn
Box KDS
Snowville, New Hampshire 03849
Telephone: 603-447-2818
General Manager: Ginger Blymyer

This country inn is set 1,000 feet up Foss Mountain in a village in the White Mountains. In winter it offers cross-country skiing and sledding; in summer, hiking, berry picking, swimming in nearby Crystal Lake. Nature is the star here: "We love children, who don't need much entertainment but enjoy the outdoors." The inn, built in 1916, has 16 rooms, 14 with private bath. In residence is a pig named Gracie who lives, as you'd expect, in Gracie's Mansion. Rates can be either for bed and breakfast or MAP— lodging, breakfast, and four-course dinner. MAP costs $69 to $83; bed and breakfast, $45 to $73 per person. For kids 2 to 6 years, the rates are $9.50 to $16.50; 7 to 12, $20.50 to $27.50; 13 to 15, $26 to $33; and over 15, $36 and $44. Infants stay free, and there's no charge for a crib.

### Whitney's Village Inn
Box W
Route 16B
Jackson, New Hampshire 03846
Telephone: 603-383-6886
General Manager and Owner: T. M. Tannehill

When the Tannehills acquired the inn in 1983, they were determined to establish the inn as a family inn run by a family. To do this they offer special rates for kids, a children's menu, a kids' dinner table, a family activities room, nightly movies, and a teen room. In winter there's skiing—downhill at Black Mountain and cross-country in the backyard; ski lessons, ice-skating (they'll provide the skates), and sledding; in summer they offer swimming in a mountain pond, hiking, tennis, volleyball, badminton, croquet, fishing, and all the family-type attractions of the Mount Washington Valley. There are eight family suites, with living room, bedroom, and bath with room for six. Cribs are available, and kids under 12 stay and eat free in summer; the charge is $20 other times. The rate for adults is $64 per person double occupancy with breakfast and dinner included.

## Vermont

### Woodstock Inn and Resort
14 The Green
Woodstock, Vermont 05091
Telephone: 802-457-1100
General Manager: S. Lee Bowden

In winter, guests at the Woodstock Inn go cross-country skiing, on sleigh rides, ice-skating, dogsledding, or downhill skiing nearby; in the warm weather they offer golf, tennis, biking, swimming, horseback riding, fishing, and hiking. The Woodstock Recreation Center is close by and has supervised playground activity Monday through Friday from 9:00 A.M. to noon. There are 120 rooms in all. A "Summer Sports Package" costs $197 per person triple, which includes two nights of accommodations, breakfasts, dinners, three days of greens fees, unlimited play on tennis courts (available midweek only). A one-bedroom suite costs $290. Kids 14 and under stay free in the same room as an adult and have free skiing privileges. Baby-sitting can be arranged for $3 per hour with 12 hours advance notice.

# APPENDIX 2
## Publishers

Note: There are two catalogs of travel books compiled especially for families. The first and most comprehensive is called *Families on the Go,* a list of 200 books in all. Write to 1259 El Camino Real, number 147, Menlo Park, California 94025, for a free copy; or call 800-367-2934 or, in California, 800-752-9955. The second, *Family Travel Guides,* is published by Carousel Press, costs $1, but it's free to our readers. It can be ordered from P.O. Box 6061, Albany, California 94706.

Following is a list of publishers of books listed in *Great Vacations with Your Kids.*

Addison-Wesley
1 Jacob Way
Reading, Massachusetts 01867

Adventure Guides
36 East 57th Street
New York, New York 10022

Anais Press
P.O. Box 9635
Denver, Colorado 80209

Bantam Books
666 Fifth Avenue
New York, New York 10019

Bobbs Merrill
630 Third Avenue
New York, New York 10017

Carousel Press
P.O. Box 6061
Albany, California 94706

Chronicle Publishers
1 Hallidie Place
San Francisco, California 94102

Congdon and Weed
298 Fifth Avenue
New York, New York 10001

Dolphin-Doubleday
245 Park Avenue
New York, New York 10167

East Woods Press
429 East Boulevard
Charlotte, North Carolina 28203

Educational Graphics
404 Park View Drive
Pflugerville, Texas 78660

Fielding/William Morrow
105 Madison Avenue
New York, New York 10016

Globe Pequot Press/East Woods
Old Chester Road
Chester, Connecticut 06412

Harvard Common Press
535 Albany Street
Boston, Massachusetts 02118

Hearst Professional Magazines
60 East 42nd Street
New York, New York 10017

Houghton Mifflin
52 Vanderbilt Avenue
New York, New York 10017

Prentice-Hall
Route 9W
Englewood Cliffs, New Jersey 07632

Sierra Club Books
730 Polk Street
San Francisco, California 94109

Simon & Schuster
1230 Avenue of the Americas
New York, New York 10020

Times Books
201 East 50th Street
New York, New York 10022

Vee Jay Press
P.O. Box 1029
Pompano Beach, Florida 33061

Writing Works
3441 Thorndyke Avenue West
Seattle, Washington 98119

Yankee Publishing
Main Street
Dublin, New Hampshire 03444

# United States Tourist Offices

Listed here are the addresses and telephone numbers for the tourist offices of every U.S. state and Canadian province. When you write or call one of these offices, be sure to request a map of the state and a calendar of events. If you will be visiting a particular city or region, or if you have any special interests, be sure to specify them as well.

## STATE TOURIST OFFICES

Alabama Bureau of Tourism and Travel
532 South Perry Street
Montgomery, Alabama 36104
205-261-4169 or 800-252-2262 (out of state) or 800-392-8096
 (within Alabama)

Alaska Division of Tourism
Pouch E
Juneau, Alaska 99811
907-465-2010

Arizona Office of Tourism
1480 East Bethany Home Road
Phoenix, Arizona 85014
602-255-3618

Arkansas Department of Parks and Tourism
1 Capitol Mall
Little Rock, Arkansas 72201
501-371-7777 or 800-643-8383 (out of state) or 800-482-8999
 (within Arkansas)

California Office of Tourism
1121 L Street, Suite 103
Sacramento, California 95814
916-322-1396

Colorado Office of Tourism
625 Broadway
Suite 1700
Denver, Colorado 80202
303-592-5410 or 800-255-5550

Connecticut Department of Economic Development-Vacations
210 Washington Street
Hartford, Connecticut 06106
203-566-3948 or 800-243-1685 (out of state) or 800-842-7492
  (within Connecticut)

Delaware State Travel Service
99 Kings Highway, P.O. Box 1401
Dover, Delaware 19903
302-736-4271 or 800-441-8846 (out of state) or 800-282-8667 (in
  Delaware)

Washington, D.C. Convention and Visitors' Assoc.
Suite 250
1575 I Street, N.W.
Washington, D.C. 20005
202-789-7000

Florida Division of Tourism
107 West Gaines Street
Tallahassee, Florida 32301
904-487-1462

Georgia For Information
Tourist Division
Department of Industry and Trade
Box 1776
Atlanta, Georgia 30301
404-656-3590

Hawaii Visitors Bureau
2270 Kalakaua Avenue, Suite 801
Honolulu, Hawaii 96815
808-923-1811

or

New York Office
441 Lexington Avenue, Room 1407
New York, New York 10017
212-986-9203

Idaho Department of Commerce
Capitol Building, Room 108
Boise, Idaho 83720
208-334-2470 or 800-635-7820

Illinois Office of Tourism
310 South Michigan Avenue
Suite 108
Chicago, Illinois 60604
312-793-2094 or 800-252-8987 (within Illinois) or 800-637-8560
  (neighboring states)

Indiana Tourism Development Division
1 North Capitol, Suite 700
Indianapolis, Indiana 46204-2288
317-232-8860 or 800-2-WONDER

Iowa Development Commission
Visitors Group
200 East Grand
Des Moines, Iowa 50309-2882
515-281-3679

Kansas Department of Economic Development-Travel and
  Tourism Division
400 West 8th Street
Fifth Floor
Topeka, Kansas 66603
913-296-2009

Kentucky Department of Travel Development
22 Floor Capitol Plaza Tower
Frankfort, Kentucky 40601
502-564-4930 or 800-225-8747 (out of state)

Louisiana Office of Tourism
Inquiry Department
P.O. Box 94291
Baton Rouge, Louisiana 70804-9291
504-925-3860 or 800-231-4730 (out of state)

Maine Publicity Bureau
97 Winthrop St.
Hallowell, Maine 04347
207-289-2423

Maryland Office of Tourist Development
45 Calvert Street
Annapolis, Maryland 21401
301-269-3517

Massachusetts Division of Tourism
Department of Commerce and Development
100 Cambridge Street—13th Floor
Boston, Massachusetts 02202
617-727-3201 or 800-343-9072 (out of state)

Michigan Travel Bureau
Department of Commerce
P.O. Box 30226
Lansing, Michigan 48909
517-373-1195 or 800-543-2 YES

Minnesota Tourist Information Center
375 Jackson Street
Farm Credit Service Building
St. Paul, Minnesota 55101
612-296-5029 or 800-328-1461 (out of state) or 800-652-9747 (in
  Minnesota)

Mississippi Division of Tourism
P.O. Box 22825
Jackson, Mississippi 39205
601-359-3414 or 800-647-2290 (out of state) or 800-962-2346
  (within Mississippi)

Missouri Division of Tourism
P.O. Box 1055
Jefferson City, Missouri 65102
314-751-4133

Montana Promotion Division
1424 9th Avenue
Helena, Montana 59620
406-444-2654 or 800-548-3390

Nebraska Division of Travel and Tourism
P.O. Box 94666
Lincoln, Nebraska 68509
402-471-3796 or 800-228-4307

Nevada Commission on Tourism
Capitol Complex
Carson City, Nevada 89710
702-885-4322

New Hampshire Office of Vacation Travel
P.O. Box 856
Concord, New Hampshire 03301
603-271-2343 or 800-258-3608 (in the Northeast outside of New
   Hampshire)

New Jersey Division of Travel and Tourism
C.N. 826
Trenton, New Jersey 08625
609-292-2470

New Mexico Travel Division
Joseph Montoya Building
1100 St. Francis Drive
Santa Fe, New Mexico 87503
505-827-0291 or 800-545-2040

New York State Division of Tourism
1 Commerce Plaza
Albany, New York 12245
518-474-4116 or 800-225-5697 (in the Northeast except Maine)

North Carolina Travel and Tourism Division
430 North Salisbury Street
Raleigh, North Carolina 27611
919-733-4171 or 800-VISIT N.C. (out of state)

North Dakota Tourism Promotion
State Capitol Grounds

Bismarck, North Dakota 58505
701-224-2525 or 800-472-2100 (within North Dakota) or
  800-437-2077 (out of state)

Ohio Office of Tourism
P.O. Box 1001
Columbus, Ohio 43266-0101
614-466-8844 or 800-BUCKEYE (out of state)

Oklahoma Division of Tourism
215 N.E. 28th Street
Oklahoma City, Oklahoma 73105
405-521-2409 or 800-652-6552 (in neighboring states)

Oregon Economic Development Tourism Division
595 Cottage Street, N.E.
Salem, Oregon 97310
503-378-3451 or 800-547-7842 (out of state) or 800-233-3306
  (within Oregon)

Pennsylvania Bureau of Travel Development
Department of Commerce
416 Forum Building
Harrisburg, Pennsylvania 17120
717-787-5453 or 800-847-4872

Rhode Island Department of Economic Development
Tourism and Promotion Division
7 Jackson Walkway
Providence, Rhode Island 02903
401-277-2601 or 800-556-2484 (East Coast from Maine to
  Virginia, also West Virginia and Ohio)

South Carolina Division of Tourism
1205 Pendleton Street
Columbia, South Carolina 29201
803-734-0127

South Dakota Division of Tourism
Capitol Lake Plaza
711 Wells Avenue
Pierre, South Dakota 57501
605-773-3301 or 800-843-1930

Tennessee Tourist Development
P.O. Box 23170
Nashville, Tennessee 37202
615-741-2158

Texas Tourist Development
P.O. Box 12008
Capitol Station
Austin, Texas 78711
512-463-7400

Utah Travel Council
Council Hall
Capitol Hill
Salt Lake City, Utah 84114
801-533-5681

Vermont Travel Division
134 State Street
Montpelier, Vermont 05602
802-828-3236

Virginia Division of Tourism
202 North 9th Street
Suite 500
Richmond, Virginia 23219
804-786-4484

Washington State Department of Commerce and Economic
  Development
Tourism Promotion and Development Division
101 General Administration Building
Olympia, Washington 98504
206-753-5600 or 800-541-9274 (out of state) or 800-562-4570
  (within Washington)

Travel West Virginia
West Virginia Department of Commerce
State Capitol
Charleston, West Virginia 25305
304-348-2286 or 800-CALL W.VA

Wisconsin Division of Tourism
P.O. Box 7606
Madison, Wisconsin 53707
608-266-2161 or 800-372-2737 (within Wisconsin and
  neighboring states)

Wyoming Travel Commission
Frank Norris, Jr. Travel Center
Cheyenne, Wyoming 82002
307-777-7777

# INDEX

# TELL US ABOUT YOUR OWN GREAT VACATION.

We want to hear about the places you've discovered so that we can include them in our next edition. Please take a minute to complete the following form and return it to: *Great Vacations With Your Kids,* c/o TWYCH, 80 Eighth Avenue, New York, New York 10011.

Your Name: _____

Your Address: _____

Your Telephone: _____


Name of Property/Tour Operator: _____

Address: _____

Telephone: _____

Contact Person: _____

Describe your "find." We'll contact them directly for details.

*Many, many thanks.*

# TELL US ABOUT YOUR OWN GREAT VACATION.

We want to hear about the places you've discovered so that we can include them in our next edition. Please take a minute to complete the following form and return it to: *Great Vacations With Your Kids*, c/o TWYCH, 80 Eighth Avenue, New York, New York 10011.

Your Name: _____

Your Address: _____

Your Telephone: _____

Name of Property/Tour Operator: _____

Address: _____

Telephone: _____

Contact Person: _____

Describe your "find." We'll contact them directly for details.

*Many, many thanks.*

# FAMILY TRAVEL TIMES®

If you enjoyed reading

**Great Vacations with Your Kids,**

you'll love reading **Family Travel Times®**

– the only newsletter dedicated to helping parents

plan fun and successful family vacations.

Come, travel with us across North America and

around the globe.      Don't let folks tell you that you can't take an

exotic or romantic vacation with your kids.  Find out where and how in

**Family Travel Times®**.  Having read this book you know that the

vacation possibilities are endless and, that with proper planning, you

can go anywhere you want on vacation, bring the kids along, and *all*

come home having had a great holiday.

After all, isn't this what family vacations were meant to be?

Precious time

with our children

enjoying,

learning,

growing,

and being together.